British Regionalism 1900-2000

British Regionalism 1900-2000

Edited by *Patricia L. Garside*
and *Michael Hebbert*

MANSELL

LONDON AND NEW YORK

First published 1989 by
Mansell Publishing Limited, *A Cassell Imprint*
Artillery House, Artillery Row, London SW1P 1RT, England

British Library Cataloguing in Publication Data

British regionalism 1900–2000.
 1. Great Britain. Regionalism, history
 I. Garside, Patricia L.   II. Hebbert, Michael
 352'.0073'0941

 ISBN 0–7201–2013–6

Library of Congress Cataloging-in-Publication Data

British regionalism, 1900–2000 / edited by Patricia L. Garside and
 Michael Hebbert.
     p. cm.
 Papers presented at a joint conference of the Planning History
 Group and the Regional Studies Association held in Salford,
 Lancashire in 1987.
 Includes bibliographies and index.
 ISBN 0–7201–2013–6 : $54.00 (U.S.)
 1. Regionalism—Great Britain—Congresses. I. Garside,
 Patricia L.   II. Hebbert, Michael.   III. Planning History Group.
 IV. Regional Studies Association (London, England)
 JN297.R44B74   1989
 320.8'0941—dc20   89–33005
                                                                    CIP

This book has been printed and bound in Great Britain
by Redwood Burn Limited, Trowbridge, Wiltshire
from camera-ready copy supplied by the volume editors
and printed on Pegasus Book Wove

Contents

Preface

The idea for this book originated at a joint conference of the Planning History Group and the Regional Studies Association held in Salford, Lancashire in 1987. The Planning History Group is an international association of people who share an interest in the history of town and country planning. Regionalism has always played a prominent part in that history. The Regional Studies Association is an interdisciplinary group, with branches throughout the British Isles, that provides a forum where regional issues can be discussed and the results of research published. Its interest in the regional idea is firmly fixed in the present and the future.

There is an obvious mutuality in the groups' interests. Even the most cloistered student of the history of regionalism must hear its echoes in today's newpapers. The present prospects for regional decentralization are incomprehensible without reference to the precedents. That was why in organizing of the Salford conference we planned the event eclectically, bringing together speakers and participants from quite different spheres in a programme that tried to look forwards as well as backwards.

As with most experiments in cocktail-making the results were mixed, but at its best the mix was heady and produced interestingly unexpected ways of seeing things. The participants at Salford were unanimous in feeling that our perspective on the past, present and future of British regionalism was worth offering between hard covers to a wider audience.

All the material here, with the exception of Chapters 1 and 10, was first seen at the Salford conference. The editors wish to thank Sally Parkinson of the RSA whose efficiency and commitment ensured the success of the conference, and Professor Gordon Cherry of PHG for his helpful support throughout.

We gratefully acknowledge the kind permission of Penguin Books to reproduce Figure 1.2 from J.P. Mackintosh (1965) p.57 and of the Acton Society

Trust to reproduce Figure 1.3 from Smith (1963) Vol. 2, p.11. The map for Chapter 9 was drawn by Margaret Dunn. Chris Tivey at Salford University helped with photographic reproduction. Kristina Ferris of the LSE Drawing Office drew Figures 1.1 and 8.1 and prepared all artwork for publication. Our thanks to them.

Jutta Muller earned our warmest respect for the professionalism with which she word-processed and indexed the book and prepared the camera-ready copy.

Finally, we were most appreciative of the unflagging assistance and encouragement provided by our commissioning editor Penelope Beck of Mansell.

P.G.
M.H.

Notes on Contributors

Michael Burgess

Senior Lecturer in Political Science at Plymouth Polytechnic, Michael Burgess's research interests encompass the history of federal ideas and comparative federalism. He edited *Federalism and Federation in Western Europe* (Croom Helm, 1986) and his book *Federalism and European Union 1972-1987* is being published by Routledge in 1989.

Patricia L. Garside

She is Senior Lecturer on Environmental Health and Housing at the University of Salford. Her research interests have revolved around the development of environmentalism, especially in the context of the social and political history of London. With Ken Young, she co-authored *Metropolitan London: Politics and Urban Change 1837-1981* (Edward Arnold, 1982), and she has contributed a chapter on the growth of the metropolis to the forthcoming *New Social History of Britain* (Cambridge University Press). She is the Membership Secretary of the Planning History Group and an Associate of the Centre for Metropolitan History.

Dennis Hardy

Trained as a geographer and town planner at Exeter and London Universities, Dennis Hardy is Head of the School of Geography and Planning at Middlesex Polytechnic. His previous work includes *Alternative Communities in Nineteenth Century England* (Longman, 1979), and a history of holiday camps, *Goodnight Campers* (with Colin Ward, Mansell, 1986). His study of plotland development *Arcadia for All - the Legacy of a Makeshift Landscape* (with Colin Ward, Mansell, 1985) was awarded the Angel Literary Prize in 1985. He currently edits *Planning History* and is writing the official history of the Town and Country Planning Association.

Michael Hebbert

After reading History at Oxford University Michael Hebbert did doctoral research under Professor Peter Hall in the Department of Geography at Reading University. He teaches town and regional planning at the London School of Economics, where his research interests have covered the history of the planning movement and present planning issues in Japan, Spain and London. Recent work includes *The London Government Handbook* (with Tony Travers, Cassell, 1988), *How Tokyo Grows* (with Norihiro Nakai, STICERD, 1988) and *Unfamilar Territory - the Reshaping of European Geography* (edited with Jens-Christian Hansen, Gower, forthcoming).

Michael Keating

Before his appointment to the Chair of Political Science at the University of Western Ontario in 1988, Professor Keating had studied and worked at the University of Oxford, Glasgow College of Technology and the University of Strathclyde. He is co-author of nine books on urban and regional politics, amongst them *Regional Government in England* (edited with Brian Hogwood, Clarendon Press, 1982), *Regions in the European Community* (edited with Barry Jones, Clarendon Press, 1985), and *State and Regional Nationalism: Territorial Politics in Western Europe* (Harvester, 1988).

David Massey

He holds degrees from the Universities of Leicester and Cambridge and is currently a lecturer in urban studies at the University of Liverpool, where he teaches postgraduate courses in planning history. His research interests include the history of regional planning, the planning and management of coastal areas and the role of innovation in town development. For a number of years he has been involved in editing the journal *Town Planning Review*. He is Treasurer of the Planning History Group and over the period 1987-89 played the role of Secretary to the newly established Association of European Planning Schools (AESOP).

Jonathan Owen

Now with the Association of District Councils, Jonathan Owen graduated with a first in History in 1984 from Bristol University, where he has since been researching a doctoral thesis entitled 'Defending the County: the reorganization of local government in England and Wales 1935-1950'.

Diana C. Pearce

A graduate in Building Engineering and Civic Design at Liverpool University, she spent a short spell in Brazil in 1976 before joining the Department of the Environment as a researcher in the Yorkshire and Humberside Region during the last years of the Regional Economic Planning Council. She moved to the Northern Region in 1986 as Housing and Planning Principal. Active in the Regional Studies Association, she contributed to its 1983 Inquiry into Regional Problems in the U.K.

Urlan Wannop

Professor Wannop holds the Chair of Urban and Regional Planning at the Centre for Planning in the University of Strathclyde. He was formerly Senior Deputy Director of Planning for Strathclyde Regional Council and Director of the West Central Scotland Plan. His earlier career as a professional planner has involved new town and sub-regional planning in both public and private practice, and he has worked as an adviser to the Scottish Development Agency, the Department of the Environment, the Scottish Development Department, and the Regional Councils for Nord-Pas de Calais and the Rhône-Alpes. He chaired the Royal Town Planning Institute's Working Party on Strategic and Regional Planning and has written widely on Clydeside and urban renewal, including chapters in *Regional Cities 1890-1980* (Harper and Row, 1986), *Land Policy* (Gower, 1985) and *Regenerating the Inner City: Glasgow's Experience* (Routledge & Kegan Paul, 1987).

Michael Wise

He is Professor Emeritus of Geography at the London School of Economics and Political Science where he taught from 1951 to 1985. As a lecturer in Birmingham University 1946-51 he was involved in the work of the West Midland Group on Post-War Reconstruction and Planning and has maintained his interest in regional and urban planning problems. He was an active member of the British Group for Regional Planning and Development, the fore-runner of the Regional Studies Association. Professor Wise was Chairman of the Ministry of Agriculture's Committee of Inquiry into Statutory Smallholdings 1964-68 and has been since 1971 (Chairman 1981) a member of the Landscape Advisory Committee of the Department of Transport. He is currently Chairman of the Governors of Birkbeck College London. His writings include papers on industrial location, transport and urban problems.

1

Introduction

Patricia Garside and Michael Hebbert

Regionalism - an eclectic movement

When the Salford conference which gave rise to this book was drawing to its close and the participants were raking again the dying embers of the regional idea, everyone's attention was captured by one elderly man. Seizing the floor after some academic had wittily suggested that the regional idea failed in Britain because it had never been much of an idea, he passionately avowed his belief in regionalism and his life-long involvement in promoting it. To him, the regional movement represented a continuing crusade for more efficient and accountable government. To highlight past lack of success and question the future was defeatism to him. He was genuinely angered by participants' lack of conviction for a cause which, he hoped, would before too long lead to the setting up of a regional assembly for the North West in neighbouring Manchester.

There could have been no clearer demonstration of the power of the regional idea, nor of the difficulty of assessing it. From its origins in Britain at the turn of the century to the present moment, when it happens to be the topic of a lively correspondence in a national daily,[1] regionalism has provided a favourite debating topic for enthusiasts and sceptics, without making any lasting mark on the system. Much of the debate has been internecine. Advocates of regional reform have differed fundamentally among themselves over its purpose and its methods, and the appropriate areas and powers for regional institutions. England has been a unified kingdom for far longer than any other European country. There are no historical precedents since the Anglo-Saxon Heptarchy, which left no trace in the national memory except as revived in the romantic novel. Despite the efforts of geographers regional divisions have seldom appeared as the 'natural' building blocks of a system of government for the U.K. On the one

1

side, the concept of the centralized nation state has held sway and on the other, local democracy has been associated with county, town, and even parish level institutions. Except in the peripheral national communities of Scotland and (to a lesser extent) Wales, the politics of Westminster, and of the locality have proved difficult to supplant, and regions have never realized themselves as 'definite groupings of people with common interests, emotions and thoughts'.[2] Yet as the journalist John Osmond reminds us in *The Divided Kingdom* (1988), the differences in culture, identity, political allegiance, prosperity and power are evident enough as one travels around Britain, for all that they lack a means of expression through the system of government.[3] Regionalism, as an *ism*, tries to express these latent differences. It involves an act of faith - faith in the prime importance of the hidden patterns and a strong element of hope, hope for the institutional change that will unlock and reveal regional identity and give it a political voice and/or administrative form.

Political ideas tend to perish unless they can draw sustenance from practice. The continued vitality of the regional idea, in the absence of durable practical experiments, is mainly due to a succession of writers and thinkers who have presented it freshly and persuasively. (Sceptics will say that it is persuasive precisely because it has never left the drawing board).[4] At the turn of the century, we find H.G. Wells anticipating the development of 'new urban regions' whose elected authorities would deliver modern functions and services efficiently, governing a complete community of the new type, and capable of dealing with absurdities that left his own house on the south coast without electricity.[5] The underlying principles of the nascent regionalist movement were derived from the new sciences of geography and biology as expressed by writers such as C.B. Fawcett and Patrick Geddes,[6] its aesthetic credentials established in the remarkable sequence of holistic regional plans, masterpieces of prose and draughtmanship now much prized by book collectors, prepared by regional planners such as Thomas Adams, Patrick Abercrombie and Raymond Unwin.[7] Fabian intellectuals, especially G.D.H. Cole and William Robson, wrote polemically on the inadequacies of existing structures of local government and the need for replacements on a regional scale.[8] The region's practical value in providing the necessary structure for managing the grave urban problems of slums, overcrowding, congestion and industrial decline was acknowledged by successive government inquiries from the Unhealthy Areas Committee of 1920-1921, to the Special Areas Commission (1935-38), and the Barlow and Scott Commissions (1940-42).[9]

During the 1940s the regional idea was to feature prominently in thinking about reconstruction, the Tennessee Valley Authority offering a much-cited practical demonstration.[10] There was a lull in the 1950s, though as Michael Wise shows below, specialists continued to meet and write. Politically, the Scottish and Welsh nationalist movements helped to keep alive the issue of the territorial concentration of power within the United Kingdom even if it was little more than a glimmering spark.[11] Then, quite suddenly, regionalism was bought back onto the agenda in the 1960s and 1970s by the combination of physical planning concerns (linked to major programmes of urban renewal and roadbuilding) and the electoral advances of Celtic nationalism. A new literature appeared, presenting the regional idea in fresh contemporary terms. Maurice Ash, Peter Self and Peter Hall - amongst others - were persuasive advocates for planning;[12] John Banks, the late J.P. Mackintosh, and (subsequently) Vernon Bogdanor, for regional devolution.[13] Once more the great and the good in government inquiries reflected an altered climate of opinion in a new readiness to consider, and in some cases recommend, regional or provisional solutions. In the present decade we have seen another lull. The time will soon be ripe for a further round of writing and action - and perhaps some practical experiment.

Several good accounts have been written of the history of the regional idea.[14] All emphasize its heterogeneity. We shall be following many disparate strands in this book, arising from the quite distinct preoccupations of individuals ranged along a spectrum from the severely practical (e.g. highway engineers) to outright visionaries and ideologues, with architects, land use planners, local politicians, and administrative reformers along the way. Some have been concerned with regionalism as a general model, others with particular regions. L.J. Sharpe, explaining the emergence and waning of regionalism in the 1960s, notes how the 'movement' (his inverted commas) comprised many separate purposes and objectives.[15] He groups them under three broad concerns:

Regional Planning The regionalization of national economic planning to suit the different economic conditions in each region so as to ensure faster economic growth nationally and reduce the economic gap between the poorer and the more prosperous regions.

Local government modernization: The improvement of land use planning and related functions, and exploiting economies of scale for other services by enlarging local government areas so as to embrace cities and their hinterlands.

Devolution: The decentralization of legislative or executive power from central government to a regional level of elected representative bodies on ethnic, efficiency or democratic grounds'.[16]

Each of these concerns is distinct and has had its own literature and reform agenda. Often they pull in different directions. But one of the enduring characteristics of twentieth century British regionalism, and a source of strength, has been the combination of the three. The strands were woven together in the original manifestoes of C.B. Fawcett and Patrick Geddes, and in the most recent schemes they receive serious political consideration: 'regional government ... can provide an important role for planning at a more local level. By bringing together the various activities of central government and quangoes currently unco-ordinated, it can provide a better focus for concerted action. It will also bring decision centres to the regions - helping to create an element of regional growth which has proved very beneficial in the case of West German cities'.[17] The vision of a regionalized Britain appeals because, like a master key, it promises to serve more than one task. The intermediate tier, midway between Westminster and the town halls, is to provide both a framework for planning and service provision, and a counterweight to central government. Broad though the spectrum of regionalism may be, this vision gives it coherence.

Drawing the map

We suggest that the regionalist tradition in twentieth century Britain has revolved around a relatively stable set of propositions. They can be summarized in Neville Johnson's words:

a) 'The concentration of power at the centre in the British system of government is harmful and should be reversed. Decentralization to regionally-based institutions is the most effective way of bringing about a genuine dispersion of powers.'

b) 'The practices of government in Britain are insufficently democratic, particularly in respect of the extent of participation by citizens.'

c) 'The rate of economic development has been inadequate and it has been unequally distributed over the country as a whole, with some regions notably worse off than others. Decentralization of government would encourage more effective economic development and planning, and indeed is a necessary condition of such progress'.[18]

It is one thing to agree on decentralization as a matter of general principle but quite another to define it on a map. The delimitation of government areas always proves an intractable problem.[19] At the drawing board, experts disagree about criteria to be used for the size and boundaries of units. On the ground, any scheme is liable to offend a public that wants to be on the other side of new lines or to keep its old ones. Scores of proposals for regionalizing Great Britain have been devised over the past century, and the main models have been well compared and contrasted.[20] Interest in this question of area delimitation was especially strong during the early 1940s when - as explained in Chapters 3 to 6 below - thought about reconstruction once hostilities were over tended to run along regional lines. War also encouraged a technocratic optimism in the ability of experts to devise solutions, and a good deal of back-room work was done, despite the constraints of the time, analyzing water-catchments, shopping hinterlands, postage flows, labour markets and traffic movements, to discern areas that met what the distinguished historical geographer Professor Eva Taylor (of Birkbeck College and the Association for Planning and Regional Reconstruction) called the two cardinal principles of *intrinsic wholeness* and *social unity*. She convened a meeting of experts in these matters at the Royal Geographical Society in January 1942. Various slides of regional divisons were shown. In the ensuing discussion, G.D.H. Cole of Nuffield College expostulated 'what are we all talking about?':

'It is easy enough for anybody - I have often done it myself - to make fancy maps of England divided up in various ways and into various regions. I know all the snags, or enough of them, in the attempt to do that; so, I expect, do most of those in this room. But the question, when you start to draw a map of that sort, is what are you drawing it for? I confess I still do not know for what we are at present discussing the suitability of the various areas.'

Cole went on to argue that the word 'region' was being used in two quite different senses, to denote an area of decentralization from Whitehall, and an area for bringing together numbers of local authorities for planning purposes; challenging the central myth of regionalism, he put it that the requirements for top-down and bottom-up regionalism were entirely different. The former needed to be large and few and headed by a first class servant, the latter numerous and small enough to allow direct democratic management. The two types of region should never be confused, although he envisaged that they might eventually be superimposed with several 'local government unified regions' nested within the ten or so 'national decentralized regions'.[21] Writing earlier on this topic in his book, *The Future of Local Government* (1921), Cole had also identified a third basic category of region, the area of operation of an ad hoc single purpose board superimposed on the existing unreformed local government structure. It is not always appreciated that this is what the Fabian Society's Committee on the Reform of Local Government had in mind when, in 1905, it called for the establishment of joint boards for public utilities which would operate on a regional scale - a 'New Heptarchy'.[22] Though G.D.H. Cole generally rejected the excessively functional and administrative ethos of the Fabians, he too supported the creation of functionally-oriented ad hoc boards as an interim step to 'real' regionalism[23] and the idea was used repeatedly to produce units as varied as the Unemployment Assistance Boards of the 1930s, the Area Hospital Boards of the 1940s, and a cartography-defying proliferation of regional boundary systems by quangoes and central government departments in the post-war years.[24]

Most of the regional experiments discussed in the following chapters can be identified with one of these three tasks; rationalizing small-scale local authorities, dividing central administration, and constructing areas for specific, limited purposes such as water supply and transport. Regionalism's vision, the root ideal that makes it an *ism*, is a structure versatile enough to reconcile the three classes of objective. Regionalization in practice has reflected the concrete choices and trade-offs that have to be made between them. Different priorities yield different maps.

For some regionalists, including G.D.H. Cole and W.A. Robson, the starting point was 'the coat of shreds and patches' set up by the Local Government Acts of 1888 and 1894. Like all patterns of local government inherited from the nineteenth century, the structure was highly fragmented in relation to modern work and living. It also had a distinctive problem, not present in France for example, of unevenness of powers. In the mosaic of local government, some urban authorities were subordinate to County Councils whilst others, the County Boroughs, had full top-tier status in their own right. The pattern was equally problematic in a region dominated by a single great metropolitan centre such as London and in areas of dispersed urban settlement, or conurbation, like Lancashire (Figure 1.1). As we shall see below, diagnoses of problems of underbounded urban authorities could point to a number of solutions, depending on the balance struck between respect for existing local government boundaries, and closeness to modern patterns of interaction.[25] The most radical application of the concept of the *city-region*, a unit of government and planning combining central places with their tributary areas regardless of historic boundaries, was made by Derek Senior (free-lance local government specialist and gardening correspondent) in his brilliant Minority Report to the Royal Commission on Local Government in England (1969).[26] Figure 1.2 shows the whole of Britain divided on this basis into more than 40 regions. To meet objections that the solution was more elegant than practicable because of the diversity of central places at the nucleus of each region (ranging from metropolises with many millions of population to middling market towns) various hybrid arrangements could be devised that provided for the special problems of the larger metropolitan areas while retaining the general principle of reuniting cities with their regions.[27]

A regionalism which starts from the other end, with the aim of devising a suitable set of receptacles for the decentralization of central government will focus on a few, substantial provincial capitals. C.B. Fawcett's was the classic division on these lines and it is worthwhile setting out the principles he followed in *Provinces of England - A Study of Some Geographical Aspects of Devolution* (1919) as well as the map he arrived at (Figure 1.3):

1. The provincial boundaries should be so chosen as to interfere as little as possible with the ordinary movements and activities of the people.
2. There should be in each province a definite capital, which should be the real focus of its regional life. This implies further that the area and communications of the province should be such that the capital is accessible from every part of it.
3. The least of the provinces should contain a population sufficiently numerous to justify self-government.
4. No one province should be so populous as to be able to dominate the federation.
5. The provincial boundaries should be drawn near watersheds rather than across valleys, and very rarely along streams.
6. The grouping of areas must pay regard to local patriotism and to tradition.[28]

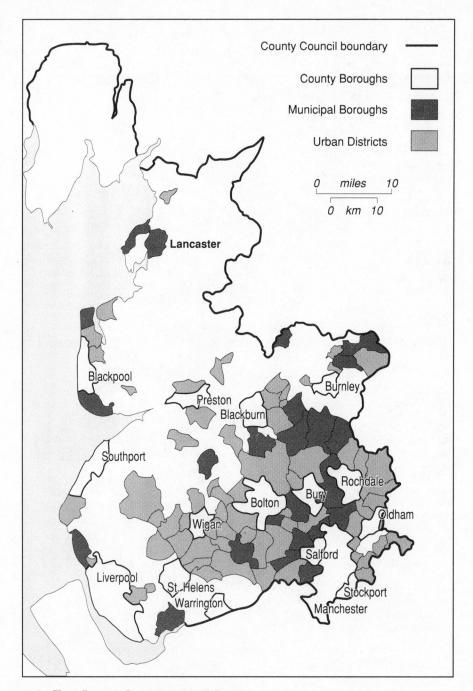

County Council boundary

County Boroughs

Municipal Boroughs

Urban Districts

0   miles   10

0   km   10

Lancaster

Blackpool

Burnley

Preston

Blackburn

Southport

Rochdale

Bolton

Bury

Oldham

Wigan

Salford

Liverpool

St. Helens

Stockport

Warrington

Manchester

1.1 The Local Government Mosaic
Lancashire County Council prior to reorganization in 1973

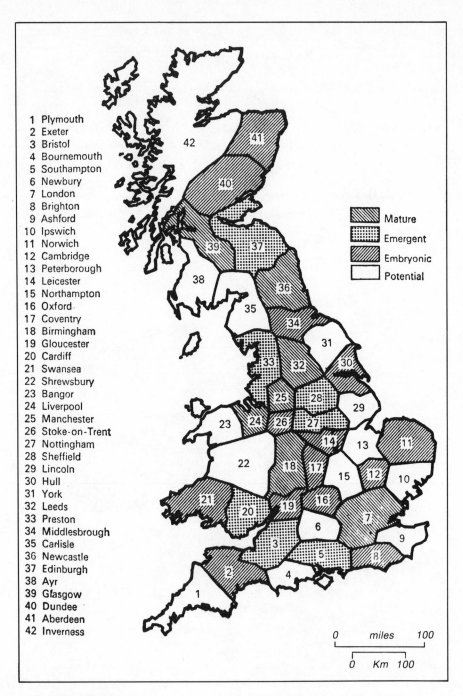

1   Plymouth
2   Exeter
3   Bristol
4   Bournemouth
5   Southampton
6   Newbury
7   London
8   Brighton
9   Ashford
10   Ipswich
11   Norwich
12   Cambridge
13   Peterborough
14   Leicester
15   Northampton
16   Oxford
17   Coventry
18   Birmingham
19   Gloucester
20   Cardiff
21   Swansea
22   Shrewsbury
23   Bangor
24   Liverpool
25   Manchester
26   Stoke-on-Trent
27   Nottingham
28   Sheffield
29   Lincoln
30   Hull
31   York
32   Leeds
33   Preston
34   Middlesbrough
35   Carlisle
36   Newcastle
37   Edinburgh
38   Ayr
39   Glasgow
40   Dundee
41   Aberdeen
42   Inverness

Mature
Emergent
Embryonic
Potential

0   miles   100

0   Km   100

1.2 City Regions
Derek Senior's scheme for the reorganization of local government

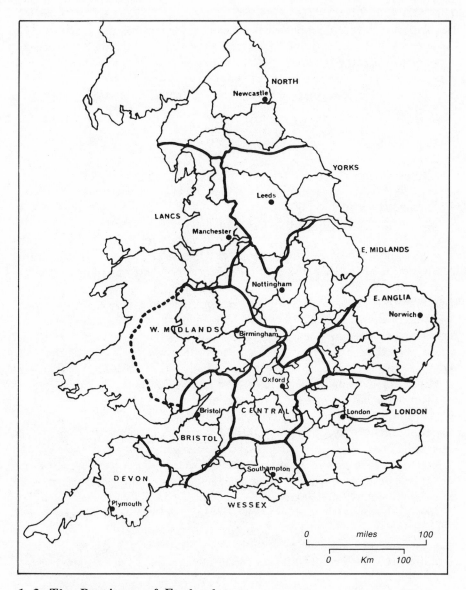

1.3 The Provinces of England

Scheme of division proposed by C.B. Fawcett in the Association for Planning and Regional Reconstruction Broadsheet 'Regional Boundaries of England and Wales', November 1942

Fawcett's scheme broadly resembles the set of standard regions used by Government today, though slightly more elaborate because of its inclusions of a Central Province (based on Oxford), and a Province of Wessex (with its capital at Southampton) as well as its subdivision of the South West into 'Bristol Province' and 'Devon'. Like Government, and almost all schemes for provincial devolution, it considers Scotland and Wales to be single units.

The treatment of the Celtic nations marks the fullest difference between the city-region and large-province approaches to regionalism. In their treatment of London, on the other hand, the two can converge completely. The capital's peculiar role in regionalism deserves further consideration.

The problem of London

As Britain's largest and most complex city, the national capital and world metropolis, London has proved a match for even the most committed reformers. In the nineteenth century, ignored by the 1835 Municipal Corporations Act, it effectively remained in the hands of the City Corporation, the J.P.'s, the vestries and the 300 or so ad hoc boards and trusts with responsibility in specific areas for paving, lighting and maintaining the peace. Even after the Metropolitan Local Management Act of 1855, the vestries remained the centre of gravity of London government, and it was they who were responsible for electing the newly created Metropolitan Board of Works. When reform finally came in 1888, the capital was treated almost as an afterthought, and Britain's most populous and extensive urban area received the status not of a city, but of a county. Furthermore, it was again ignored in 1894 when second-tier authorities were created for all the other counties, and the metropolitan borough councils were established separately in the London Government Act of 1899. The irony of London's position as capital of the Empire, home of the mother of Parliaments and at the same time the most chaotically governed city in Britain, could not be overlooked. Nevertheless for the next half century, the prospect of reforming London government was repeatedly lost in local, regional and national conflict and rivalry.[29]

What was clear was that the problem of governing London's sprawling and heterogeneous area would not resolve itself - the necessary social and political integration and identify singularly failed to emerge. Since London would not define itself for the purposes of government, subjective construction was necessary and here regional reformers clearly had a critical role to play. With a population several times greater than the other conurbations, and reaching almost 9 million in 1939, the London conurbation fitted ambiguously into any regional structure, whether based on city-regions, conurbations/counties or provinces. It presented particular problems of definition, size and dominance. C.B. Fawcett, for example, initially proposed a narrowly circumscribed province for London, with a separate region to the south and east centred (somewhat quaintly) on Brighton.[30] To the north, the proposed East Anglian region initially included

Cambridge. Fawcett revised these boundaries before the publication of his book in 1919 expanding the London region south to the Channel coast, and north into Cambridgeshire, to leave Norwich as the focal point of a truncated East Anglian province. Even so, he remained unhappy because the revised boundaries gave London fully 25% of the total population. In the Preface to his book, Fawcett explained that his principles delimited the provinces with varying degrees of clarity. He organized his discussion, therefore, so that 'the most distinct natural units i.e. those which are more clearly marked off by natural features and population distributions have been considered first and the less definite ones last'.[31] Not surprisingly, this placed the North first, and London eleventh (out of 12), the last position being reserved for 'central England'. The problem of London continued to dog the small band of inter-war British geographers in their efforts to establish the relevance and influence of their discipline through regionalization exercises.[32]

If the size and status of London hindered reform of intermediate-level government in Britain, a consequence was to reinforce its significance as the hub of national economic, cultural and political life and so enhance the prevailing centrism of the state. Too much of the history of twentieth century Britain can be written in terms of the capital's continuing, progressive domination of all aspects of the national life.[33] Economic historians such as Lee and Rubinstein have shown the concentration of personal wealth in London even in the heyday of provincial industrial prosperity in the mid nineteenth century.[34] Victorian London's separate, self-generating and highly successful economy, based on consumer oriented industries such as paper, printing, publishing, clothing and furniture and on 'high-tech' instrument and electrical engineering industries, was both cause and product of a large affluent society enjoying high levels of conspicuous consumption and generating a wide range of labour intensive service jobs. By 1900, London was well on the way to becoming the world's first large-scale consumer society.

The success of the metropolis in generating wealth and in providing the financial, legal and other services required by the owners of wealth reinforced its competitive advantage over provincial centres, which in turn reinforced the general trends to concentration within the economy.[35] The trends run parallel in banking and financial services, in manufacturing and in retailing. However it is measured (and there is debate about the appropriate measures) ownership has been concentrated in fewer hands, principally by mergers and absorption of smaller enterprises into large corporations, facilitated by a permissive tradition of regulation. The effect has been a strong flow of business control from the regions to the capital. Hannah and Kay comment:

'In Britain the danger of overcentralization is particularly clear. Virtually all leading firms, many of which once had head offices in provincial cities, have moved them to London. In the United States, by contrast, only a proportion of corporations have head offices in New York: other are found in California, the Midwest, and throughout the north-eastern states.... Highly centralized control of a society's resources has had formidable implications for the quality of political and social life in Britain'.[36]

The same story of metropolitan domination is true of political life in twentieth century Britain. To a degree unique in Western democracies, British political life has been channelled through monolithic nationally organized parties with a strong statist bias. 'Unionism' - a commitment to the hegemony of Westminster - is written into the basic constitution of the Conservative Party. As early as the 1920s the Labour Party had also aligned itself squarely with centralism, shaking off earlier syndicalist and anti-statist leanings.[37] Party behaviour at both ends of the ideological spectrum, reflecting the rules of political life laid down by the unwritten constitution, has accorded a low priority to territorial issues - to the politics of place.[38] And that in turn has allowed the forces of economic concentration a freer rein than elsewhere. Whereas in the United States, state governments have actively used anti-trust legislation to curb concentrations of corporate power damaging to their economies, British mergers policy gives little or no weight to the territorial effects of concentration.[39]

Metropolitan dominance has likewise been a primary factor in the slow, painful decline of local government in Britain. At the turn of the century, British provincial cities led the world in public service provision and municipal enterprise, setting a high standard for local government as a whole.[40] Only a part of the blame for its current predicaments can be attributed to secular trends in economic geography that have leached away population and employment from the older, larger urban authorities, traditional flagships of the local government system.[40] More important have been the three centralizing factors analysed by Diane Dawson and Alan Alexander in their contributions to *Half a Century of Municipal Decline 1935-1985*; the pressure on local government, from both Labour and Conservative governments, to implement national policies of all kinds, especially macroeconomic; the pressure, part bureaucratic and part political, for standardization and uniformity in local service provision; and, since 1980, the distinctively Thatcherist emphasis on the paramountcy of national over local goals in a unitary state.[41] Over the long perspective of the century British local government has been stripped of functions, denied (especially since 1965) any voice in schemes for its reorganization or dismemberment, and subjected to progressively harsher financial controls culminating in the poll tax and business rate legislation which leave only a shred of fiscal autonomy at the local level.

We have mentioned the trends of political, economic and fiscal centralization. The catalogue can be continued through other spheres of activity - education, music, publishing, the arts, advertising, commercial services, finance:

'Not only does London and the South-East dominate every sector of national life outside agriculture and certain extractive industries, it is also the home of practically every important institution, public or private, and if the whole institution is not located there its headquarters will almost certainly have to be. Even those in the upper reaches of the status system who do not live in the South-East were mainly educated there and in many senses feel themselves to be part of it. Their 'local' paper is *The Times*, they speak with a southern English accent and many of their values are rooted in the peculiar bogus-rural, rentier society of the Home Counties'.[42]

Perceptions of the degree of centralization in a society are based on a complicated mixture of factors in which the physical growth of the metropolis has generally played an important part. For William Cobbett in 1820s, London's sheer scale and appetite for building land betrayed the *all-devouring Wen's* invisible parasitism through the mechanism of the National Debt, redistributing tax-revenues to metropolitan fund-holders at the expense of farmers, small-businessmen and the poor.[43] The great spreading blot of the built-up area, and a rising population graph, played an equally important part in the anti-metropolitan polemic of Frederic Osborn and the Town and Country Planning Association, a hundred years later, and in Jean-François Gravier's famous and influential post-war denunciation of centralization in France, *Paris et le desert français* (1947).[44] With its poisonous smogs, water stoppages and traffic jams, Mexico City - still spreading its built-up area and enlarging its population despite the earthquake of 1985 - directly expresses the maldistribution of wealth and power in Mexican society today.

Because post-war London has had a steadily declining population and been physically curbed by a green belt to more or less its 1939 boundaries, the British metropolis has not offered such a tangible symbol of centralization as it once did. The innocuous stability of a capital city with a falling population and no new building (or hardly any) around its edge for fifty years has perhaps served to conceal the extent of the continuing process of concentration in British society. The tremendous growth that has occurred in the South-East has been artfully distributed around the region and absorbed into the predominately green setting of the Home Counties. A considerable feat of regional planning has helped to keep regionalist dissatisfaction in check.

That equilibrium, if such it was, has been dislodged in the 1980s. It seems likely, for reasons explored in the final chapter of this book, that the geographical divisions and inequalities of Britain will tend to become more pressing and politically salient during the closing decade of the century. There will be debate about the strategy for renewal - whether through electoral reform or through new, more polycentric structures of government. Advocates of regionalism have a highly attractive vision to offer of Britain in the year 2000 - geographically decentralized, economically competitive, politically pluralist, with a refreshed democratic life that draws upon the country's diverse provincial and national identities. In most scenarios, Scottish nationalism is identified as the redeeming force that, by domino effect, will bring devolution first to Wales and them to English regions - so achieving the quasi-federal solution of 'Home Rule All

Round' which - as explained in the next chapter - was first canvassed a century ago as a solution to the Irish question.

Critics argue that Scottish and Welsh nationhood is belittled by schemes for English regional government. The goal of decentralization can be won more directly through electoral reform and a revival of existing local authorities. They argue that the government which follows Mrs. Thatcher will have work enough on its hands without embarking on complicated territorial reorganizations that have no basis in popular feeling. The historical record of British regionalism provides some important points of reference for this debate. We hope our book will be found timely.

The contents summarized

It is not the purpose of this book to provide a general history of regionalism, and others have already written of the interplay between individuals, organizations and the wider policy. Rather, what follows are a series of essays exploring aspects of the fortunes of British regionalism in the present century.

Michael Burgess opens by questioning the characterization of the United Kingdom as a unitary state. He argues that its political tradition has at times involved a vigorous and explicit federalism. Burgess traces the historical evolution of the federal idea through Lord Rosebery, Joseph Chamberlain, Lord Milner, Austen Chamberlain and (unexpectedly) Winston Churchill, showing its appeal as a means of accommodating two of the dominant concerns of late nineteenth and early twentieth century English politicians, the Empire and Ireland. Though his narrative ends with Lloyd George shrinking back from practical federalism at the end of the First World War, he points to the continuing strand which was to lead, through the revived Federal Union movement in the late thirties, to Gaspar Altieri who read and was inspired by its literature whilst imprisoned by Mussolini and went on to translate Anglo-Saxon precept into a practical federalist militancy with ultimate European integration as its aim.

British regionalists have always found it easier to agree on the general need for reform than to specify the shape and functions of their preferred units. Jonathan Owen traces the failure of successive initiatives to tackle the multiplicity of small local authorities - especially the *Royal Commission on Local Government in the Tyneside Area* (1937), and the National Association of Local Government Officers' *Reconstruction Committee on the Reform of Local Government Structure* (1943). Regionalism, he concludes, was more of an intellectual reflex to the problems of the 1888 structure, than a politically coherent substitute for it.

Perhaps the people best able to transcend the 1888 structure were the drawing board professionals, architects and engineers, commissioned as consultants to prepare regional advisory plans for groups of small local authorities struggling to get a purchase on the modern, low-density urbanization straggling across the patchwork quilts of their areas. David Massey, in Chapter 4, shows how these planning regionalists, or rather regional planners, tackled their task, highlighting both their intellectual debt to the work of Patrick Geddes (with its emphasis on the importance of preliminary regional survey to give empirical and policy substance to cross-boundary planning efforts) and the sheer elegance and aplomb of their plans. Attention is paid to the role of individuals such as Sir George Pepler, at the Ministry of Health and Sir Patrick Abercrombie, doyen of the consultants, in the highly successful promotion of regional planning in this period.

The chapter shows the proliferation of plans from 14 in 1923 to 105 in 1931, when they covered almost all parts of Britain subject to urban development pressure. Local governments' acceptance of regional *planning* contrasts with the resistance to *reform* described in the previous chapter. Advisory regional plans were acceptable precisely because they did not challenge the fragmented status quo. When presented, as they sometimes were, in leather bindings with gold tooling on the spines, they rather conferred a touch of dignity and credibility upon it. They demonstrated the potential for joint action within existing structures, albeit on a limited geographical scale ('regions' generally meant parts of counties) and for a limited and uncontroversial policy purpose.

Dennis Hardy next traces the contribution of one London-based reform group, the Garden Cities and Town Planning Association, later renamed the Town and Country Planning Association, towards relatively stronger regional planning of post-war years, manifested especially in strictly enforced green belts around urban areas and a public programme of new town construction. From single-minded late nineteenth century beginnings as an idealistic experiment in the construction of an alternative urban community, the Association developed into a modern-style pressure group, lobbying government and business to promote its concept of a regional balance between town and country. Though such thinking indisputably became, and still to some extent remains, a government orthodoxy in Britain, Hardy (the official historian of the TCPA) is guarded in alloting credit for the policy shift.

Patricia Garside's focus in Chapter 6 is on the impact of the regional idea on town planning and municipal reform in London. Garside recounts how the broad regional planning philosophy of consultants such as Patrick Abercrombie was rebuffed by London County Council politicians and officers in favour of tried and tested approaches to zoning and slum clearance. Regional planning theory sought bold schemes of population redistribution across the region regardless of anachronistic local authority boundaries; municipal practice, scrupulously boundary-respecting, rather took the form of limited and localized interventions, chiefly via slum clearance and housing projects, in areas known to be politically amenable. She analyses the interaction of these two antagonistic conceptions of policy. Regionalism initially 'failed' in the early 1940s in the sense that Sir Patrick Abercrombie's grand plan was used cynically but successfully by the LCC leadership as a lever with which to win (in the 1944 'Blitz and Blight Act') stronger powers for its own more limited ends. Regionalism appeared to have a last laugh when the incoming Labour government of 1944 brought to the Ministry a former LCC member, Lewis Silkin, who had been inspired by the Abercrombie plan and appalled at the way in which it had been subverted for narrow municipal ends. Silkin's planning legislation, however, was not based on any reform of local authority areas. His New Town Commissions were a separate creation of central government which in practice became a device for postponing reform because they were able to achieve redistribution of population and industry *without* changing the status quo.

Hopes that post-war reconstruction would usher in radical regional reforms were soon disappointed. Bevan chose never to put it to Cabinet his scheme to replace existing local government units with 240 all-purpose authorities. Ten years later, in 1958, a Conservative government again considered and ruled out wholesale reorganization of the structure of local government. Against this background of immobilism, the regional idea continued to retain its interest for a wide range of specialists who were eventually to converge on the Regional Studies Association, founded in 1965. Michael Wise traces back this body's origins to the Association for Planning and Regional Reconstruction (APRR), set up during the Second World War by research-minded architects to train manpower for reconstruction according to the philosophies of Patrick Geddes and Lewis Mumford. The APRR connection is shown to lead, a decade later, to the seminal First International Conference on Regional Planning and Development held at Bedford College, London, in September 1955 with participants from over 40 countries. That led in turn to the founding and work of the International Centre for Regional Planning and Development, based in Brussels.

Wise explains how the English and Scottish branches of the Brussels organization broke away to found their own Regional Studies Association, which flourishes to this day. With the privileged insight of a participant historian, he reveals that in 1962-64 they had contemplated merger with, amongst other organizations, the Town and Country Planning Association, the International Federation of Housing and Town Planning, and America's Regional Science Association, but decided for independence so as to keep both a specifically regional focus and the right (denied to Regional Science Association branches) to comment on policy and influence legislation.

Diana Pearce's chapter offers an insider's view of one of the nine Regional Economic Planning Councils established in 1965 to participate in a Labour government's National Plan and abolished soon after Mrs. Thatcher's first election victory in 1979. The composition of the Council, its working methods, its relationships with other agencies (those with local authorities were generally strained), and its shifting policy concerns are analysed in turn. It was, in the words of its Chairman Sir Bernard Cotton 'the best club in Yorkshire', offering a meeting ground to many otherwise segregated interests; but, Pearce concludes, mere policy deliberation without either powers or resources proved in the long run an insufficient basis on which to sustain a regional body.

Urlan Wannop in Chapter 9 tells the story of the one region where a synoptic planning approach in the 1940s - The Geddesian Clyde Valley Plan - matured, via local government reorganization in the 1970s into an established and powerful regional authority. For the achieved progress of the regional idea, which encountered in Glasgow Corporation a civic enemy every inch as dogged as the London County Council, Wannop gives particular praise to Sir Robert Grieve, 'by far the most distinguished regionalist in Britain.' With Jean Mann, Sir William White, and other Glasgow administrators and politicians, Grieve is shown to have bridged that gap between regionalism and municipalism discerned by other contributors.

In Chapter 10, Professor Michael Keating reviews the proposals for regional government variously advanced in the context of constitutional reform of the United Kingdom (the Kilbrandon Commission) and local government reorganization (the Redcliffe-Maude Commission). Finally, Michael Hebbert sets British regionalism into a European context. He reviews the trend of decentralization amongst the United Kingdom's southern neighbours, highlighting the development of regional autonomy in Italy, Belgium, France and Spain, and offers a summary analysis of the failure of constitutional reform in Britain to follow a similar course during the 1970s. From an analysis of the interaction of European integration with regional decentralization it is suggested that the United Kingdom, having missed Europe's decentralist tide in the last decade, might find a less hospitable environment for regional experiment in the next.

Notes

1. *The Independent*, following Roy Hattersley's article 'Devolution to defend the Nation against elective Dictatorship', Dec. 30th, 1988.
2. Fawcett, C.B. (1922) British Conurbations in 1921. *Sociological Review* 14(2), 12.
3. Osmond, J. (1988) *The Divided Kingdom*, London: Constable.
4. 'The advocates of regional government are utopians. They plan decentralization to bodies that do not now exist and thus they can impute to regional governments virtues that may not be present in organizations when they are operational.' Jones G. and Stewart J. (1983) *The Case for Local Government*, London: George Allen & Unwin, p.86.
5. Wells, H.G. (1902) *Anticipations*. Chapman and Hall.
   Wells, H.G. (1906) The Question of Scientific Administrative Areas in *Mankind in the Making*. London: Chapman and Hall, p.219.
6. Fawcett, C.B. (1919) *The Provinces of England* (new revised edition (1961): Hutchinson).
   Geddes, P. (1915) *Cities in Evolution*. London: Williams and Norgate.
7. See Chapter 4 below, also Cherry, G. (ed.) (1981) *Pioneers in British Town Planning*, London: Architectural Press and Cherry, G. (1988) *Cities and Plans*, London: Edward Arnold.
8. Cole, G.D.H. (1920) *Social Theory* (1921). *Guild Socialism Reinstated* (1921). *The Future of Local Government* (1921). London: Cassell and Co.; Robson, W.A. (1930) *Government and Misgovernment of London*, London: Allen & Unwin (1942), *The Development of Local Government*. London: Williams and Norgate.
9. Ministry of Health (1920-21) Committee to Consider and Advise on the Principles to be Followed in Dealing with Unhealthy Areas. Interim, Second and Final *Reports*. HMSO.

Commission for Special Areas in England and Wales (1935-38) *Reports*. Cmnd 4957, 5090, 5303, 5595, 5896 HMSO. Royal Commission on the Distribution of the Industrial Population (1940). *Report* Cmnd 6153: Ministry of Works and Planning (1942). Committee on Land Utilization in Rural Areas (*Report* Cmnd 6378 HMSO).

10. Gutkind, E.A. (1943) *Creative Demobilization*, London: Kegan Paul, Vol. I, pp.226-238; Huxley, J. (1943) *TVA Adventure in Planning*, London: Archtectural Press.

11. Evans, G., Donaldson A. and Banks, J. et.al. (1956) *Our Three Nations*, Cardiff, Glasgow, London: Plaid Cymru, SNP and Common Wealth.

12. Ash, M. (1962) *The Human Cloud*, London: Town and Country Planning Association.
    Self, P. (1957) *Cities in Flood*, London: Faber and Faber
    Hall, P. (1963) *London 2000*, London: Faber and Faber.

13. Banks, J. (1971) *Federal Britain? The Case for Regionalism*, London: Harrap.
    Mackintosh, J.P. (1968) *The Devolution of Power - Local Democracy, Regionalism and Nationalism*, London: Charles Knight.
    Bogdanor, V. (1979) *Devolution*, Oxford: University Press.

14. Especially useful accounts are Bennett, R.J. (1985) Regional Movements in Britain: a review of aims and status *Government and Policy* III, pp.75-96; Keating, M. (1982) *The Debate on Regional Reform* in Hogwood, B.W. and Keating, M. (eds.) *Regional Government in England.*. Oxford: Clarendon Press pp.235-254, and the twin volumes by Brian Smith *Regionalism in England, Regional Institutions - A Guide* (1964) and *Regionalism in England 2 Its Nature and Purpose 1905-1965* (1965) London: Acton Society Trust. See also Thornhill, W. (ed.) (1972) *The Case for Regional Reform*. London: Nelson; Dickinson, R. (1964) *City and Region*, London: Routledge and Kegan Paul, and Banks J. *Federal Britain?*

15. Sharpe, L.J. (1982) 'Regional Government in Britain - the furtive tier? in Mény, Y. *Dix Ans du Régionalisation en Europe*, Paris: Cujas, pp.75-100.

16. p.77 cf. Smith (1965) Vol. 2, pp.25-40, 'The Aims of Regionalism'.

17. Richard Caborn M.P. (1988) Urban and Regional Policy - A National Strategy (unpublished submission to Labour Party Policy Review) p.12.

18. Johnson, N. (1983) Decentralization in Britain: a critique of the case in the light of West German experience, *Government and Policy*, 1 (1), p.6.

19. See Smith, B.C. (1985) *Decentralization*, London: George Allen & Unwin, Chapter 4.

20. In Banks *Federal Britain*, Dickinson *City and Region*, Mackintosh *Devolution*, Smith *Regionalism in England*.

21. 'Discussion on the Geographical Aspects of Regional Planning' *Geographical Journal* (1942), Vol. XCIX, pp.61-79.

22. Sanders, W.S. (1905) *Municipalization by Provinces* (Report of the Society's Committee on the Reform of Local Government) Fabian Tract No. 125, London: The Fabian Society. The Fabian view was that areas should be defined flexibly in relation to the function being served. However: 'It may be that in connection with the water supply, or with the supply of electricity, it will be found that the best administrative areas will be created by following the Hegelian historical spiral until we arrive at a stage with regard to the division of the country vertically above the period of the Saxon Heptarchy, and make a halt there.'

23. Cole, *Future of Local Government*. Chapter XIV discusses the circumstances in which ad hoc authorities may be preferable to general 'omnibus' authorities.

24. Hogwood, B. and Lindley, P. (1980) *Which English Regions? An Analysis of Regional Boundaries used by Government*, Strathclyde: Centre for Public Policy.

25. The issues received full treatment in Cole, G.D.H. (1947) *Local and Regional Government*, London: Cassell and Dickinson, R.E. (1947) *City Region and Regionalism*, London: Routledge and Kegan Paul.

26. Cmnd 4040-1.

27. These alternatives are discussed in Mackintosh, J.P. (1968) *The Devolution of Power: Local Democracy, Regionalism and Nationalism*, Penguin Special, Chapters 3 and 4.

28. Fawcett, *Provinces of England*, p.150.

29. The reform of London government has been explored by Young, K. and Garside, P.L. (1982) *Metropolitan London: Politics and Urban Change 1837-1981*. Edward Arnold, and for a more limited period by Davis, J. (1988) *Reforming London: The London Government Problem*. Oxford: Clarendon Press.

30. Fawcett, C.B. (1971) 'Natural Divisions of England', *Geographical Journal* XLIX 124-141.

31. Fawcett, *Provinces of England*, p.19..

32. The limited status and influence of geographers between the wars is described in Steel, R.W. (ed.) (1987) *British Geography 1918-1945*. Cambridge University Press, and this general picture is discussed with particular reference to London in Garside, P.L. 'Metropolitan Machine: Images of London Life and Organization'. Paper presented to German Historical Institute Conference. *Spell of the Metropolis*. Berlin: pp.5-7, May 1988.

33. The expansion and influence of the metropolis is the subject of Garside, P.L. 'London and the Home Counties' in Thompson, F.M.L. (ed.) *New Social History of Britain*. Cambridge University Press (forthcoming).

34. Lee, C.H. (1981) Regional Growth and Structural Change in Victorian Britain *Economic History Review* 34, pp.438-452.
   Rubinstein, W.D. (1977) The Victorian Middle Classes: Wealth, Occupation and Geography *Economic History Review* 30, pp.602-23.

35. Pollard, S. (1983) *Development of the British Economy* 1914-1980. London: Edward Arnold, pp.301-314.

36. Hannah, L. and Kay, J.A. (1977) *Concentration in Modern Industry* , p.40.

37. Jones, B. and Keating, M. (1982) *The British Labour Party - The Territorial Dimension in U.K. Politics*. London: Macmillan, pp.177-201.

38. Johnson, N. (1977) *In Search of the Constitution*. Oxford: Pergamon, pp.108-130.

39. The position is complex: see Ashcroft, B.K. and Lover, J.H. (1988) The Regional Interest in U.K. Mergers Policy. *Regional Studies*, 22, 4, pp.342-344.

40. The authors of the otherwise useful collection *Regional Cities in the U.K. 1890-1980* (edited by George Gordon (1986) London: Harper & Row) are perhaps too ready to view urban decline understandingly as a consequence of inexorable geographical trends.

41. Diane Dawson, 'Economic Change and the Changing Role of Local Government', pp.26-49, and Alan Alexander, 'Structure, Centralization and the Position of Local Government', pp.50-76, in Loughlin, M. Gelfand, D. and Young, K. (eds.) (1985) *Half a Century of Municipal Decline* 1935-85. London: George Allen & Unwin.

42. Sharpe, L.J. cited by John Osmond (1988) *The Divided Kingdom*, London: Constable p.159. Osmond's discussion of the psychic ascendancy of London and the Home Counties, and its basis in class structure, is excellent: see Ch. 6 'Identity Ascendant'.

43. See Cobbett, W. (1912 edn) *Rural Rides*, London: Everyman, December 4th 1821, January 8th 1822 and *passim*.

44. For Osborn see Dennis Hardy's chapter below, and Hebbert M. (1981) 'Frederic Osborn 1885-1978' in Cherry, G.E. *Pioneers in British Planning*, London: Architectural Press Ch. 8; Gravier, J.-F. (1958) *Paris et le desert français*, Paris: Flammarian.

2

The Roots of British Federalism

Michael Burgess

Introduction: Terminological Pitfalls

The title of this chapter seems self-explanatory. I intend to underline both the progress and the significance of the federal idea in British political development during the last century by focussing upon two interrelated problems to which federation appeared intermittently as the most appropriate solution. But this clear purpose is deceptively difficult. It is bedevilled particularly by the fact that the two dominant issues of peacetime domestic British government and politics, namely the Irish problem and the future of the Empire, changed dramatically both in appearance and reality in the period 1870-1921. As their nature and meaning altered so too did the terms used to describe them. Though the ratification of the Anglo-Irish Treaty in 1921 and the formal shift from Empire to Commonwealth occasioned by the Statute of Westminster in 1931 put the federal idea into temporary abeyance, the roots had been laid of a federalist tradition that continues to offer relevant political insights, not least for the solution of the late twentieth century Irish question and for the construction of Europe after 1992.

The question of terminological meaning and accuracy, however, further complicates our task when we focus more sharply upon the United Kingdom. Our country is of course not a federal system, but its opposite, a unitary state. Yet how far does the term 'unitary' state have a precise meaning during this period? To what extent was the constitutional theory of the unitary state outstripped by the haphazard practice of government? A political and conceptual lexicon might be appropriate here. Indeed the relationship between federalism and regionalism is a further case in point. This chapter looks primarily at British federalism but it is clear that the idea of regional devolution - of elected regional assemblies and governments - although both conceptually and empirically distinct from the federal ideal is nonetheless related to it in a broad sense. The application of the federal principle to the United Kingdom would fundamentally reconstruct the state along the lines of territorial power-sharing while regionalism would involve some measure of self-government within the territorial sub-divisions of the national state. Both tackle the territorial dispersion of power and both may incorporate a wide range of types of power distribution. Like federalism, regionalism has many faces and cannot be reduced to a single simple meaning. The difficulties alluded to above may be conveniently summarized for our purposes in three separate but intimately connected areas: the changing nature and meaning of the state; the evolving understanding of the character of the Union; and the consequent use of the term 'unitary'. It is important to clarify these terms because in this chapter image, perception and reality mingle in a highly confused and confusing manner. But a brief examination of these terminological difficulties is also crucial if we are to demonstrate precisely how and why federal ideas are more indigenous to British political culture than conventional wisdom would have us believe.

I shall look more closely at what I loosely refer to as 'the federal idea' a little later in this discussion. In order for this to make sense it is necessary first to clear the conceptual ground of some old unchallenged assumptions about the nature of what constitutes Great Britain and what is the United Kingdom. Let us briefly examine these three aspects of our preliminary analysis outlined above with this particular purpose in mind.

In Search of the State

During the last decade a burgeoning academic literature has sought to illuminate and underline the complex and subtle processes by which England's constitutional and political authority was gradually extended formally to incorporate Wales, Scotland and Ireland in the United Kingdom.[1] This literature has, *inter alia*, clarified several previously obscure issues surrounding the evolution of the United Kingdom and confirmed, via the reexamination of old received assumptions, its accidental and contingent character. One important consequence of this general conclusion has been the necessary and penetrating reappraisal of traditional political concepts and terminology applicable to the United Kingdom of Great Britain and Northern Ireland. Many myths have been dispelled about its presumed political homogeneity and the nature of its political integration, and it is now openly acknowledged that the question of the state is neither as simple nor as straightforward as we might previously have been led to expect.

The English national characteristic of skirting around awkward topics rather than confronting them, is well displayed by the studied avoidance of the question of the state.[2] Richard Rose has commented on this intellectual puzzle that constitutes the United Kingdom:

'In international law the United Kingdom is a state, that is, a Kingdom that claims sovereign authority within given territorial boundaries ... But the *state* is rarely used to describe the contemporary United Kingdom ... To describe the United Kingdom as a state is to import a continental European term to political discourse in Britain. The idea of the state as a thing in itself ... is alien to British political thinking'.[3]

The conundrum is only partly resolved by Rose when he describes the United Kingdom as a 'problematic state'. The unusual case of the United Kingdom has been tackled, as regards Northern Ireland, by denying the integrity of the United Kingdom rather that by its assertion, as would be anticipated in most contemporary states. Instead distance has been imposed by Westminster to deflect the challenge of Northern Ireland.[4]

But this underlying notion of 'statelessness', of being without an idea of the state, to which Rose refers, actually antedates the Anglo-Irish Treaty of 1921. It precedes the formal creation of the United Kingdom in 1801. As our focus upon the next section will demonstrate, this received sense of being unaware of the state is also indissolubly linked to the peculiar push and pull of incomplete political integration in Great Britain spanning several centuries before the modern partition of Ireland. Rose himself has acknowledged that the United Kingdom was not inevitable: it is 'the product of a multiplicity of historical events.' It is certainly not the product of a 'logical plan'.[5] What, then, does this suggest about the lack of perception of the United Kingdom state?

If Barker is correct (as I think he is) to argue that a description of the state is primarily about its *historical capacity* [6] then consideration of England's agonising journey along the road towards Union furnishes revealing evidence of the reluctance (some might say failure) of the state to fulfill its basic objectives of peace, order and security via formal constitutional mechanisms. In other words, and somewhat paradoxically, the historical incapacity of the English state to achieve its fundamental aims by *informal* means compelled it to implement *formal* Union. This paradox, then, suggests either that we should question the historical capacity of the English state, its assertive strength, or that its relatively passive role has been part of a deliberate accommodationist political strategy designed to achieve voluntary compliance. Let us probe a little further.

Territorial Management and Modernization: An Open Outcome

Jim Bulpitt's somewhat self-effacing 'preliminary interpretation' of the history of territorial politics in the United Kingdom also offers an implicit explanation for English obliviousness to the nature of the state.[7] Bulpitt's thesis posits an élite operational code of territorial management designed to secure the goals of the authorities in London by a tacit system of indirect rule offering considerable autonomy to local élites. It buttresses the view that the English state deliberately chose a backseat when and where possible. Put simply, it preferred a maximum of advantage with a minimum of commitment. The framework of a set of imperial-type relations between England and the periphery which Bulpitt utilizes serves to pose the key question: when should the state resort to outright annexation or incorporation? And the answer is, only reluctantly and as a last resort. Informal control was a symbol of strength and inner confidence; formal control was indicative of a perceived decline arising out of a growing inability to handle difficulties both at home and abroad.[8]

If this summary of territorial management and modernization is correct it helps us to understand that peculiar sense of being without an idea of the state and it also underlines another characteristic of the 'unplanned' Union, namely the variety of possible outcomes. Given that the idea of an intrusive, meddling and ubiquitous state was never purposely entertained, a number of alternative state scenarios merit legitimate consideration. Bulpitt's thesis serves to emphasize the flexible, accommodative nature of the state which adjusted the practice of territorial politics to achieve political settlements sufficiently attractive to rival protagonists to be lasting. Without wishing to enter the main debate about the nature of territorial politics in the overall evolution of the United Kingdom there are two observations to be made regarding the implications for the federal idea. First, the bargaining character of the state implicitly accepted 'an operational federalism' between centre and periphery 'supposedly absent from English constitutional development'.[9] Territorial practice outstripped constitutional theory. Secondly, the acceptance of rival models of territorial development in Britain, if not Ireland, suggests that indigenous federal ideas and proposals for constitutional change were neither as radical nor as utopian as their critics would have us believe. The federal idea, broadly conceived, was simply one of many possible outcomes in response to perceived challenges to the state. The idea of a fully-fledged federal system or, at least, federal instalments (such as colonial representation in the House of Commons) was, moreover, a perfectly *legitimate* alternative perspective of the reformed state. All that was required to trigger it into life as an active force in British politics was a unique conjunction of internal and external circumstances sufficient to threaten the existing conditions of peace, order and stability. In the period surveyed here it is undoubtedly the case that between 1870 and 1921 the combination of uncertainties engendered by domestic, imperial and foreign events and circumstances acted as a powerful spur to the public popularity of the federal idea in Britain. However, perhaps it is because the Unitary myth has been so dominant and resilient, and indeed so successful as far as the English are concerned, that rival perspectives of the state and its constitution have been so easily dismissed as either impractical or chimerical. What, then, is the myth and reality of the Unitary state?

The Unitary State: Myth and Reality

Among the many paradoxes which lie at the heart of the United Kingdom the phrase 'Unitary State' seems particularly perplexing. Scholars who have written recently about it seem to veer awkwardly between constitutional theory which is unequivocal and constitutional theory which is ambiguous. This is because although the United Kingdom is a state in terms of international law it nonetheless has no written constitution. As Rose argued, 'the stateless and nonconstitutional nature of government in the United Kingdom means that questions about its institutions and territorial extent are neither confronted nor resolved'.[10] But Rose remains emphatic that 'the United Kingdom meets the basic definitional criteria of a unitary state. The Crown in Parliament is the sole political authority, and its authority is formally unlimited.' Authority is clearly undivided in a unitary state and where there appear to have been departures from this axiom they have been 'more apparent than real'.[11]

Vernon Bogdanor, in his *Devolution*, also acknowledged the highly centralized and 'profoundly unitary nature of the United Kingdom, as expressed in the supremacy of Parliament', but he distinguished this from 'the spirit in which this unitary state is administered'.[12] Here centralization as a force of habit rather than of ideology has permitted a wide diversity of political relationships: 'British politicians have rarely allowed a theory of government to prevent them from constructing new relationships which, whatever the faults to be found in them by strict constitutionalists, nevertheless succeed in providing workable answers to practical problems'.[13] Rose and Bogdanor lead us inexorably to the conclusion that the United Kingdom is a unitary state without a unitary constitution. But the formal trappings of the unitary state have not in practice stifled every attempt at redefining relations between England and Scotland, Wales and Ireland during the last few centuries.

Bulpitt denies that the post-Union structure of government was unitary 'in so far as that term has any meaning.' His thesis emphasizes the reluctance of the central authorities to interfere directly in the affairs of local communities and depicts a 'peculiar structure of territorial politics ... characterized by a high degree of constitutional ambiguity'.[14] In summary, then, the authority of the Crown in Parliament has remained intact. The United Kingdom developed as a unitary state in theory but the instinct and spirit of its practice has been intermittently imaginative and flexible. As Rose remarked, the state was unitary but not uniform.[15] Hence in the absence of an overwhelming centralist ideology dedicated to cultural uniformity via a single integrated organization both the myth and the reality of the unitary state have been perpetuated, in the United Kingdom, that intellectual puzzle.[16]

The Emergence of the Federal Idea in the Mid-Victorian Era

The foregoing discussion underlines the contingent unplanned character of the United Kingdom. It is a union which defies consitutional symmetry. But what does the recent scholarship about understanding the United Kingdom suggest about the federal idea? The literature certainly indicates that elements of federal practice were far from unfamiliar in British political development. Bulpitt acknowledged this when he argued that new bargains between élites could be struck as a series of reconstructions of as much of the old indirect management of the celtic periphery as could be achieved in changed circumstances. As an élite affair such a practice depended entirely upon élite willingness to modify their management of affairs of state. They had first to be convinced that it was necessary. What, then, do these changing élite images, perceptions and realities tell us about the federal idea in British Government and politics during 1870-1918?

It would be an exaggeration to suggest that the federal idea was ubiquitous. It was not conscious federal practice consistently pursued. But we should appreciate how far historical practice had paved the way for a growing appeal and relevance of the federal idea in the nineteenth century. The making of the United Kingdom had placed it among the category of legitimate options and responses available to English élites during difficult periods of change. Its intermittent bouts of popularity derived from an underlying sense that rigid centralism was not the universal panacea for Britain's outstanding problems in the nineteenth century. During the period we shall survey the two dominant themes in British politics were Empire and Ireland. These two problems were interrelated in a close and complex fashion and provided the main wellspring for the nourishment of federal solutions.

The mid-Victorian era witnessed a sudden surge in the popularity of the federal idea about 1870. Ged Martin has drawn attention to the existence of a continuous interest in the federal nature of the Empire between 1820 and 1870 but it possessed neither the salience nor the intensity of the debate which followed.[17] It did not generate a political movement to compare with the Imperial Federation League during 1884-1893. Besides, the Irish dimension was then less menacing and intrusive. 1870 was to be an important turning-point in the growing appeal and relevance of the federal idea in British politics.[18] It furnished all of the ingredients adumbrated by Bulpitt in his hypothesis of a discernible shift from informal to formal Empire: perceived economic decline; a change in international power relations against British hegemony; the mounting menace of Ireland, symptomatic of a breakdown in élite collaboration; and the challenge the traditional political certainties posed by urban enfranchisement in 1867.[19] In short, the mid-Victorian era encapsulated a series of major challenges to the old order amounting to nothing less than the modernization of British politics.

Since the subsequent focus of this survey will be Empire and Ireland up until the end of the First World War it is appropriate to conclude this section by clarifying what I mean by 'the federal idea' before discussing its progress and significance in British politics after 1870. There are a number of important distinctions worth making in the context of Empire and Ireland. Certainly the phrase 'Imperial Federation', so widely used in the vocabulary of British politics for nearly fifty years after 1870, created many misconceptions and was the source of protracted quarrels and heated rivalries among British and colonial élites. In retrospect, it was merely a convenient rallying cry for those who sought a much more binding and regulated Empire but who could not agree upon the details of how it should be achieved. It was a useful mobilization ploy for the imperialism of consolidation rather than expansion. Most of those who sympathized with this vague ideal, however, did not necessarily believe that the utilization of the federal principle meant superimposing on the Empire the paraphernalia of a federal constitution analogous to that of the United States. Such activists who worked to this end were in a tiny minority. But this still left available a very extensive range of Empire federalist schemes which permitted numerous variations of the federal idea. As we shall see these included well-worn proposals for sending colonial M.P.s to Westminster and advisory bodies of colonial agents based in London to advise Parliament on colonial affairs.

In a general sense, then, the federal idea was ubiquitous in the public debate about how to consolidate the white self-governing Empire in the years after 1870. 'Federate or disintegrate' was the favourite slogan of the consolidationists many of whom instinctively believed that the British Empire - with Canada nominally independent and considerable local autonomy established in the Australian, New Zealand and South African Colonies - was already a federal system in practice if not in theory. The federal idea was a flexible solution to maintain imperial unity and strengthen the British state in a period of growing uncertainty. This is also why it assumed importance in relation to Ireland. Federal constitutional reform *within* the United Kingdom was indissolubly linked to federal constitutional reform *vis-à-vis* the white self-governing Empire.

Empire, Ireland and the Federal Idea 1870-1918

It would be beyond the bounds of this survey to identify every major article and speech which advocated the application of the federal principle to the Empire and Ireland during these years. Instead I shall emphasize the context of the public debate about federalism in order to convey the atmosphere which it created and within which it sustained itself. I then intend briefly to focus upon six specific case studies which demonstrate both the relevance and the attraction of the federal idea to the reconstitution of the British state. For the moment, let us grasp some idea of the political atmosphere of this period which encouraged many solutions to major problems to be channelled into a federal mould.

The evidence for the rise of the federal idea in this period is overwhelming. Throughout the 1870s the federal idea, loosely referred to as 'imperial federation', was hotly debated both in the Royal Colonial Institute (RCI) and in the plethora of articles and essays which appeared in the mid-Victorian press and review literature.[20] In Parliament, too, the federal idea began to be taken seriously. Indeed its significance in British politics at this time was such that it was able to sustain a political movement created in 1884, entitled the Imperial Federation League. When the League collapsed in 1893 the idea of incorporating closer imperial ties in political forms did not die with it. On the contrary, the federal idea proved resilient and was sustained in the variety of pressure groups which sprouted in the United Kingdom during the 1890s. Apart from the RCI, which had nurtured the idea for a generation, the Imperial Federation (Defence) Committee emerged in 1894 as clear evidence that the cause of imperial unity had been reorganized along more specific lines.[21]

The federal idea soon resurfaced in more robust shape during the first decade of the twentieth century when the Round Table movement was formed during 1909-10. Destined to dominate British intellectual thinking about Empire-Commonwealth relations until the early 1920s, the movement served as an invaluable repository for the federal idea. In this sense, 'Imperial Federation' represented a fundamental continuity of thought and action between the late nineteenth century and the early twentieth centuries in terms of the reorganization of the British state. Ireland, too, provided a persistent focus for the germination of the federal idea. Federalism was advocated in the 1870s by Isaac Butt and his Home Rule Party, but its significance loomed much larger in the mid-1880s when Joseph Chamberlain first propounded it as the solution to the Irish problem. Never far below the surface of the public debate thereafter, it received widespread publicity and support during the great constitutional and home rule crisis of 1910-1914 and it was seriously discussed by the Lloyd George coalition government as a viable proposition in 1918.

Set against this broad background of events surrounding Empire and Ireland between 1870 and 1918 it can be more fully appreciated precisely how far the federal idea had seeped into the public mind as a means of reconstituting the United Kingdom in order to retain the white self-governing Empire and Ireland. Here at least part of Bulpitt's thesis appears to be confirmed. The logical conclusion to the evolution of colonial self-government was independence - and imperial federation could prevent it by reformulating the imperial relationship - but Ireland was intrinsically part of the United Kingdom territorial periphery. The integrity of the State was paramount. Yet if Union had been only a last resort, according to Bulpitt's thesis, what circumstances would impel the English to reassess its continuing value? Since Ireland had been formally incorporated in the United Kingdom, in a sense reluctantly, then it takes little thought and imagination to appreciate why the federal idea should appear increasingly attractive as a solution to the Irish problem during 1870-1918. Union could be a troublesome nuisance. The federal idea offered the restoration of peace, order and stability via admittedly formal reconstruction of the United Kingdom but one which might retain Ireland and yet keep it at a comfortable distance from London.

Let us now briefly examine six specific examples of the federal idea in the context of British Government and politics during 1870-1918. The six short case studies identified to underline the relevance and appeal of the federal idea are: The Imperial Federation League and its federal plan, 1884-1893; Joseph Chamberlain and Ireland 1885-1886; Sir Joseph Ward and the 1911 Imperial Conference; the political ideas and influence of the Round Table Group; the Home Rule crisis of 1912-1914; and Federalism and the Irish Problem in 1918. I shall examine each one of these in the order presented above.

The Imperial Federation League and its Federal Plan, 1884-1893

Founded on 29 July 1884 at the Westminster Palace Hotel, London the Imperial Federation League sought both to publicize and to popularize the idea of 'imperial federation' and was committed to 'secure by Federation the permanent unity of the Empire.' It received its official public baptism on 18 November 1884 and under the leadership successively of W. E. Forster, Lord Rosebery and Lord Brassey was the most important public expression of closer imperial union until its abrupt collapse in December 1893.[22] Altogether thirty one branches of the League were formed in England and Scotland during these years and membership hovered at around the figure of 2,000. The membership size is, however, misleading. Since it included many relatively important and influential public figures, drawn from the élites of British and colonial societies, it represented a potentially significant force for almost any cause it might promote. Its very existence was ample testimony to the strength and progress of the federal idea in the United Kingdom in the late-Victorian period.

From the outset the League was a house divided against itself. Its adherents agreed about the urgent need to strengthen the bonds of Empire, but little else. They disagreed both on strategy and tactics. The most fundamental rift at the League's inception was between those who sought an undefined closer union by adjustments in Britain's traditional trading practices and those who wanted changes in imperial defence, especially naval defence, leaving free trade intact. The League was able to sustain itself only by avoiding any definite commitment and confining itself to vague generalities. When it eventually crossed the Rubicon in April 1893 by formulating a specific federal scheme for the Empire, Gladstone, the Liberal Prime Minister, rejected it and the League disintegrated, torn apart by irreconcilable differences and with no viable alternative policy to offer for the 1890s.

But this episode is worth a moment's reflection. Wisely or not, the League did propose a carefully considered federal scheme. It did not entertain a fully-fledged federation but an Imperial Council - a Council of the Empire for defence and foreign policy. Its composition was to include the British Prime Minister, the Foreign Secretary, the Colonial Secretary, the Chancellor of the Exchequer, the First Lord of the Admiralty, the Secretaries of State for India and War and the representatives of the governments of Canada and of Australia and South Africa when they themselves were federated. The proposals submitted to Gladstone were deemed tentative pending the convocation of an Imperial Conference representative of the white self-governing empire which would mould an acceptable scheme into shape.[23]

What are we to make of this episode? The minutes of the Executive Committee of the League have only recently been released to researchers and they make fascinating reading. They give an invaluable insight into late-Victorian thinking about the federal idea. They recognize the indispensable preconditions of timing and of political will leading to the formation of a new political organization. Theirs represented an incremental, step-by-step approach to the federal goal. Many of the details of the League's scheme were left deliberately vague in order to maximize discussion and maintain flexibility but it was their very imprecision which, ironically, allowed Gladstone to condemn them as inadequate. If the factors which are deemed *essential* and *conducive* to the creation of federations have long exercised the minds of theorists examining their success and failure the experience of the Imperial Federation League might still repay further investigation.

Joseph Chamberlain and Ireland 1885-1886

The problem of Ireland returned to the forefront of British politics in 1885 and continued to dominate it throughout 1886 until Gladstone's first Home Rule Bill was defeated and split the Liberal party. As one of the most famous and influential reform agitators of the late-Victorian era, Joseph Chamberlain was a consistent opponent of any home rule scheme which threatened the imperial connection but the Birmingham Radical was certainly not averse to constitutional or other reforms which would keep Ireland in the Union. It is here that the federal idea assumed a growing prominence in the Radical leader's mind.

Much research into the emergence and overall significance of Chamberlain's federal ideas during 1885-6 is still required. There can be no doubt that they crystallized under the sudden pressure of the Irish problem in 1885 but much remains unexplained. Chamberlain's main political strategy was to defeat the Gladstone bill rather than to promote an alternative scheme but the whole episode is a complicated one and the Irish issue certainly sparked the federal idea into existence at this time. There is, however, some consistency in Chamberlain's thinking. His support for the federal solution to Irish home rule can be traced back at least to 1874 when he approved Isaac Butt's proposal, called a 'federal arrangement' and it was firmly incorporated in the famous Radical Programme of 1885. Here the primary aim of a federal reorganization of British government was the devolution of parliamentary business which would improve the efficiency of legislation by freeing the 'imperial parliament' to confine itself to foreign affairs, trade, defence and colonial affairs.

This fundamental rationale of federalism and 'Home Rule All Round' provides the explanatory background to Chamberlain's disruptive parliamentary observations of 1886. His somewhat sudden interventions for the federal cause in April and June 1886 are perhaps less surprising and unexpected if we take into account his own private correspondence with his Radical partner, Sir Charles Dilke, and the views he expressed in two key articles in the *Fortnightly Review* for July 1885 and February 1886.[24] In his private correspondence with Dilke he acknowledged during 1885 that federation would involve 'the entire recasting of the British Constitution and the full and complete adoption of the American system.' Later, in May 1886, he reiterated his faith in the federal principle and made no secret of where he thought the central issue lay:

> 'The retention of the Irish representatives is clearly the touchstone. If they go, separation must follow. If they remain, federation is possible whenever local assemblies are established in England and Scotland'.[25]

In summary, then, Chamberlain certainly favoured a federal home rule scheme in principle. He knew, however, that it would logically involve the abolition of the House of Lords and ultimately the monarchy, and was therefore only a remote possibility from the vantage point of the mid-1880s. Two observations merit particular emphasis here. First, we should not overlook the extent to which the federal idea percolated throughout the epic parliamentary debate on Irish Home Rule in 1886. Almost every M.P. commented upon the perceived strengths and weaknesses of the federal panacea. Secondly, the nature of the connection between the Irish problem and the larger question of imperial federation is worthy of closer analysis. As we have already observed, the Irish problem could never be completely divorced from imperial unity in the late-Victorian years. And the federal idea was sufficiently malleable to be the common ingredient in two separate but confusingly interrelated political issues. Both Ireland and Empire were to test the resilience of the federal idea in later years.

Sir Joseph Ward and the 1911 Imperial Conference

If we return briefly to the problem of the British Empire shortly before the beginning of the First World War we encounter yet again the continuing relevance and the remarkable resilience of the federal idea in men's minds. With audacious enthusiasm, Sir Joseph Ward, the New Zealand Prime Minister, laid bare his detailed scheme of imperial federation as the last peacetime initiative to reconcile local self-government with imperial unity at the Imperial Conference of 1911. Ward's proposal met with the sort of indignant disbelief customarily reserved by governing élites for radical reform blueprints. In retrospect, his bold initiative seems naive. It had no real chance of being accepted. Yet it was not without significance both from the standpoint of the federal idea and as a serious proposition directed at imperial reintegration.

The 1907 Colonial Conference had recognized the need to convene regular conferences in order to discuss questions of common interest among the white self-governing members of the Empire. At this time, the balance of the imperial relationship, according to Hancock, consisted of two main elements: the local autonomy of individual governments and the broad authority possessed and exercised by the United Kingdom.[26] The 'Imperial Problem' for those who sought a more formally regulated and binding union of states was to arrive at a new institutional arrangement which would facilitate common defence and foreign policies and thereby reverse the trend towards decentralization. Their aim, in short, was to centralize the direction of local affairs. They deemed the Conference system to be too weak to arrest the process of decentralization which they viewed as leading ultimately to the disintegration of the Empire into wholly independent states. As a political institution the Imperial Conference lacked both legislative and executive authority; it was merely a forum for consultation and cooperation.

Ward's plan symbolized the desire to reconstitute the imperial relationship by the reintegration of the parts into the whole. The details of his federal scheme were put forward as tentative suggestions designed to create a favourable atmosphere and to demonstrate that a new central authority, empowered to legislate on specific subjects, was feasible. It would halt imperial disintegration, widen the burden of imperial defence and give the Dominions a voice on subjects hitherto the sole responsibility of the United Kingdom. What, then, did Ward propose to the sceptical representatives assembled before him? How would his version of imperial federation work?

If the long and tortuous speech introducing his plan did not endear him to his audience, his failure adequately to clarify its institutional details did not augur well for support. Indeed, if read today the discussion appears unreal. Ward's defence of his proposal sounded like an apology. But while criticism is easy, initiatives are not. Ward's scheme, despite its deficiencies, was founded upon a logical, coherent argument: the need to co-ordinate and harmonize naval defence by establishing a uniform system which would formally accommodate the component units of the Empire in the decision-making centre. To achieve this, Ward advocated an 'Imperial Parliament of Defence' composed of two houses: an 'Imperial House of Representatives' elected for five year terms with one member for every 200,000 of the constituent populations of the United Kingdom, Canada, Australia, New Zealand, South Africa, and Newfoundland; and an Imperial Council of Defence or 'Senate' providing equal representation to the six Governments, resulting in a Council of twelve and having only limited consultative and revisory functions. The executive would consist of up to fifteen members of whom not more that one would be chosen from the Senate. In this way the Dominions would acquire an entrenched voice in naval defence, treaty negotiation, foreign relations and questions of peace and war, but without seriously threatening British supremacy.[27]

According to Hancock, the Prime Minister took 'less than an hour to discuss the proposal', but with hindsight we should not be so dismissive.[28] The British Prime Minster, Asquith, was compelled to confess to the Dominion premiers that he had received a memorial signed by some 300 British M.P.s who had called for the formation of a representative advisory council. And we should also remember that the Dominion premiers did not approach the issue with identical motives. Ward's initiative clearly never stood a chance of acceptance in 1911; no government was prepared to sacrifice local interests for the sake of a common policy. Hancock's conclusion was both accurate and succinct: 'The Empire had become too decentralized to permit 'imperial solutions' to 'imperial problems'.[29] Yet we should be reminded here that the federal idea was not a vague abstraction. It had once again entered the arena of practical politics discussed by national leaders. Although rejected its very presence indicated a significance which was not ephemeral.

The Political Ideas and Influence of the Round Table Group

Sir Joseph Ward's proposal discussed above must not be viewed as a fatuous initiative propounded by an eccentric individual isolated from his contemporaries. To do so would be to overlook and misunderstand the important context within which public debate about the federal idea took place. This context was provided by the Round Table movement, formed in 1909-1910, which was dedicated to closer imperial union. Destined to dominate British intellectual thinking about Empire-Commonwealth relations until the early 1920s, the movement served as a crucial repository of imperial federationist ideas which represented a basic continuity of thought and action between the late nineteenth and early twentieth centuries in terms of the reorganization of the British State.[30]

Imperial federation was the link which ran beneath the surface of the activities of public men like Lionel Curtis and Philip Kerr, later Lord Lothian, who were among the founders of the new political movement in Edwardian England. This connection was expressed by the nebulous phrase 'organic union' but it is clear that 'the discovery of some form of federation which shall be at once effective and acceptable' was the main focus for their energies.[31] Their main strategy, like that of the Imperial Federation League, was to popularize the federal idea and to influence official thinking; but there the similarity ended. They avoided the mistakes of their predecessors. Concentrating less on mass agitation than on influencing leadership, they recognized that popular support was valuable only after politicians had raised the issue. This, as Ged Martin observed, determined their tactics: 'Major policy problems, like the role of India in a federal union, were thrashed out in secret memoranda. Lobbying was confined to the powerful'.[32] And as the historian of the movement, John Kendle, remarked 'the movement, particularly the London group, did have some influence in governmental circles in Great Britain and in the Dominions, not least because its members came from the affluent, the well-placed, the intellectual, and generally the most acceptable members of society'.[33]

Curtis and Kerr worked diligently to disseminate the federal idea both at home and abroad. Curtis, a former town clerk of Johannesburg, dubbed 'the Prophet' by his admirers, launched himself with single-minded determination on the path towards a federal reconstruction of the Empire. The movement aimed at a form of imperial federation which would guarantee the separation of domestic and imperial affairs. In an attempt to maximize the impact of its newly published manifesto Curtis toured the Dominions in 1910, helping to establish Round Table Groups among the élite and professional classes and encouraging them to reappraise their relationship with Great Britain as regards defence and foreign policy. His influence appears to have been greatest in Australia and New Zealand where he was able convincingly to depict 'the Imperial Problem' as 'the Empire in danger', successfully exploiting Antipodean anxieties about German and Japanese expansionist designs. It comes as no surprise that many of the ideas and details associated with Sir Joseph Ward's federal scheme of 1911 derived from Lionel Curtis.

The Round Table Group was unanimous in its belief that the Dominions should have an effective voice in imperial policy, particularly defence and foreign policy, and that the quadrennial imperial/colonial conferences were palpably inadequate. There existed in their view a constitutional void which could be successfully filled only by new executive machinery devised to respond smoothly in times of crisis. That crisis arrived in 1914 with the onset of the First World War. The moment for the Round Table appeared to be at hand. In 1915 Curtis published *The Problem of the Commonwealth* which emphasized the urgent need for a common foreign policy. With Lord Alfred Milner, the Round Table's inspiration and idol, entering Lloyd George's War Cabinet in 1916, the prospects for the federal idea at the forthcoming Imperial Conference to be summoned in 1917 seemed highly promising. No supreme federal organ emerged, however. The Conference did produce the Imperial War Cabinet with (briefly) executive powers in which all autonomous governments were represented. It just outlasted the war, to represent the Empire at the peace conference. With it faded the vision of a common imperial government. It would be difficult to take issue with Ged Martin's conclusion: '1917 marked both the greatest triumph and the final defeat of the imperial federation movement'.[34]

The Home Rule Crisis of 1912-1914

We have already examined the significance of the federal idea in the public debate about Irish Home Rule in the mid-1880s. Gladstone's second Home Rule Bill had successfully traversed the House of Commons in 1893 but was rejected by the House of Lords. During 1912-1914 the Irish issue began to dominate British government and politics once again, threatening the survival of Asquith's Liberal government and dividing the Conservative Party along several lines of strategy and tactics.[35] The third Home Rule Bill received the royal assent in September 1914 but was held in abeyance for the duration of the war. In these troubled years the federal idea was also prominent in the protracted discussions about Ireland's future and the Round Table Group played an important role in its reshaping and reappearance as 'Home Rule All Round'.[36]

In 1910 federal solutions were canvassed in the Constitutional Conference, assembled to resolve the conflict between the Commons and the Lords. Austen Chamberlain, a leading member of the Conservative Opposition, resurrected his father's old policies and became the leading exponent of federalism in the party and, later, in Lloyd George's Coalition Government in 1918. There is a direct link between the influence and activities of certain members of the Round Table Group and the growing significance of the federal idea in Unionist circles. Both Lionel Curtis and Philip Kerr were busy behind the scenes attempting to exert pressure at home and abroad in their quest to forge links between constitutional reform in the United Kingdom and organic union of the Empire. But it was above all the persistence of Frederic Scott Oliver, a Unionist and much respected political thinker, which ensured that federalist solutions remained on the agenda in this period.

Oliver had immersed himself in the problem of constitutional reform in 1910, becoming convinced that the federal idea was the panacea for the complexity of problems confronting the United Kingdom. Along with J. L. Garvin, editor of *The Observer*, he carried his personal campaign right into the heart of Unionist circles. While Garvin used his newspaper to support the federal cause and kept up a fierce bombardment of leading Unionists with lengthy letters and memoranda on the Irish question, Oliver inflitrated the Unionist camp with his federalism by approaching Austen Chamberlain and Arthur Balfour directly. Using the pseudonym 'Pacificus' he also published a short series of letters in *The Times* calling for a truce between the political parties at odds over Ireland. His influence in helping to shape the intellectual climate favouring federalism was clearly considerable and Kerr remarked he had 'ploughed the hard soil' in preparation for Round Table ideas.[37]

Curtis, meanwhile, had scored a great success on his own terms. He persuaded the young Winston Churchill to consider the federal ideas circulating within the Round Table. As First Lord of the Admiralty who had introduced the second reading of the Government of Ireland Bill in the House of Commons, Churchill was an obvious target for Round Table activists. However, his willingness to listen to Round Table opinions must have come as a surprise. They could not have anticipated Churchill's apparent conversion to their cause in a major public speech during September 1912 in which he urged his Dundee constituents to consider a federal United Kingdom. His conception of a reconstructed Albion included national parliaments for Ireland, Wales and

Scotland and regional legislatures within England - all subordinate to an Imperial Parliament. Churchill's own version of 'Home Rule All Round' would, he argued, solve the Irish problem and facilitate the Dominions in a new central government of the Empire. Empire, Ireland and federalism were thus indissolubly connected in his mind. Kendle noted that Churchill spoke speculatively and not as a Cabinet representative but his speech had 'wide reverberations' and he 'helped in making federalism a major talking-point once more in party intellectual circles; and it remained at the forefront of the political stage until the early summer of 1914'.[38] The scene is now set conveniently to investigate our sixth and final case study.

Federalism and the Irish Problem in 1918

We have already seen how the federal idea received widespread consideration by British politicians during 1912-1914, although it obtained insufficient support across the political party spectrum. The outbreak of war in 1914 effectively halted the public debate about Ireland and wider constitutional reform for the United Kingdom. What, then, caused these issues to be resurrected in 1918?

According to Kendle, 'it was only with the virtual breakdown of negotiations over the home rule question in early 1918 and the apparent need to introduce conscription to Ireland that federalism began to seem a reasonable alternative to many British politicians'.[39] But the personal influence of Frederic Scott Oliver upon leading Unionists in general and upon Lloyd George, Austen Chamberlain, and Edward Carson in particular seems to have been crucial. Once again his personal contacts were of vital importance and his single-minded commitment to the federal cause ensured that 'the main topic of conversation was federalism.' Chamberlain was especially amenable to the idea which he regarded as 'the best compromise available.' Federal schemes received wide coverage in the British press and figured prominently in both Scottish and Welsh home rule circles. Indeed, such was the ubiquity of this style of thinking in the United Kingdom that Oliver himself estimated that about fifty Unionists, ninety Liberals and an uncertain number of Labour M.P.s wanted 'federalism for its own sake'.[40]

This assessment of support for the federal idea in March 1918 may indeed have seriously underestimated the real figure. A personal survey conducted for Lloyd George in May 1918 to weigh the strength of the federalists put their numbers at around 340 M.P.s spanning virtually the entire party political spectrum. And on the Irish Committee set up by the Prime Minister to draft a home rule bill acceptable to all the interested groups, discussion and negotiation on political and financial issues alike took place 'constantly within an ideological framework of federalism'.[41]

It is clear that by April 1918 both Lloyd George and Austen Chamberlain were agreed upon a scheme of Irish home rule which would 'fit in with a Federal plan' - it would facilitate 'Home Rule All Round'. But the Prime Minister was exposed to conflicting views within the War Cabinet. Whilst opinion within his Irish Committee hardened in the direction of a federal system, the War Cabinet had no desire to embark upon a full-scale overhaul of the United Kingdom. Their interpretation of a home rule bill 'consistent' with federalism was at odds with its general applicability within the United Kingdom. Moreover, Lloyd George did not believe that a public discussion of federalism during the war was feasible, while its viability after the conclusion of peace would be undermined by the overriding priority of reconstruction.

Conclusion: The Dog That Did Not Bark?

The federal idea did not peter out at the end of the First World War. The Speaker's Conference on Devolution, created in October 1919, ensured that reform of the constitutional structure of the United Kingdom remained at the forefront of British politics in the immediate postwar era. The aim of the Conference was not the discussion of general principles but 'the consideration of practical schemes of devolution.' Alluding to these in broad terms as 'Federal Devolution', this all-party conference of Lords and Commons reached agreement upon four out of five separate sections in the Report and recognized the federal principle underlying the division of powers between the United Kingdom Parliament and the subordinate parliaments. Indeed, as one expert commentator upon the Speaker's Conference wrote in 1926 'the result of this will be federalism in the broader sense, for the common features of all federal states is the division of power'.[42]

From these beginnings Liberal thinking on federalism and devolution evolved during the interwar years into a consistent advocacy of radical decentralizing reform of the British constitution. Already in the Liberal Party Manifesto of 1929 Lloyd George claimed among the watchwords of the Liberal programme, 'the devolution of purely national questions within the nation to the nationalities concerned', and number eighteen of the *20 Point Manifesto of the Liberal Party* in 1945 could justifiably boast that it had 'long been in favour of suitable measures of devolution'.[43]

It is true that the relevance of federalism both to Ireland and Empire diminished somewhat during the inter-war years but it was re-routed as a direct consequence of Britain's changing relationship to Europe in the 1930s. The new constellation of power relations in Europe during these years sparked a number of innovative public organizations into existence in Britain, the most important of which was the Federal Union.[44] Formed in 1938 by a committed group of Oxford graduates, the new movement was originally animated by the desire to prevent war. It came to propound federalism as a theory of political organization and towards the end of the war as a strategy for reconstruction both in Europe and throughout the world. As Walter Lipgens' account of its development demonstrates, the movement reached the peak of its effectiveness during 1940-

1941, 'having grown with astonishing speed and produced an equally astonishing output of books and pamphlets'.[45] If we consider that its active local organizations numbered just over 200 in February 1940 and that these had grown to 225 branches totalling 12,000 members by June 1940 we can appreciate once again just how far the federal idea had retained its vitality, resilience and relevance in British political life during the twentieth century.[46]

The significance of the Federal Union as a channel through which distinct British federal ideas made an important intellectual contribution to post-war European integration has only recently been underlined. The links between the 1930s and 1940s and the current debate about European Union in the 1980s have at last been made.[47] The shift from Ireland and Empire towards Europe is at last complete. Yet the federal idea has also surfaced in its more familiar arena of domestic constitutional relations in recent times. The Kilbrandon Report on the British Constitution of 1973 inevitably attracted federal ideas as part of a genuinely multinational perspective. Anthony Birch observed that 'eight of the thirteen members of the Commission favoured the creation of legislative assemblies for Scotland and Wales' and the logical concomitant of this proposal was 'the creation of an assembly for England, or several assemblies for the regions of England, thus giving the United Kingdom a federal or quasi-federal form of government.' Birch was surprised that it was 'rejected outright' by the Commission; in his view 'the merits of federalism ought to be carefully weighed against the alternatives'.[48]

We must not, in summary, make exaggerated claims for the federal idea in British government and politics. There is a sense in which it was a dog that did not bark. It altered attitudes and perceptions towards government and politics without directly affecting policy. To this extent the federal idea remained an idea. But we should equally not overlook its existence as a legitimate part of the British political tradition. The federal idea was itself indicative of how widespread was the concern for a major overhaul of the United Kingdom. Both the Kilbrandon Report of 1973 and the proposals of the New Ireland Forum of 1984 indicate that federalism will always merit at least intermittent attention in British political theory and practice.

Notes and References

1. Among those referred to here are: Bogdanor, V. (1979) *Devolution*, OUP; Rose, R. (1982) *Understanding the United Kingdom*, London; and Madgwick, P. and Rose, R. (eds.) (1982) *The Territorial Dimension in United Kingdom Politics*, London; and Bulpitt, J. (1983) *Territory and Power in the United Kingdom*, Manchester.

2. Barker, R. 'The Rise and Eclipse of the Social Democratic State', Chapter 1, pp. 1-18 in Borthwick, R L. and Spence, J. E. (eds.) (1984), *British Politics in Perspective*, Leicester University Press.

3. Rose, *Understanding the United Kingdom*, p.47.

4. Rose, 'Is the United Kingdom a State? Northern Ireland and a Test Case', Chapter 4, p.128 in Madgwick and Rose, *Territorial Dimension*.

5. Rose, *Understanding the United Kingdom*, p.5.

6. Barker, 'Rise and Eclipse', p.6 in Borthwick and Spence, *British Politics in Perspective*.

7. Bulpitt, *Territory and Power in the United Kingdom*.

8. Bulpitt, *Territory and Power*, Chapter 3.

9. Bulpitt, *Territory and Power*, p.83.

10. Rose, *Understanding the United Kingdom*, p.48.

11. Rose, *Understanding the United Kingdom*, p.52.

12. Bogdanor, *Devolution*, pp.7-8.

13. Bogdanor, *Devolution*, p.8.

14. Bulpitt, *Territory and Power*, pp.96-99.

15. Rose, *Understanding the United Kingdom*, p.54.

16. Rose, 'The United Kingdom and an Intellectual Puzzle', in Jaensch, D. (eds.) (1977) *The Politics of 'New Federalism'* Chapter 3, pp.21-34 Adelaide.

17. Martin, G. (1973) 'Empire Federalism and Imperial Parliamentary Union 1820-1870, *The Historical Journal* volume XVI, I , pp.65-72.

18. See Burgess, M. 'Imperial Federation: Continuity and Change in British Imperial Ideas 1869-1871' *The New Zealand Journal of History* Volume 17, 1., (April 1983) pp.60-80 in which I challenge Martin's thesis of continuity.

19. Bulpitt, *Territory and Power*, p.88.

20. See Reese, T. (1968), *The History of the Royal Commonwealth Society* 1868-1968, London.

21. See Miller, M. G. (1980) 'The Continued Agitation for Imperial Union, 1895-1910: The Individuals and Bodies Concerned, Their Ideas and Their Influence', unpublished doctoral thesis, Corpus Christi, Oxford.

22. For an explanation of the League's appearance in 1884 see, Burgess, M. 'Forgotten Centenary: The Formation of the Imperial Federation League in Great Britain, 1884', *The Round Table*, Volume 289 (January 1984), pp.76-85.

23. The full report on the proposals was published in the League's journal, *Imperial Federation* volume VII (December 1892) and Gladstone's comments are in *Gladstone Papers* Add. Mss 44775, ff, pp.114-125, British Museum London.

24. See Escott, H. S. and Fottrell, G. 'Local Government and Ireland', *Fortnightly Review*, (July 1885) and Chamberlain, J. 'A Radical View of the Irish Crisis', *Fortnightly Review*, (February 1886).

25. Chamberlain to Dilke, 26 December 1885, Gwynn, S. and Tuckwell, G. (1917) *The Life of the Rt Hon Sir Charles Dilke* Volume 2 (London), pp.199-201, and Chamberlain to Dilke, 3 May 1886, *Dilke*, Volume 2, p.217.

26. Hancock, I. R. 'The 1911 Imperial Conference', *Historical Studies: Australia and New Zealand* Volume 12 (October 1966) pp.356-372.

27. For the details of Ward's scheme together with the debate in his proposals, see Keith, A.B. (1933), *Selected Speeches and Documents on British Colonial Policy*, 1763-1917 , London, Volume 2, pp.247-303.

28. Hancock, 'The 1911 Imperial Conference', p.359.

29. Hancock, 'The 1911 Imperial Conference', p.372.

30. See Kendle, J. (1975) *The Round Table Movement and Imperial Union* (University of Toronto Press).

31   Kendle, *Round Table Movement* p.64. On Lothian, see Butler, J. R. M. (1960) Lord Lothian (Philip Kerr) 1882-1940, London.

32. Martin, G. 'The Idea of Imperial Federation', Chapter 6, p.133 in Hyam, R. and Martin, G. (1975), *Reappraisals in British Imperial History*, London.

33. Kendle, *Round Table Movement*, p.305.

34. Martin, 'The Idea of Imperial Federation', p.134

35. See Murphy, R. (1986) Faction in the Conservative Party and the Home Rule Crisis, 1912-1914, *History*, Volume 71, 232, pp.222-234.

36. See Kendle, J. 'The Round Table Movement and Home Rule, *The Historical Journal* Volume 11, 2 (1968) p.332-353.

37   Kendle, J. 'Round Table Movement', p.337.

38. Kendle, J. 'Round Table Movement', p.349.

39. Kendle, J. 'Federalism and the Irish Problem in 1918', *History* Volume 56, (1971) p.207.

40. Kendle, J. 'Federalism and the Irish Problem in 1918', pp.213-214.

41. Kendle, J. 'Federalism and the Irish Problem in 1918', pp.217 and 222.

42. See Chiao, W.H. (1926) *Devolution in Great Britain* (New York, AMS Press), pp.184 and 190. See also the brief description in Banks, J. C. (1971) *Federal Britain?*, London: Harrap & Co Ltd , pp.82-85.

43. Craig, F.W.S. (1970) British General Election Manifestos, 1918-1966, Chichester, PRP, pp.62-110.

44. On the emergence of these new groups and Federal Union, see Lipgens, W. (1982) *A History of European Integration, 1945-1947*, Oxford: Clarendon Press, Volume 1, pp.142-153.

45. Lipgens, *A History of European Integration* p.142.

46. The most recent published research on Federal Union is Bell, P.H. and Pinder, J. 'British Plans for European Union, 1939-45', Part One, pp..23-155 in Lipgens, L. (ed.) (1986) *Documents on the History of European Integration* Volume 2, Berlin: de Gruyter.

47. On these links see, Burgess, M. 'Altiero Spinelli, Federalism and the EUT', Chapter 9, pp.174-185 in Lodge, J. (ed.) (1986) *European Union: The European Community in Search of a Future* , London: Macmillan.

48. Birch, A.H. (1977), *Political Integration and Disintegration in the British Isles*, London: Allen & Unwin, pp.156-169.

49. See Collins, N. 'Federal Ideas in Contemporary Ireland', Chapter 6, pp.99-126 in Burgess, M. (ed.) (1986) *Federalism and Federation in Western Europe*, London: Croom Helm.

3

Regionalism and Local Government Reform 1900-1960

Jonathan Owen

Introduction

One of H. G. Wells' less bizarre predictions at the turn of the century was that British local government would have to adjust its boundaries to take account of improvements in transportation and changed patterns of residence.[1] Surprisingly, his more outlandish predictions (such as tanks) proved to be correct whilst local government areas remained virtually unchanged. This article examines the failure of regionalism to transform local government. It will identify inherent weaknesses in the concept, discuss the motives underlying regionalism and examine alternative responses to the local government problem which made regionalism redundant. It will elaborate on these themes with particular reference to three occasions when regionalism and local government reform were placed on the political agenda, as a result of the 1937 report of the Royal Commission on Local Government on Tyneside,[2] during the 'reconstruction debate' of World War Two, and as a result of Aneurin Bevan's 1949 plan for local government reform.

The problems of local government have rarely been off the political agenda throughout this century. Even though reorganisation has taken place, often at great intervals, there has been a continuing dissatisfaction with the existing system. No reorganisation has quite got it right. Some problems have been solved but all too often the goal posts have been moved and within a few years dissatisfaction returned. The trauma of the reorganisations of the 1970s have only recently calmed yet the whole question of reform is in the air again.[3]

This sense of dissatisfaction with earlier reorganisations has bred a feeling that at some point an opportunity was missed. That a bold, courageous reorganisation could have created a rejuvenated system of local administration which would have both increased interest in local government and made it a system able to support a range of services which would have counteracted the twentieth century drift towards centralisation.[4] Regionalism is often portrayed as this vision, as the opportunity which was missed. If only central government policy makers or major political figures had grasped the nettle and created wide units of local administration then local government would be healthier than it is today. This failure to regionalize has often been explained by lack of political will (indeed it is used by the American political scientist Douglas Ashford as a case study to examine how effective twentieth century British policy making has been[5]) or it has been explained in terms of pressure group politics. Local vested interests represented by the all powerful local authority associations have impeded rational progress.[6] There is certainly some truth in these explanations, but as a result there has been less attention paid to either the inherent wisdom of regionalism, the coherence of its proponents or to alternative solutions to the local government problem which were taken in default of any major reorganisation.

Precisely because of this context of expectation of change there has been little critical analysis of the call for larger areas. John Dearlove[7] has provided a stimulating marxist critique of the general 'orthodoxy'; the call for larger areas is explained in terms of political exigencies rather than neutral, rational service needs. Larger administrative areas would swamp 'working class' dominated urban areas with the more 'responsible' suburbs and hence exercise control over expenditure levels. But what Dearlove fails to do is explain the failure to create such large areas. Also, by attributing them all to the same political quarter and without examining what these proposals meant in terms of the existing structure he underplays significant differences within the call for large areas. The delineation of boundaries, the areas they enclosed and the internal structure of the proposed new unit could have a range of political, territorial and cultural implications which were rarely the same.

Closer analysis of regionalism and what regional proposals meant for the existing structure help to fill this gap. Not all calls for large areas lumped together under the umbrella term 'regionalism' represented a common, coherent demand. Regionalism was never as convincing as that. Rather it was a broad church linking a range of interests from the Left as well as the Right. It encompassed those who saw in regionalism the roots of a democratic revival of British society and those whose thinking ran on purely administrative lines. It could as well be inspired by an urban based vision of the social organisation of society as by one that was rural dominated. Regionalism could be invoked equally to defend the county as to make the town triumphant.

In this chapter we shall look at the background to the regional idea, examine the motivations behind its exposition, and argue that its failure to transform local government must be in part explained by its eclectic nature. The internal inadequacies of the policy-making machine and the cowardice of political leaders is pushed into the background as an explanation of non-reform.

Regionalism: Background and Motives

The diagnosis of local government's illness has always been easier than finding its cure. Two major areas of malady have been identified; areas and finance. Uppermost in the 1980s has been an understandable preoccupation with financial weakness but for the period under consideration the area problem predominated. No barren field of administrative detail, this question of areas has tremendous significance for the political organisation of the state at sub-national levels and is revealing of the broader (and continuing) conflict between town and country.[8]

The area problem existed for two reasons. Firstly, the 1888 Local Government Act, which established democratic local government in England and Wales rapidly became outdated as a result of population and transport development. Regionalism was the response to the territorial strain caused by these developments.

Secondly, as the services which local government was expected to perform increased and national standards became expected[9] there was a question mark over whether the 1888 areas provided a sufficiently stable, financially secure base upon which services could be built. Regionalism was designed to create areas with the resource base to support 'modern' expectations of local services.

The Territorial Imperative

The 1888 settlement established an administrative system which buttressed perceived social and cultural divisions between town and country. England and Wales were divided into two tier County Council and one tier all purpose authorities - the County Boroughs. This static system was placed under strain because urban growth and transport developments changed the distribution of population. Towns which had been relatively small in 1888 grew in population and aspired to County Borough status. Existing county boroughs faced with a transport led movement of population outwards into the suburbs and the surrounding County attempted to extend their boundaries so as to regain mobile population and fleeing rateable value. The desire for boundary reform was rarely reciprocated by new suburbs.

A territorial conflict arose between the County and the Town over the suburbanizing population which had implications for service provision. There was a reluctance on the part of local authorities to cooperate with each other in the provision of services at these territorial margins because to do so would open an authority to the accusation that it could not cope on its own and thus could not justify its existing status. But the implications were more general and related to whether the political organisation of society at the local level was to be rural or urban.

In many ways the logical trend would have been to allow County Borough extension, to enable towns to expand administratively to capture those areas which looked to them for services, amenities and community. But this solution was far from ideal. There was a continuing tension within the local government debate over the relative merits of single and multi-tier authorities. Single tier authorities were seen as being more democratic as they were closer to the people but only in a context which kept their size restricted. There were fears about the potential loss of electoral interest in single tier authorities which became too large and accusations that they were susceptible to bureaucratic domination. The two tier County system sought to combine size with efficiency with a second tier for local interest, but ran up against the problem of intra-authority disputes. The regional debate was permeated with such considerations, being conducted not in an administrative vacuum but with the implications in terms of the existing structure very much in mind.

Certainly this territorial battle and the associated lack of cooperation was a fundamental cause of much regional comment. For H. G. Wells, one of the earliest and most influential regionalists, the realisation that larger areas were needed sprang directly from personal experience. It was the difficulties of building a new house in one of these frontier areas, and of getting cooperation between local authorities that led to his 1902 paper to the Fabian Society which spelt out how existing local government units were incompatible with a rational planned society.[10]

In the first edition, in 1931, of his standard text *The Development of Local Government*, William Robson envisaged large scale coordination being achieved through the joining together of existing units in ad hoc combination. Like Wells he became a convert to regionalism as a result of direct experience of local authority in-fighting, gained whilst researching his study of *The Government and Misgovernment of London* (1939).[11] At just this time the Royal Commission on the Distribution of the Industrial Population (the Barlow Commission) was preparing its Report, which was to become the bible of post-war regional planning. Though unable to make any direct recommendation on a matter so clearly beyond their already well-stretched terms of reference, the Commissioners showed their dissatisfaction with the existing fragmentary structure, with its attendant dangers 'that an authority in embarking on a particular policy or course of action may have insufficient regard to the interests of its neighbours' and their preference for larger, regionally-based units.[12]

Regionalism, within this territorial context, was a response to the expansion of urban society. Whereas the preferred solution of urban authorities themselves was territorial expansion, regionalists posed an alternative organisation which would remove the need for piecemeal boundary changes. The major flaw for them in County Borough extension was that it perpetuated the divide between town and country which they perceived as no longer relevant. Regionalism became a total solution rather than the piecemeal adjustment of urban expansion. C. B. Fawcett stressed that there was nothing new in the underlying principle that local government areas ought to match the communities they represented, and that boundaries should where necessary be moved to achieve this. The novelty of regionalism lay in its greater scale and consistency. It meant 'the consideration of the problem of the adjustment of local government divisions *as a whole*, instead of the fragmentary treatment is has received in the past'.[13] But what were the new units to be? In the absence of any readily definable (in the sense of culturally distinct) British regions, the schemes of regionalists could differ extensively on the basis of their own predilections. Within those services, both public and private, that did develop some form of large scale organisation there was no standard. E. W. Gilbert tabulated twenty-five different existing regional divisions of England and Wales in 1939.[14] The reality of administrative regionalism which did develop was highly diverse and a confusing guide for local government reform.

There were disagreements about the size, internal structure and relative weight to be given to urban and rural interests within the regionalist lobby. This made regionalism more exciting - geographers especially could develop ever more intricate means of defining areas of common interest - but reduced the chances of its successful implementation. Disagreement existed at the general level of areal definition; Wells based his regions on watersheds,[15] Robson on Civil Defence areas,[16] the Labour Party on Counties.[17] Was the regional body to be executive or (as G. D. H. Cole envisaged) merely coordinatory, a third planning tier above the County and County Borough?[18] Were regional units to be simply enlarged local government units or would they draw powers from central government as C. B. Fawcett implied in his contribution to the Home Rule All Round debate?[19] There might have been a general demand for larger areas which centred on 'regionalism' but the small print of proposals reveal little unanimity about their definition. Regionalism was more a response to existing problems than a clearly defined and articulated proposal for the future.

The ambiguity of the regional alternative encouraged central policy makers to manage territorial conflict by a strategy of minimum change. This took the form of defending the County against the piecemeal encroachment of the town. The Royal Commission on Local Government, established in 1922, recommended, not changing the existing system, but limiting the creation and extension of County Boroughs. Whereas between 1889 and 1922 23 new County Boroughs had been created, post 1926 there was only one new addition, Doncaster.[20] After the Second World War the Local Government Boundary Commission was set up expressly to put a stop to disruptive claims for boundary extensions caused by the demographic impact of the war.[21] Moreover, the development of services tended to buttress the County. Responsibilities were placed increasingly upon upper tier authorities - the County and County Borough. Many urban districts lost powers, as a result of the 1944 Education Act and the 1946 Police Act. This in effect reduced their claims to County Borough status.

Local Government as Community: The Question of Balance

The second result of suburbanization was that local government areas ceased to be 'balanced'. People were able, in the words of Wells, to 'live in one area, work in another, and shop in a third.' Local units no longer reflected community. This process of delocalisation led to a loss of interest in local government as people consumed services in one area and paid rates in another. Local units ceased to be, in Wells' words 'complete minor economic systems.' By this he meant that communities were being split into rich and poor: local authorities becoming homogenous not heterogeneous.[22]

This was precisely the situation that the Tyneside Royal Commission commented upon. In Hebburn, for example, out of a population of 24000 only 50 'belonged to the employing class and there were no professional men, except the doctors and clergymen whose work more or less compelled them to reside in the town'.[23] For the Royal Commission this imbalance led to extravagant expenditure policies as local councils responded irresponsibly to the needs of a predominantly working class electorate. Their 'regional' solution was designed to restore a socially balanced community at the metropolitan scale in much the same way as Mackinder (the father of modern geography) saw regionalism based on devolution to provinces as a solvent of class division within the national life.[24]

The creation of such 'balance' through large areas was not politically neutral, as John Dearlove has pointed out.[25] The demand for large areas reflected both establishment concern over the perceived excesses of working class dominated councils, and a reformist concern to strengthen the redistributive element of municipal government.

Progressives, such as Wells and Robson, saw the reintegration of rich areas as a means of financing local expenditure policies. Wells described the separation as 'a cruel injustice on the poor',[26] Robson wanted those living in suburbia to pay for the amenities they enjoyed in the town.[27] Spreading the burden, subsidising services used by the poor was as much a motivation behind regionalism as political control, though it would become less salient as expectations grew of welfare policy at the national rather than local level. The Labour politician Ellen Wilkinson, whilst broadly supporting the redistributive element in the Tyneside proposals called for it to be the responsibility of central government.[28]

Regionalism therefore had a mixed political appeal. All that was common to left and right was a desire to create units which reflected a broader social reality than the existing ones, and restored to urban areas the 'balance' that suburbanization across municipal boundaries was somehow felt to have upset.

The flaw in this social planning exercise was that it was to be imposed from the top. External observers were to create balanced units based on rational requirements. But there was no common definition of these rational requirements or of the geographical boundaries of a balanced urban community. This was to prove a particularly intractable problem for the Commissioners on Tyneside.

The Functional Imperative

The functional requirements of local government services pointed towards larger areas if not regionalism. For the early Fabians and of those in the Chamberlainite tradition alike, larger areas were crucial to the success of municipal (and not necessarily socialist) endeavour. They appreciated, of course, that different services needed different areas and that the ideal units for electricity and water supply were not necessarily congruent.[29] Webbs[30], Robson[31] and NALGO[32] were unanimous in their willingness to consider both patchwork arrangements of smaller territorial units joining together in a range of combinations for different services, and ad hoc single-purpose boards. But the trend in early twentieth century local government structure was away from functional organisation and towards the consolidation of service provision as first the School Boards (1902) and then the Poor Law Guardians (1929) were abolished.

Ironically, however, such consolidation proved to be only a small victory in a longer campaign between the needs of functions and territory. Policy developments on the left, of which the Fabians were a part, moved away from local to state socialism and reached their apogee in the activities of the post-war Labour government which created new central state machinery to meet the demands of individual services (such as health) instead of using or combining existing local government units. For Herbert Morrison (whose general silence on the territorial question was vocal) these developments were the strongest argument against regionalism as he declared during the debate on the 1944 White Paper on Local Government:

'What was the real case for regionalism? It was the case that a number of services were beyond the capacity of the average local authority, even the county borough council, even the county. But these services were largely economic in character - municipal passenger transport, electricity, gas, water, drainage ... I suggest to the House that these economic questions ...are tending more and more to be settled on some sort of national basis'.[33]

It was this functional approach, in the ascendancy during World War Two, which effectively ruled out consideration of regionalism as a model for reorganisation during the deliberations of the post-war Labour government.

The Royal Commission on Local Government in Tyneside: A Bold Vision of the Region?

An analysis of Tyneside provides an illuminating case study of the territorial background to regionalism. Here was an area which could be considered a textbook example of all that was irrational and inefficient in the pattern of local government. It cried out for regional treatment, but the remedy proved to be surprisingly elusive.

The problem was placed on the agenda by the 1930s depression (itself an important influence on perceptions of the nation as a collection of regions. Government investigators were sent out to certain areas where the depression was most acute and instructed to comment upon the causes and extent of unemployment and the chances of recovery.[34]

The investigations of Tyneside, culminating in the Royal Commission,[35] drew attention to local government as a contributory factor in the depression. These reports indicted the existing system as an anachronism and an impediment to any coherent industrial planning for the area. Tyneside, broadly defined, consisted of the administrative counties of Durham and Northumberland. Clustering around the Tyne and on both sides of the river were four independent county boroughs, including Newcastle, and a number of lesser urban authorities. Industrialization and the growth of population had changed the river area from a group of distinct communities into one contiguous unit. It was a classic conurbation. Workers, shoppers and residents flowed between areas, criss-crossing the arbitrary but obstinate boundaries of the local government structure. In an area with a population of just over 800,000 there were 15 authorities; in the similarly sized Liverpool or Birmingham there was only one. The investigators detected a wasteful duplication of services: elementary education was the responsibility of 10 local authorities on Tyneside; in Liverpool of only one.[36] Conflict between the authorities was acute. There was a disinclination to cooperate for public works of large scale because to do so would admit dependency on another authority. The urban districts of Gosforth and Longbenton for example developed their own costly sewage systems to avoid draining into Newcastle as to do so would have given Newcastle a potential justification for boundary extension. Wallsend refused to cooperate in the building of a tramway with Newcastle unless the latter promised not to use it in any subsequent territorial bid.[37]

The Royal Commission agreed that the existing organisation was inefficient. As outside observers they set about creating a new social unit which would make the area more efficient in its provision of services, less dominated by single-class interests and generally more attractive to the outside world. Their solution was to divide local government services into regional and local categories. Regional services - public health, education, public assistance, fire and highways - were to be entrusted to a new regional body.[38] This solution was described by *The Economist* at the time as a 'bold vision',[39] but, how bold was it?

The Commissioners (under the chairmanship of Sir Angus Scott) were shocked in equal measure by the administrative chaos which they perceived to exist on Tyneside and by the evidence that local people not only accepted the state of affairs but were prepared to justify and defend it.[40] If the Commissioners wanted change they were forced to impose a solution from above. Drafting it, however, opened up dissension within their own ranks. This was always going to be the problem with any 'rational' outside plan. The Commission agreed that coordination was needed over larger areas for certain services but disagreed what this area was to be. Indeed their disagreement came close to making it impossible to frame a report.[41]

There were two strong, coherent plans. The first was to unite the geographical counties of Northumberland and Durham. But this was seen as politically impractical since Durham with its 'peculiar political complexion'.[42] would have come to predominate. The alternative which became the basis for a minority report of the Royal Commission was to expand Newcastle's boundaries to achieve a degree of metropolitan integration.[43] But this was opposed by County interests on the Commission who were fearful that this would effectively destroy the shire counties. These interests preferred making the geographical county the administrative unit, extending Durham and Northumberland to the Tyne - a course which would have resulted in the diminution in status and responsibilities of the riparian county boroughs, and left the Tyne a dividing line rather than the spinal column of a unified region. The final compromise, outlined in the majority report (and therefore still unacceptable to the author of the minority report, Charles Roberts) was to extend Northumberland across the Tyne to include some of the south bank authorities.

The rational construction of a regional area was subject to clear territorial and political constraints - territorial in that there was preference for the County, political in that there was a desire to limit the influence of Durham. The proposals were criticized at the time for offering a vision not so much of regionalism as of the County triumphant:

'Is that what regionalism will come to mean? Will it resolve itself into a mere reorganisation of County boundaries, and the establishment of the County Council as the major local authority of our system'?[44]

The reaction of central government to the Royal Commission was lukewarm. It declined the opportunity offered by this report to create new, balanced, and therefore in a Dearlovian sense, politically responsible areas. In part this was due to realisation of the weaknesses in the report. But, more generally, such a reorganisation would have had implications for the country as a whole. The ministry was loathe to embark on widespread local government reform to solve the peculiar problems of Tyneside.[45] If anything it came to support the minority report proposals and subsequent limited action was taken to this end.

But even this was only half-hearted and there was no political lead from the Minister of Health, Kingsley Wood. The minority proposals would have involved the Ministry in complex and controversial local boundary extension discussions. It would have been difficult to achieve without liberal application of the financial oil-can to ease the financial consequences of boundary shifts. This the government would not do as they did not want to become further financially embroiled in an area where they felt they were already overstretched and overused.

The Impact of the Second World War

War is often portrayed as a positive force for change. It acts as a test which reveals weaknesses in existing organisations, and opens new opportunities for the pursuit of national policy against the opposition of vested interest groups. Perhaps the classic exposition of this is Titmuss's explanation of the evolution of post-war social policy: war revealed the poor state of existing provision and generated new organisational forms, notably the Emergency Medical System, which became the basis of the National Health Service.[46]

The world of local and national government was not immune from this force. Bombing and the requirements of civil defence harshly exposed the problem of coordination between local authorities and devolved agencies of central government. Moreover, the war revealed the top-heavy nature of the British state. Strategists became aware that if communications between London and the provinces were broken there was no machinery for coordinating the actions of central departments at a sub-national level. These problems forced a unique experiment in 'intermediate government' in the U.K. in the shape of the Regional Commissioners for Civil Defence. The country was divided into 12 regions each headed by a prefect-like figure whose task was to coordinate the actions of central and local government.[47]

This experiment has been portrayed as a model on which a post-war regional organisation could have been built. It might have been expected that opposition to regional institutions would have broken down as the efficiency benefits and the potentialities of regionalism were revealed. This was certainly the hope of W.A. Robson;[48] throughout the war he called for the Regional Commissioner system to be the direct basis for post-war elected regional government. Within the dominant historical tradition that sees war as leading to change there has been an emphasis on this period as the one when the opportunity for local government reform was missed. There was, so the argument goes, plenty of discussion of regionalism which it is claimed amounted to a consensus for change which could have been forced through against the opposition of vested interests in the context of war as opportunity. Alan Alexander, for instance, quotes the Regional Commissioners, the Barlow Report, the Abercrombie Plan for London and the Labour Party and NALGO reconstruction deliberations (which called for 'regional' government) as evidence of this general groundswell. Reform was only avoided because of lack of political will, because of an 'unshakable reluctance to adopt radical solutions'.[49]

A study of reactions to the Regional Commissioners, an analysis of the regional proposals that did emerge (with a realisation of their implication in the territorial battle between authorities) and an understanding of the working out of long-term functional trends suggests that war did not provide such an opportunity. Political courage is always in short supply but the regional proposals that did emerge did not make it any easier for policy makers to act.

There is no doubt that the war generated much debate about the post-war machinery of government. This would have occurred even without the experiment in Civil Defence. But it would be wrong to suppose either that there was a majority in favour of change or that the solution reflected any more than a fragile consensus.

The Regional Commissioners provoked vehement opposition both as an institution and because of their perceived potential for reform. They were referred to as Gauleiters and the question was asked whether the war was being fought for the installation of these regional 'dictators'.[50] As a potential model they served to confuse and exacerbate the issue. Confuse in that their primary task was to co-ordinate the field services of central government. Exacerbate because regional proposals became viewed as a centralising replacement for local government. Even William Robson's advocacy of regionalism, resting though it did on a concern for the health of local government, had far more to say about the administrative advantages of large areas than about their democratic aspect.[51]

There was little agreement over the areas or functions that new regions ought to have. Those regional proposals which were floated remained as wide ranging as ever. Organisations which did submit regional proposals were often internally split. The making of the Labour Party's 1943 Regional Plan revealed a continuing split between those who favoured a system of city-regions based upon enlarged county boroughs and the victorious pro-county regionalism.[52] The 1943 Party Conference revealed how deep the divisions remained and the vehement opposition of the Lancastrian county boroughs effectively ruled out any further action on its recommendations.[53] Alec Spoor has described the similar wranglings which took place in the production of the report of NALGO's Reconstruction Committee on the Reform of Local Government Structure (1943), which resulted in the resignation of their pro-county President, Lieutenant-Colonel F. N. Stead who feared the territorial implications of the report for the county councils.[54]

Within government too the question of regionalism was on the agenda. Two enquiries into the significance of the civil defence system for the post-war organisation of central and local government were held as part of its own internal reconstruction debate.[55] But these internal government enquiries showed little enthusiasm for either the regional devolution of central government along the lines of the Regional Commissioners or for a regional system of local government. It appeared that attitudes had been surprisingly little changed by the war. Indeed, changes in service provision related to the war and expectations of the creation of the welfare state led to a downgrading of the question of local government reform. The first priorities in reconstruction were housing, health, economic management and social welfare, not esoteric changes in the machinery of government.[56] Of course, such fear is close to political cowardice but it was sensible too. Morrison recalled during the debate over the 1945 Local Government White Paper:

'I lived through the application to London of the 1929 Local Government Act ... It took years to frame the legislation and quite a period to fight through the House, and more years for the local authorities to absorb and organize the transferred functions'.[57]

This 'realistic' attitude was evident outside government too. In the early stages of the war, both within and outside government, there was much optimism which saw local government reform as the starting point for a whole range of reconstruction policies. G.D.H. Cole, in a Cabinet memorandum of 1941, had identified it as the necessary prerequisite for the improvement of post-war services.[58] But within two years he had come to adopt a more realistic position and the conference held at Nuffield College, Oxford in 1943, to discuss reform epitomized this change in attitudes as speaker after speaker, culminating in the pronouncement of Beveridge, declared that reform must wait.[59]

While ministers weighed the sure political costs and uncertain benefits of regional reform, civil servants were naturally disposed to favour working through the established machinery of central government. Departments such as the Board of Education or the Ministry of Health were intent on developing their own services and were loathe to enter into wide ranging interdepartmental discussion of the machinery of government. Indeed they cooperated to ensure that reform of local government was deferred. This suited ambitious Ministers such as R.A.B. Butler who 'was not troubled at ... the extent to which local government affected his problem'.[60]

The war and reconstruction then, were ultimately to offer an unfavourable environment for regionalism. Their combined effect was to enthrone the primacy of the functional over the territorial approach to local public service provision. The review of education, health and police functions removed responsibility for them from the smallest authorities without entrusting them to a reformed local government system. As individual services were modernized and new machinery for their implementation was developed, one of the major justifications of regionalism disappeared - the need for more extensive boundaries for the provision by all-purpose local governments of services such as transport, electricity, gas and hospitals. The solution to the problem of coordinating these services increasingly became a national one. The 1945-51 Labour Government intensified this trend with its centralist policies especially with regard to health, a reflection of the continuing shift in Labour policy from municipal to centralist socialism.

The Bevan Plan

The nationalization of health and power and the transfer of education and police to larger authorities weakened the functional justification for regionalism post-war while allowing the territorial conflict between authorities to continue unabated. By the end of 1946 the Local Government Boundary Commission had received applications from county boroughs which would have reduced the population of county government by 6 million and its rateable value by 25%.[61] The Commission was convinced that a mere tinkering with boundaries would not be sufficient and its 1947 report stepped outside its terms of reference and called for a reorganisation on the basis of an essentially two tier structure consisting of 67 new counties. The County Borough was to be integrated within the County, would retain certain powers and would be renamed the 'new County Borough'.[62]

Aneurin Bevan, as Minister of Health was not attracted to this scheme. He felt the structure threatened to be overly bureaucratic and feared that reorganization would divert political energy from more pressing tasks. His immediate solution was to suspend the activities of the Local Government Boundary Commission, arguing that they were not the right body to initiate such a reorganisation. As Minister of Health, however, he had to protect himself against accusations of neglecting local government,[63] and so proposed the delaying device of a Royal Commission.[64] This course was opposed by Herbert Morrison who believed the only way to achieve reorganisation was for the government to settle its own proposals and implement them early in the next parliament, and by Lewis Silkin, Minister of Town and County Planning, whose responsibilities were being disrupted by the continuing territorial conflict. Morrison was victorious and the Cabinet concluded that an interdepartmental committee should be established under Bevan's chairmanship to 'consider the main principles which should govern the reorganisation of local government in England and Wales'.[65]

The deliberations of this committee (though conducted too near to the general election to have any hope of implementation) are interesting in that they reveal how the agenda of reorganisation had shifted. Regionalism, in the sense of creating wider units, was a ruled out of consideration, though its aim of resolving the conflict between town and country continued to be influential. The interdepartmental committee noted the trend towards centralisation and the effect that this had upon local authorities' 'power to initiate action and to take full responsibility'.[66] It was felt that the reduction in local government functions pointed towards a single tier local structure rather than the two tier model outlined by the Local Government Boundary Commission. This would have created at least 240 authorities and satisfied one of the criteria of regionalism in that it would have linked town and country and put a stop to the 'hostility between the county and county boroughs'.[67]   But the proposed system was to be based on towns and not regions.   Such a reorganisation could be envisaged precisely because the functional scope of local government had been trimmed.   There was no plan to regionalize in order to create a new system capable of administering nationalized services,[68] rather a realisation that these services had been lost by local government.   Indeed, Bevan went further and argued that if existing services could not be administered by his proposed units without recourse to joint-authorities then a more fundamental question should be posed:

'If we accept certain units as satisfying the general principles on which the conception of local government can be founded in practice then if a particular service requires that those units should everywhere be made larger, it must be because that service is fundamentally not of a kind which can properly be run by elected local government bodies'.[69]

The Bevan Plan aimed to rejuvenate local government by linking town and country and creating small units which recognized the realities of the changed patterns of community caused by transport and population changes.   The stress in the discussion was upon community and harnessing war-time experience of local action.   These local units were to be given extra permissive powers such as retail distribution, hotels, laundry, and taxis.[70]   The strait-jacket of *ultra vires* was to be loosened.   Here was a vision of local government based not upon the Fabian tradition of municipal industry but on the consumption services, the washing basket and the food hall.

Conclusion

Explaining failure is the task of any study of the impact of regionalism upon local government reorganisation.   This article has explained failure not in terms of an opportunity missed but rather in terms of the 'mythical' nature of regionalism.   In the absence of any political expression of regional identity or demand for provincial autonomy, regionalism was never a clearly articulated proposal and the influence of its proponents was restricted to specialist circles.   For local government's structural problems, alternative responses held sway, which at least had the merit of some degree of coherence if not imagination.   The transfer of services to central government solved the problem of lack of cooperation between local authorities and met the functional requirements of the services concerned.   The management of the territorial question through the machinery of Boundary Commissions (which continued into the 60s) combined with loss to urban authorities of many services ensured practical coexistence of counties and county boroughs.   These were predominately administrative solutions to the problems of local government (though not necessarily neutral ones) and are often contrasted with regionalism which is seen as the intellectual, visionary response. But the disparate, incohate nature of the term made it a vision without substance: a chimera.

References and Notes

1. For the broad affect of transport developments ('locomotion') on social and political structures see Wells, H. G. (1924) 'Anticipations and other papers' in *The Works of H. G. Wells*, London: T. Fisher Unwin Ltd.

2. *Report of the Royal Commission on Local Government in the Tyneside Area* Cmnd 5402 London: HMSO, 1937.

3. For a discussion of this see Rhodes, R. A. W. (1987) 'The Reform of Local Government-Revival of an Industry', *Public Administration*.

4. See Robson, W. A. (1966) *Local Government in Crisis*. London: George Allen & Unwin.

5. Ashford, D. E. (1983) 'At the pleasure of parliament: the politics of local reform in Britain' in Studlar, D.T. and Waltman, J.L. (eds.) *Dilemmas of Change in British Politics* London: Macmillan, pp.102-126.

6. Brand, J. (1974) *Local Government Reform in England*. London: Croom Helm. Especially ch. 3; The Local Government Associations and Reform, pp.88-129.

7. Dearlove, J. (1979) *The Reorganisation of British Local Government* Cambridge: CUP. Part One; The Boundary Problem, pp.21-106.

8. The classic study is Lipman, V. D. (1949) *Local Government Areas 1834-1945*. Oxford: Basil Blackwell.

9. Hennock, E. P. (1983) describes the growth of this national dimension in 'Central-Local Relations in England: an outline 1800-1950' *Urban History Yearbook*, p.38.

10. Wells, H. G. 'Locomotion and Administration: A Paper on Administrative Areas Read Before the Fabian Society' in *Works of H.G. Wells*, pp.283-304.

11. Compare Robson, W. A. *The Development of Local Government*, 1st edition (1931) and 2nd edition (1949) London: George Allen & Unwin. See also his *Government and Misgovernment* of London (1939) London: George Allen & Unwin.

12. *Royal Commission on the Distribution of the Industrial Population*, Cmd 6153 London: HMSO, 1940, p.76.

13. Fawcett, C. B. (1919) *The Provinces of England*, London: Hutchinson 1960 (re-publication) p.70, emphasis added.

14. Gilbert, E. W. (1939) 'Practical Regionalism in England and Wales' in *Geographical Journal*, vol xciv.

15. Wells, H. G. 'Locomotion and Administration', op.cit.

16. Robson, W. A. (1942) ('Regionaliter') *Regional Government*, London: Victor Gollancz and the Fabian Society.

17. Labour Party, (1942) *The Future of Local Government: The Labour Party's Post-War Policy*, London.

18. Cole, G. D. H. (1947) *Local and Regional Government*, London: Cassell.

19. Fawcett, C. B. *Provinces of England*, pp.26-30.

20. Lipman, V. D. *Local Government Areas*, p.185.
21. According to the Permanent Secretary of the Ministry of Health, Sir John Maude, the Commission was established to 'get sensible decision on County Borough extensions and ... (it) ... has been welcomed by the County Councils as being likely to afford proper protection to the interests of County Government' Note for Minister dated 19/12/44, Public Records Office (PRO) Prem 4 88/3.
22. Wells, H. G. op.cit. pp.291-2.
23. Cmd 4728 p.88.
24. Mackinder, H. J. (1945) *Democratic Ideals and Reality*, London: Pelican (reprint of 1919 original) p.135.
25. Dearlove, *Reorganization of British Local Government* passim.
26. Wells, H. G. op.cit. p.299.
27. 'Regionaliter' op.cit. p.18.
28. Labour Party (1937) *Annual Conference Report*, p.188.
29. See *Municipalisation by Provinces* (1905) Fabian Tract No.125, London: Fabian Society.
30. See Webb, B. and S. (1920) *A Constitution for the Socialist Commonwealth of Great Britain*, London: Longmans Green.
31. In Robson, W. A. *The Development of Local Government* (1931) London: George Allen & Unwin, but not the 2nd edition (1948).
32. NALGO (1943), *Report of the Reconstruction Committee on the Reform of Local Government Structure* , London.
33. Hansard vol.408, col. 511, 15th February 1945.
34. See *Reports of Investigations into the Industrial Conditions in Certain Depressed Areas*, Cmd 4728 London: HMSO, 1934. Euan Williams on Tyneside, pp.86-96.
35. *Report of the Royal Commission on Local Government in the Tyneside Area* Cmd 5402 London: HMSO, 1937.
36. Cmd 4728 p.87.
37. Ibid pp.86-88.
38. Cmd 5402 p.41.
39. In *The Economist* 30th March 1937.
40. The evidence which is not published is in (P R O) H L G 11/4-20.
41. H L G 11/40 outlines the problems of drafting a report.
42. H L G 52/352 Minute entitled *Tyneside* 23rd March 1936.
43. Charles Roberts's Minority Report in Cmd 5402 pp.78-89.
44. Warren, J. H. (1937) 'The Significance of the Proposals for Reorganization of Tyneside Government' *Public Administration* p.372.
45. For an overview of the Central Government's reaction see H L G 30/21.
46. Titmuss, R. M. (1976) 'War and Social Policy' in *Essays on the Welfare State* London: George Allen & Unwin, 3rd edition p.83.
47. O'Brien, T. H. (1955) *Civil Defence* London: HMSO and Longmans, Green & Co.
48. His numerous articles on this theme, often under the pseudonym 'Regionaliter' are catalogued in Hill, C.E. (1986) *A Bibliography of the Writings of W.A. Robson* London School of Economics, Greater London Paper No. 17.

49. Alexander, A. (1982) *The Politics of Local Government in the U.K.* New York: Longman p.13.

50. The question was forcefully asked by the Lord Mayor of Birmingham, Norman Tiptaft in *The Times* 17/3/42.

51. 'Regionaliter' op.cit.

52. The victorious position was articulated by Charles Latham against the pro-County Borough representations of Susan Lawrence. See Labour Party Archive *Machinery of Local Government Sub-Committee Minutes* especially 13/11/41.

53. Labour Party (1943) *Annual Conference Report* pp.90197.

54. Spoor, Alec (1967) *White Collar Union* London: Heinemann pp.215-6.

55. The Sir William Jowitt Inquiry dated 4/2/42 in Cab 127/167 and the Sir Thomas Sheepshanks Inquiry dated 7/4/43 in Cab 87/72.

56. For a discussion of this see Young, K. and Garside, P. (1982) *Metropolitan London: Politics and Urban Change 1837-1981* London: Edward Arnold pp.234-243.

57. Hansard vol.40, col.501 15th February 1945.

58. Cole, G. D. H. (1941) 'A Memorandum on the Reorganization of Local Government in England' in Cab 117/223.

59. See report of conference dated 18/10/43 in Nuffield College Social Reconstruction Survey Archive LG 138. Beveridge saw local government as a means not an end, the crucial aim was to rid Britain of Five Giants.

60. According to his parliamentary secretary's (James Chuter-Ede) diaries. *British Library Additional Manuscript* 59696 vol.7. 31 March 1943 p.185.

61. Quoted in Cole (1947) op.cit. px.

62. *Report of the Local Government Boundary Commission* London: HMSO March 1948, pp.19-22.

63. The Economist would declare: 'Mr Bevan's reputation deserves to suffer severely for his offhand treatment of the Commission and of local government in general' 25/5/49.

64. 'The course favoured by governments which shirk difficult decisions' Herbert Morrison in a memorandum entitled *Local Government* 4/5/49 Cab 129/34.

65. Cab 128/15, 12/5/49.

66. Cab 134/470 First Meeting 31/5/39 p.2.

67. Cab 134/470 Memorandum by Minister of Health entitled *Organisation of All Purpose Authorities in England and Wales* 14/10/49 p.2.

68. As Bevan would later claim in his article 'Local Government Management of the Hospitals is Best' in *The Municipal Journal* March 1954.

69. Bevan (1954) p.3.

70. Cab 134/470 Memorandum by Minister of Health *Extending Permissive Powers* 28/6/49.

4

Regional Planning 1909-1939:
'The Experimental Era'

David Massey

Introduction

The purpose of this chapter is to introduce and consider the early experience of regional planning in England and Wales from the origins of statutory planning in 1909 to the establishment of the Barlow Commission in 1937. This early period of regional planning is somewhat forgotten today and what is remembered is not altogether well regarded. Ashworth's incisive comment that 'regional planning remained in Britain so unpractised a subject, so seldom fertilized by the necessity of translating paper propositions into actions, that its influence on the progress of opinion, both professional and lay, was bound to be limited' is characteristic of this view.[1]

Ashworth's conclusion certainly reflected one line of thought among those who had been involved in regional planning; but there were other opinions too. At the Town and Country Planning Summer School in 1938 the division surfaced in an exchange between F.J. Osborn and Thomas Adams. Osborn was reported as saying that 'Regional and Advisory committees do not work. Very little notice has been taken of Advisory Committee Reports.' Adams countered by stating that: 'I should flatly like to contradict Mr. Osborn, and to say that Advisory Reports in my own judgement, have proved worthy of representation as practical and useful.'

Regional planning in the interwar decades was indeed a novelty (as was town planning itself as a public activity) and was poorly placed to be the embodiment of wider aspirations. Nonetheless it provided an opportunity for the development of planning techniques, policies and procedures, which statutory town planning by itself would not have provided and which were to contribute towards the realization of a 'new era' of planning in the 1940s.

57

Recent studies have tended to draw out some of the more positive aspects of the early experience of regional planning and to give some attention to the local experiences of regional planning efforts.[2]   Cherry notes how 'this form of practice gave the Institute its first professional recognition...it was perhaps through regional understanding that the wider context of planning became apparent'.[3]   Cherry's approach is not uncritical, however, rather it is one of reappraising the usual point of view based on a longer time perspective and a deeper knowledge of the development of planning ideas and practice. In his 'interim review' of interwar regional planning schemes he writes that 'certainly many of the high hopes of the 1940s lay dormant in the 1930s, frustrated in their full potential'; but, he concludes 'it is clear that the inter-war Regional Reports can shed important light on the development of British planning thought and practice in that period'.[4]

Sheail has provided a pioneering exploration of the role of regional planning in rural conservation efforts between the Wars.[5]   His case study of the South Downs Preservation Bill, he says, 'is a story of the failure of regional planning', but failure he notes, 'is just as instructive as success' for the purposes of his analysis.[6]   This reaching beyond the success/failure divide for a deeper understanding provides the hallmark of recent historical approaches to the early decades of planning thought and practice.

The purpose of my chapter is to discuss some aspects of the history of regional planning from 1909 to 1937 in the light of this renewed interest. The general theme it pursues is that suggested by Thomas Adams's comment that the period from 1909 to 1931 'may be regarded as an experimental era in town planning'. In 1931 planning was, he considered, 'entering upon a new era in which we could build on the foundations of past experience and accumulated knowledge'.[7]   Adams certainly thought of his town planning as incorporating regional planning, and his idea of an 'experimental era' as applied to the early decades of regional planning is a helpful one.[8]   For the purposes of this chapter I have extended the era under consideration, since I do not think that the 1932 Town and Country Planning Act brought quite the sea change to planning affairs that Adams envisaged, but rather served to extend the period of experiment while allowing for a measure of consolidation.

The idea of an experimental period suggests attempts to develop something new and original in which knowledge and skills are accumulated through a process of trial and error. It suggests that regional planning itself could have been a vehicle for testing the objectives and instruments of planning and also its limits and that in such testing there will be failures as well as successes. In this way we can perhaps begin to understand the difference of opinion between Osborn and Adams, the frustrations of informed professional opinion and why Ashworth reached his rather negative conclusions. It is also helpful in directing attention to the major groundwork undertaken during this period in establishing Adams' foundations of past experience and accumulated knowledge on which the achievements of the new era of the 1940s were to be built.

The discussion initially focusses on the practical origins of regional planning in groups of local town planning authorities who felt the need to co-operate in the preparation of general advisory plans and to link regional survey work with statutory town planning. It then briefly considers four dimensions of experiment: first, the development of administrative structures; secondly, the diffusion and timing of regional planning activities; thirdly, the role of techniques during a 'craft' era of planning methodology; and, lastly, the extension of the scope of regional planning in terms of policy content and policy instruments during this period.

Local authorities and regional schemes

Planning regions are a type of spatially-defined administrative unit . They do not necessarily fit into other definitions of functional, natural or geographic regions, although there is frequently quite proper debate about whether they should. The scale of such administrative regions depends on the nature of the units to which they are regional and to their functions. For the United Nations for instance, the scale of regions is a continental one. Within nation states the definition of the regional boundaries expresses the political and administrative purposes of national government bodies, or collections of local government bodies, or a mixture of both.

In this case, the reasons why British town planners of the 1920s and 1930s turned to the regional aspects of their work were mostly quite narrowly and locally conceived, and in general owed little to the broader issues and ideas of regionalism. Admittedly there were some connections between regionalists and town planners in terms of the development of techniques and general philosophical approaches; and there was also a common interest in the form of regional administrative arrangements. But for the most part regional work was seen in terms quite unlike the geographical conception of regions as natural entities. For town planners, they were a convenient form of overview or context for the primary task of local regulation.

In the period under consideration planning regions were formed from below, using building blocks based on existing town planning powers. These powers derived from below, using the 1909 Housing, Town Planning, etc., Act and consequently rested primarily with the country's 1400 housing authorities i.e. the county boroughs, municipal boroughs, urban and rural districts. Not until the 1929 Local Government Act were county councils given statutory powers to engage in town planning and thus become involved in regional planning although in practice in many cases they had hitherto been informally involved. Planning regions for the most part during the period under discussion were therefore developed on a locally ad hoc 'bottom up' basis and reflected local political rivalries and abilities to co-operate. Cherry comments how town (and regional) planning was rooted in the interwar period in achieving effective statutory planning at a local level.[9] This gave it a secure base in professional practice but 'it lacked the vitality of a wider imagination that could be released outside local government procedures'.[10]

The attitudes of county borough councils and their relationships with adjoining county boroughs and with county councils provided the local political contexts in which the more urban planning regions of the 1920s and 1930s had to be formed; in more rural counties the context was largely set by the relationships between the county council and their smaller boroughs and districts. Patterns of local rivalry across traditional boundaries might frustrate the formation of rational planning regions as in Tyneside and Teesside; elsewhere, as in Manchester and the West Midlands, there might be a greater willingness to co-operate (at least in plan preparation). The regions formed under this approach were thus ad hoc arrangements; there was no general model or systematic structure to which they had to conform.

From the beginning of statutory planning there had been an awareness that the boundaries of local planning authorities would not be adequate for planning purposes where developments or issues crossed those boundaries. For this reason local planning authorities were given the rather unusual power to include relevant parts of adjacent authorities within their own schemes. It was envisaged for instance that the comparatively well-resourced and staffed county boroughs might prepare such schemes for adjacent and potentially suburban urban and rural districts. Other wider-ranging planning issues came quite quickly to the attention of the Local Government Board (LGB) and provided some background experience and precedents for later action. Central as well as local government, was to play a role in the establishment of the 'experimental era's' planning regions.

Area-wide precedents - Town Planning Conferences

The newly developing South Yorkshire coalfield around Doncaster presented one of the first challenges to the existing planning and administrative framework. Gaskell has discussed how the 'rather county nineteenth century atmosphere of Doncaster had been struck to its roots by the development of the surrounding coalfield'.[11] The problems were characteristic of those of rapidly developing mineral resource regions: rapid in-migration, overcrowding, pit villages built as ugly terraces without community amenities. These seemed just the sort of problems which the new town planning powers might tackle, but where there was a need for the relevant authorities to work together. As a first step a Town Planning Conference was held in Doncaster in January 1911.

Thomas Adams, then Town Planning Inspector at the LGB, later recorded how during the years 1911 to 1914 he had investigated the housing and sanitary conditions of the 'great mining field' in the area and concluded that 'the situation must be dealt with comprehensive treatment of the whole problem'.[12] Although the planning authorities and speakers at the 1911 Conference confirmed their support in principle for the planned development of the area, 'the rural districts failed to make any plans and Doncaster Corporation continued to prevaricate'.[13] The initiative for action was lost before 1914 and Adams departure for Canada, but it did not disappear from the collective memory of the LBG and its newly-appointed town planner - George Pepler. The Board's annual report for 1914-15 noted that 'during the year our attention has again been directed to the industrial developments which are taking place in the South Yorkshire coalfields...(although)..progress is likely to be delayed owing to depleted staffs and the additional duties devolving upon them in consequence of the war'.[14]

Much of Pepler's early work at the LGB was concerned with the London Arterial Roads Conferences. The origins of these conferences lay in the growing number of motor vehicles in the national capital and its outskirts and the complete inadequacy of the existing road network to cope with the traffic they generated and were expected to generate. The Board of Trade's London Traffic Branch began a detailed study of the arterial road problem in 1909 under Colonel Hellard.[15] Hellard's proposals of 1910 and had both clear local implications for the new town planning authorities of the Greater London area as they began to consider their suburban schemes and also highlighted the cross-boundary implications of motor traffic and highways and the need to deal with them on a co-ordinated basis.

This proved difficult to achieve, however, and it took a deputation to the Prime Minister in July 1913 and the organization of a Conference in November of the involved authorities convened by the LGB President John Burns to take matters forward. Hellard's proposals were circulated to seven sectional conferences for consideration including how far what was necessary or desirable in this direction could and ought to be secured by town planning schemes. Buchanan records how by 1916 the 'way had been largely cleared for a concerted effort at tackling London's road problem, if not in the centre, at least on the outskirts where most of the growth was taking place'.[16]

The general relationships between traffic, arterial roads and land use planning and development which emerged from the Conferences were of general interest as factors promoting subsequent regional planning not only in Greater London but also in other metropolitan regions.[17] Not only were the lines and scale of future highways and improvements significant components of planning Schemes, but their inclusion in the Regional Reports and Schemes gave them a statutory definition helpful to highway surveyors and decision makers.

Furthermore, the successful working of the procedural administrative device of a conference for a wide area established a precedent which might usefully be applied in other local government functions, particularly town planning. Consideration had also been given to the general relationships between roads and town planning and the need to work in a co-ordinated fashion at both a Greater London scale and in terms of sections (or sub-regions) of the metropolitan region. Moreover the LGB (and local planning authorities elsewhere) had been given a framework in which to consider the future co-ordination of the patchwork of local town planning schemes being prepared by the 140 or so local planning authorities in Greater London.

Regionalism and Regional Plans

The derivation of a specifically 'regional' formula within which to treat such emerging town planning issues came from a quite different source than the rather arid world of central and local government administrative procedures. The source contains two separate strands, both of which are connected with the application of the ideas of Patrick Geddes. First, there was his use of 'the geographical concept of the region, as a unit for the study of social, cultural and environmental factors'. Drawing on the work of French social scientists Geddes 'began to feel his way towards the idea that the city and its region were intimately related and that to understand the one, it was necessary to understand the other'.[18] For town planners, this organizing concept of the region could be of immediate interest. It might enable them to picture their parochial suburban schemes within a framework of the entire town and its adjacent rural area.

Geddes' other contribution was the idea of 'survey', that is of a wide-ranging, field-based investigation of the various elements constituting civic and regional entities, their nature and interactions, as a means of understanding the city and the region and their policy issues and remedies. Whilst Geddes 'thankfully recognized in the town planning movement the kind of milieu in which his interpretation of social service might flourish',[19] a few leading town planners also saw his ideas of survey as providing them with the sort of approach they needed to begin to understand the urban areas whose suburban extensions they were to plan under the 1909 Act. In theory at least, Geddes' approach to survey took deep root in individual planners such as Patrick Abercrombie, but it was too idiosyncratic to be easily made operational in a practical sense for the routine, technical conduct of town planning in local authorities up and down the country. A period of experiment and experience was required before planners routinely adopted the survey as a component of their existing technique.[20]

The development of civic and regional surveys owed more to the practical efforts of groups of Geddesian enthusiasts and some planning consultants and academics than it did to local authority town planning staff: their technicians, who were few in number, felt that the specialist nature of the survey lay beyond their competence and they were anyway swamped with the detailed work of Scheme preparation. Nevertheless, in the tumult of the First World War and with a view to post-war reconstruction, architects, surveyors, planners and voluntary bodies such as the London Society joined together, to promote 'civic surveys' in Greater London, South Lancashire and South Yorkshire, obtaining government funds to help undertake the work.[21]

Those professional town planning consultants who were interested in considering how surveys could contribute to town planning, drew H.J. Fleure into the Town Planning Institute's 1917 programme to lecture on "The Regional Survey, Preparatory to Town Planning". In the subsequent discussion Abercrombie took the opportunity to put regional survey in a wider context of the planning challenges of reconstruction. In particular he noted the embryonic idea of what was to become the 1919 "Homes for Heroes" housebuilding campaign, and expressed his worries that with half a million houses being mentioned there was a special need to build them where they were wanted. The LGB had gone about things in the wrong way by asking each local authority to estimate their housing needs, a task they could not realistically undertake. Regional surveys, however, which would take other, particularly local economic factors into account, could give a scientific basis to resource allocation. 'They must therefore devise some means whereby the study of this regional survey work was connected with Town Planning, and he would like to see the words "Regional Planning" introduced'.[22] He also saw the need to embody this proposal in suggestions for new legislation. The separate term 'regional planning' had thus been established, conceptually linked with regional survey, but what the new activity was to consist of and how it would be practised remained to be discovered.

The Development of Administrative Structures

The legislative mechanism sought by Abercrombie to enable regional planning to be explored, was established in Part II of the Housing, Town Planning, etc., Act which completed its Parliamentary passage at the end of July 1919. The new machinery was to be overseen by George Pepler as Chief Planning Inspector at the newly-established Ministry of Health, which replaced the Local Government Board. Cherry has described the 'remarkable achievement' of Pepler's pioneering role in regional planning work, which often included the stage managing of the inaugural meetings of Regional Advisory Committees during the 1920s and 1930s.[23]

Under the provisions of the Act local planning authorities were enabled to come together to constitute Joint Committees. These Committees were quite often termed 'Regional Town Planning Committees' indicating their origins and the lack of a clear identity for the new form of planning. There were two main types of committee. The first enabled its authorities to come together to provide a common source of advice. This might be in terms of expertise, for instance, on the procedures, contents or policies appropriate for local Scheme preparation, to co-ordinate ideas for a particular arterial road, or, more ambitiously to undertake a regional survey and prepare an outline regional planning report which would set out a co-ordinated basis for the preparation of schemes. The second type of joint committee enabled the authorities to transfer their planning powers to the committee itself, which could then act on their behalf and that of others on an executive basis to prepare a 'regional' Town Planning Scheme. It was possible to arrange for variants of these basic types to meet differently required delegations of powers and to incorporate pre-existing planning Scheme work.

The membership of the committees themselves was generally provided by local politicians - aldermen and councillors, with their senior officers - mostly the clerks and surveyor/engineers - forming technical sub-committees. The Manchester and District Committee for instance began by establishing sub-committees to promote town planning schemes among its members, to consider building development (including standards, open space, and zoning), roads, and civic and regional survey. The committees shared their expenses out among their members and this and the membership constitution of the committees often proved delicate points of negotiation and local protocol. Occasionally too the politicans would rein in their officers and establish voting rights more precisely.

One difficulty before the 1929 Local Government Act was to find a formal way of associating the County Councils and their major highway interests and broad-base of rateable value with joint committee work. The 1929 powers, which enabled local planning authorities to cede their planning powers to the county councils, were not always welcomed as local interests felt threatened by the prospects of control from county or shire hall. One method of extending membership came through co-option. The South-West Lancashire Joint Town Planning Advisory Committee for instance co-opted a local representative and the County Surveyor from Lancashire together with Professors Abercrombie and Roxby from the Liverpool and District Regional Survey Association, two representatives from the Roads Improvement Association, and a volunteer from the Land Agents Society.

In a paper to the 1928 International Geographical Congress C.B. Fawcett stressed that 'the proper unit-area for the planning of the human occupation of our country is not the town but a much wider "region",' but he also drew attention to some significant trends which had resulted from the legislation. First, that the establishment of local committees was permissive (although the preparation of planning Schemes had been made obligatory for towns of more than 20,000 in the 1919 Act); secondly, of the 55 committees that had been estalished he noted, two only were 'executive' committees, although he thought that the 'advisory' nature of the majority of committees tended to encourage discussion, since 'they must convince the Local Authorities of the soundness of their plans'.[24] Fawcett's review revealed a clustering of regional committees in the suburban areas around London, a second metropolitan cluster established around Birmingham, and a general extension of smaller local regions in the industrial and mining areas of the Midlands and northern England (Figure 4.1).

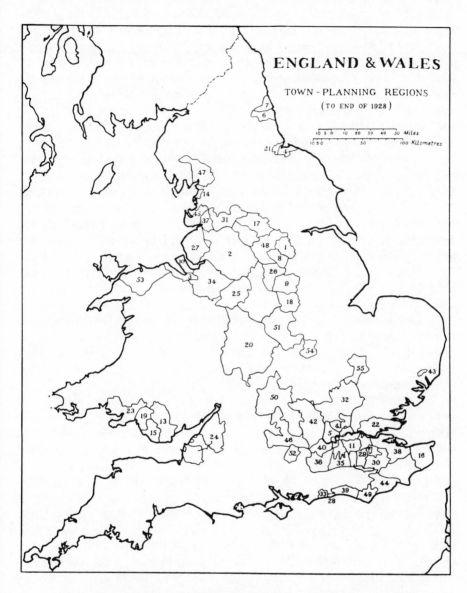

The numbers on the map are those employed by the Ministry of Health. The map gives the position at the end of 1928 and includes three additional Regions: (53) North Wales, (54) Mid-Northampton, (55) Cambridgeshire. Regions 11, 29 and 30, also 5 and 12 overlap.

4.1 Regional Planning in 1928

from Fawcett, C.B. 'Regional Planning in England and Wales'
(see note 24 below)

The regions established by the mid 1920s fell into four general categories: resource-exploitation urban regions, such as Doncaster; industrially-based urban regions, such as South Teesside; developing suburban regions, such as Wirral and West Middlesex; and, metropolitan regions, such as Manchester and District in north west England. Maps prepared by the Ministry of Health, whose Annual Reports regularly catalogued the establishment of new planning regions and reviewed their surveys and proposals as they were published, showed the emergence of a fifth type of planning region - the rural county region, such as East Suffolk - and a general thickening up of the coverage of regions in and around the country's urban-industrial 'axial belt' (Figure 4.2). The major exceptions to this pattern were found in the still deeply rural counties of Eastern England, in central Wales and adjacent English Marcher counties, and in South West England from Somerset to Cornwall. Regional planning had little to offer these areas before the extension of planning powers to rural areas in the 1932 Town and Country Planning Act and the effective definition of a "Rural Zone" in 1938. The Ministry of Health's maps portray a varied, even anarchic, patchwork of town planning regions far removed from any rational or ordered subdivisions. Nevertheless, those alert to the quickening of change in the country and to objectives of countryside protection seemed aware of the potentialities of the regional adea. The Council for the Protection of Rural England, for instance, published regional surveys of Cornwall (1930) and Devon (1932), and in the North Riding of Yorkshire the County Clerk encouraged a positive interest in the introduction of country planning.[25]   Overall, however, the ambiguities of inter-war regionalism remained, embroiling regional planning in the confusion, which in its turn added to, rather than resolved the conflicts.

The establishment of a region and a committee was in itself no guarantee of any published report. In the 1920s particularly regional planning expertise was in short supply and many of the committees appointed one or more consultants to undertake their regional survey and prepare a regional report/advisory plan. Abercrombie was associated with 16 projects;[26] the firm of Adams, Thompson and Fry was associated with a dozen or so more, 'drawn up largely by Thompson, though Adams paid occasional "state visits" to the regions and no doubt cast an eye over the draft plans'.[27] Other leading consultants included S.D. Adshead, W.R. Davidge, R.H. Mattocks, Thomas Mawson and J.H. Forshaw. With so many demands on their expertise, the work of the consultants was not of a consistently high quality, nor did it find universal favour. The employment of a consultant was certainly no guarantee of acclaim and the geographer E.C. Willatts commented on the example of the South Essex Joint Town Planning Committee, which with S.D. Adshead as consultant had ignored 'the finest tract of market-garden land within reach of London as yet not severely mutilated' and 'proceeded to regard it as a tract of virgin country that exists to be commandeered for urban use'.[28]

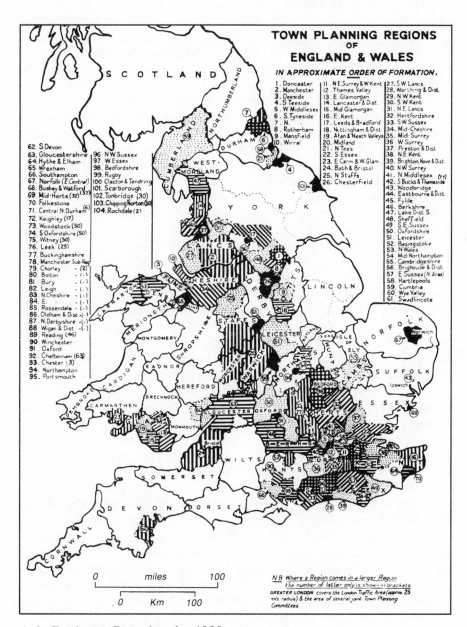

TOWN PLANNING REGIONS
OF
ENGLAND & WALES

IN APPROXIMATE ORDER OF FORMATION.

1. Doncaster
2. Manchester
3. Deeside
4. S Teeside
5. W Middlesex
6. S Tyneside
7. N.
8. Rotherham
9. Mansfield
10. Wirral
11. N E Surrey & W Kent
12. Thames Valley
13. E Glamorgan
14. Lancaster & Dist.
15. Mid Glamorgan
16. E. Kent
17. Leeds & Bradford
18. Nottingham & Dist
19. Afan & Neath Valleys
20. Midland
21. N Tees
22. S Essex
23. E Carm & W Glam.
24. Bath & Bristol
25. N Staffs.
26. Chesterfield
27. S W Lancs
28. Worthing & Dist
29. N W Kent
30. S W Kent
31. N E Lancs
32. Hertfordshire
33. S W Sussex
34. Mid-Cheshire
35. Mid-Surrey
36. W Surrey
37. Preston & Dist
38. N E Kent
39. Brighton, Hove & Dist.
40. N W Surrey
41. N Middlesex (77)
42. S Bucks & Thameside
43. Woodbridge
44. Eastbourne & Dist
45. Fylde
46. Berkshire
47. Lake Dist S.
48. Sheffield
49. S.E. Sussex
50. Oxfordshire
51. Leicester
52. Basingstoke
53. N Wales
54. Mid-Northampton
55. Cambridgeshire
56. Brighouse & Dist
57. E Sussex (N Area)
58. Hartlepools
59. Cumbria
60. Wye Valley
61. Swadlincote

62. S Devon
63. Gloucestershire
64. Hythe & Elham
65. Wrexham
66. Southampton
67. Norfolk (E.Central)
68. Bushey & Watford
69. Mid-Herts (32) (32)
70. Folkestone
71. Central N.Durham (6)
72. Keighley (17)
73. Woodstock (50)
74. S Oxfordshire (50)
75. Witney (50)
76. Leek (25)
77. Buckinghamshire
78. Manchester Sub Reg
79. Chorley . (2)
80. Bolton . (-)
81. Bury . (-)
82. Leigh . (-)
83. N.Cheshire . (-)
84. E. . (-)
85. Rossendale -(-)
86. Oldham & Dist -(-)
87. N.Derbyshire -(-)
88. Wigan & Dist . (-)
89. Reading (46)
90. Winchester
91. Oxford
92. Cheltenham (63)
93. Chester (3)
94. Northampton
95. Portsmouth

96. N W Sussex
97. W Essex
98. Bedfordshire
99. Rugby
100. Clacton & Tendring
101. Scarborough
102. Tonbridge (30)
103. Chipping Norton (50)
104. Rochdale (2)

N.B. *Where a Region comes in a larger Region the number of latter only is shown in brackets.*
GREATER LONDON *covers the London Traffic Area (approx. 25 mls. radius) & the area of several joint Town Planning Committees.*

miles   0 — 100
Km   0 — 100

4.2 Regional Planning in 1930

from Pepler, G.L. 'Twenty-one Years of Town Planning in England and Wales', Journal of the Town Planning Institute, XVII, No.3 (Jan. 1931), p.65.

Other joint committees (particularly the largest provincial ones e.g. Manchester and District and the Midlands) used their own staff. Occasionally they employed a 'regional planning assistant' as a specialist. Thomas Sharp, who had worked with Adams, Thompson and Fry on their outer London commissions was appointed to such a post with the South-West Lancashire Committee.[29] The role of these internally managed regional planning studies is understated in comparison with the attention given to the leading consultants and further work is required before an assessment can be made of their contribution.

The first generation of regional planners had little by way of established techniques to use in their novel task. To that extent they were very much part of what Long has called the 'craft' stage of town planning. Simpson describes the output of the Adams, Thompson and Fry partnership as being 'representative examples of their genre, notable for their lucid if wooden exposition, relatively unsophisticated analyses of physical, economic and social conditions in the sketchy surveys and straightforward recommendations which unashamedly had more to do with common sense than environmental science. British regional planning had little intellectual rationale...'.[30]

One possible source of ideas was United States practice. Brownell has described how 'by 1911 the planning survey became the most specialized tool in general use. By the 1920s the survey technique had been expanded considerably to include data on economic activities and population projections...this was still, however, largely an endeavour of collecting and displaying large amounts of data'. He sees transportation as providing 'a new dimension for technique' and recounts how not only could large amounts of data be collected, but how 'certain "laws" of traffic movement and street design also evolved'.[31] They were not he argues 'theoretical formulations', but were far more esoteric and technical than general surveys and layout designs. The basic techniques and methodology of the modern land use/transportation study had been established by the late 1920s, although its wider application had to wait for another 30 years or so.

Adams, of all the British planners, was best equipped to bring more sophisticated techniques such as those developed in the New York Regional Survey and Plan in the 1920s to bear on regional efforts in Britain. Among the particular contributions made by those working on the Plan noticed by Johnson were developments in population projection methods, the beginnings of economic base theory, and developments by Robert Murray Haig and Roswell McCrea in 'economists' theories of the interurban location of economic activity through their path-breaking empirical studies of the accessibility requirements of firms and households. Haig and McCrea also demonstrated the validity of the view that the city was important as a production unit as well as a consumption unit in the national economy'.[32]

However, with no British regional plans funded on the scale of that of New York, little seems to have filtered across the Atlantic towards British practice. Moreover there was very little support available from the British social or engineering sciences by way of intellectual rationale with which planners could work. Once the contributions of the civic and regional surveyors in data collection had been exhausted, there was little beyond intuition, commonsense and experience to guide the planner in correlating the various factors which were neatly tabulated, mapped and graphed.[33] It was not merely that the techniques were at a rudimentary stage of evolution, but the basic data were usually not available either. Either they had not been collected systematically or had simply never been collected at all. Although voluntary bodies could contribute a good deal, for the most part there was a need for the public authorities to organize their own surveys.

Sir Henry Maybury, Director-General of Roads at the then newly-established Ministry of Transport, for instance told the Manchester and District Committee at their 1922 Conference that 'road design in its broadest sense can only be securely based on traffic-statistics and charts of traffic-currents'. He then went on to express his hope that comparable data would be collected on a yearly basis in the future and to congratulate Manchester for its contribution to the first nationally organized traffic census in August 1921. 'In Manchester your census was conducted with greater thoroughness than in most other centres', he stated, 'and as the outcome you will be rewarded with data of unrivalled scope for study by Town Planning experts and road designers'. However, it was not clear how the data was to be used in such a study other than by visual inspection of mapped quantities of traffic flow. 'When the statistics...are collated the road engineer will gain a bird's eye view of the traffic-streams flowing along all the great channels of communication', he added.[34]

The early regional planners did their best as such data became available, producing maps of traffic flows along main roads and of projected change in traffic volumes over time. No doubt when set against capacity standards (the early regional plans are full of diagrams of different road widths configurations), they were of some help in justifying improvements, but there is little to suggest that highway engineering had much intellectual rationale to add to the regional planning debate. Further maps were produced showing accessibility to main centres by public transport, using perhaps one quarter or one half mile walking distance to bus routes as a standard. They also depicted the changes in these conditions which might be expected if new routes were built and services extended.

The position over the regional economy was no better. Cherry has commented on how there was virtually nothing said in the inter war regional planning reports on economic problems, and instances the Abercrombie and Kelly 1932 Cumbrian Regional Planning Scheme, which concentrated on the preservation of Lakeland from bungalows, road-houses and petrol filling stations, but 'could offer little more than the palliative of zoning for the acute problems of the industrial coastal strip'.[35] But neither geographers nor economists at the time had much to offer. The South-West Lancashire Committee organized a survey of the larger manufacturers in the region in 1927 asking them 14 questions ranging from the numbers employed and the percentage travelling to work by public transport from other districts, to the type of power used and whether they would be interested in a scheme of decentralization of industry and population into new satellite towns. The returns, analyzed for the team by its brilliant young assistant Thomas Sharp and subsequently Dr. Caradoc Jones of Liverpool University's Social Survey of Merseyside, seem to have had little bearing on the Committee's recommendations.[36]

If the analytical content of the regional advisory plans was thin, their presentation, artwork and typography were often very fine. Regional planning was, interestingly, a preserve of architecture rather than engineering, and many of those involved had been trained in the tradition of the arts and crafts movement. The leading consultants' plans were published in folio format, on good uncut paper, with scrupulous attention to quality of binding, typeface and illustration. Patrick Abercrombie set a high aesthetic standard for this type of report with the elegant, slightly archaic penwork that adorns the maps and diagrams of his inter-war plans. Observations about landscape or townscape might as often be supported by an effective sketch drawing as by a (sepia) photograph. The accompanying prose had, again, a slight hint of eighteenth century mannerism. Despite their predominantly descriptive, empirical content, the plans were drafted more in the spirit of literary essayism than of the Blue Books.

Regional Planning for Greater London

The development of ideas for the regional planning of Greater London in the decade between 1925 and 1935 provides a salutary example of both the potential of regional thinking and also the frustrations of those who tried to apply it in the circumstances of the time. Their contribution is often overlooked in the degree of attention given to Abercrombie's most famous production, the *Greater London Plan 1944*; but just as invention comes only to the prepared mind, so this paradigm planning report owed much to the well-established foundations and accumulated knowledge of an earlier experimental era. Gordon Stephenson, who was a member of the Greater London Plan team, puts it like this: 'The Greater London Plan 1944 may be seen as the conclusion of work begun by Unwin and continued by Abercrombie'.[37] Unwin's Second Report (1933) for the Greater London Regional Planning Committee 'provided a challenge and a brief for Abercrombie, after lying dormant for a decade'.[38]

From the days of the Greater London Arterial Road Conferences there had been ideas that a wider planning context was needed for the national capital region than could be provided even by quite extensive regional associations of its suburban local authorities. The position was complicated, however, by the presence of a predominant authority at the core of the region in the shape of the London County Council (LCC), whose fiscal resources, territorial and development ambitions beyond its boundaries aroused suspicion and hostility among its neighbours.[39]   At the same time in regional planning terms the suburban authorities could not manage without the LCC; and when the Council turned inward in the mid 1930s and withdrew its financial underpinning of the fragile wider area efforts, they faltered despite the manifestation of a regional planning strategy for Greater London which included many of the main elements which were to appear later in the 1944 Plan.

The Greater London Regional Joint Town Planning Committee was established in 1927 after much background work and prompting from professional bodies, voluntary societies and special interest groups.   The Committee was made up of 45 members representing the LCC and other local authorities.   The intention was to formulate a comprehensive plan for the 1,846 square miles that it covered.   Gwilym Gibbon, Principal Assistant Secretary at the Ministry of Health, wrote in a background minute for the first meeting of the Committee that 'the master question is that of decentralization and it is desirable that measures should be taken immediately for a thorough consideration of this question.   The problem is one of such difficulty and importance that it will require the best Committee that can be got together...this fact will the more onerous,' he emphasized, 'because there is unfortunately no body of doctrine with a firm basis of fact giving conclusions which could be applied in the case of Greater London.'   There might he thought, 'also be some advantage if the co-operation of some competent economist could be secured'.[40]   In his usual incisive way, Gibbon put his finger on regional planning's lack of principle and coherence, and also its narrow and restricted intellectual base.   The scale of London and its problems challenged and mocked the resources of the Greater London Regional Joint Town Planning Committee.

In practice it was left to Raymond Unwin (an architect-planner, with a decade or more of gifted public service in the housing field and now reaching the end of his official career) as Technical Adviser to the Committee to try and organize some basis of fact.   In terms of one of the basics - industrial location - he had practically to invent the subject, to originate his data and analyse it as best he could.   The Committee's Interim Report on Decentralization (1931) indicates the nature and scope of his enquiries.

'While we cannot claim to have made any complete analysis of industry in the London Region,' he wrote, 'conditions in regard to 40 or 50 manufacturing firms have been studied and discussed with their heads or managers.   These firms have included a large proportion who have moved their industries, started new industries in the areas, or have considered the question of moving and decided against it for the time being.   Collating the results of these enquiries...there emerge a few predominating considerations which mainly determine their movement and location'.[41]   The pioneering academic study of industrial growth in the northern and western sectors of outer London by the geographer D.H. Smith based on a survey of 627 factories was not to be published until 1933. With it came a foreword by Unwin in which he commented that '...the results are helpful and enlightening to the planner..'.[42]

It was as well that some enlightenment based on empirical study was at hand, because the alternative (as one suspects Gibbon feared) was a doctrine based on ideology. The leading view came from the Garden City Movement, whose advocates such as C.B. Purdom, had attempted to apply its ideas to the wider London region in the immediate post-war period. Through his close association with Letchworth Garden City in the early 1900s, Unwin was well aware of their basic concerns and in the early 1920s set out his reformulation of 'satellite town' approach as possessing the basic elements for the realistic wider-area planning of a great industrial city.

Foley has discussed how although it would be inaccurate to attribute the basic ideas of the 1944 Plan exclusively to garden city doctrine, it was nonetheless of the first importance: 'the concepts of Green Belt (although at first a narrow and irregular one), a ring road, and satellite towns evolved gradually, with new proposals building on parts of earlier ones'.[43] Since the early regional planners could not rely on Gibbon's doctrine with a firm basis of fact, they had essentially to work on a basis of ad hoc data collection, informed by instruction, common sense and an ideological doctrine based on a set of convictions about desirable spatial form and relationships.

This gradual evolution of regional planning technique tested the proposals of garden city doctrine and related proposals (especially those concerned with major road developments) against political, technical and administrative opinion, local circumstances and the capacity of the planning system to provide effective policy instruments. The experimental methodology of regional plan-making of the late 1920s and early 1930s consisted not only of developing and testing the individual components of the plan proposals, but also bringing the various elements together into new types of pattern, under the aegis of new forms of organization, central as well as local, voluntary as well as official.[45]

No effective administrative method existed, however, to harmonize the Regional Advisory Committee's proposals with the second tier of regional advisory reports for the sections or sub-regions of Greater London and the third tier local planning schemes. Nor were there appropriate implementationary organizations in place despite repeated pleas and demands from Unwin for a regional planning authority with sufficient power and permanence to revise, modify and promote the plan over a long period of time. After 1934, the LLC drew largely apart, hostile to any follow-up action. Unwin found the setbacks hard to bear, despairing of the 'persistent desire to cling to the haphazard'.[46] In the event there were organizational changes rather than implementating actions - notwithstanding the LCC's own Green Belt purchase scheme. The Greater London Committee was replaced in 1937 by a Standing Conference on London Regional Planning, which published its first report in 1939, 'calling once again for the preparation of a regional or master plan for London'.[47] Stephenson comments that the new Standing Conference proved to be cumbersome and slow to reach conclusions, but its Technical Committee was later to assist in the preparation of the Greater London Plan of 1944. Harry Stewart remained as

Chairman of the Technical Committee when he acted as Abercrombie's 'office manager'.[48] Furthermore, Abercrombie himself paid tribute to Unwin's reports 'on which, if action had been taken, the planning problems of Greater London would have been vastly more measurable today'.[49]

Conclusions

The early years of regional planning in Britain can be divided into three and possibly four phases: first, the period from 1909 to 1919 during which statutory town planning by local authorities was established, the case for regional planning was promoted and regional survey technique was linked to regional planning. The second phase from 1920 to 1932 provided the first period of statutory regional survey and planning with an emphasis on the preparation of regional advisory reports which included survey material and outline planning proposals. The third period from 1933 to 1937 was marked by increasing activity on the part of regional executive committees in preparing planning schemes on behalf of the authorities in their area (and in the meantime exercising an 'interim' form of controlling development) and an increasing involvement of county councils under powers granted in 1929 and 1932. Following Adam's suggestion, these second and third phases may be regarded as an experimental era of 'regional town planning' efforts.

A fourth period may also be dimly discerned from 1937 until the inauguration of the 1947 Act system. It was a transitional period, however, largely devoted to the definition of a 'new era' of planning and its inauguration following government's acceptance of the radical and far-reaching recommendations of the members of the Royal Commission on the distribution of the Industrial Population (the Barlow Commission), which reported in late 1939, although the Report as such was not published until earlier the following year. The 1943 Town and Country Planning (Interim Development) Act had extended interim development control throughout the country. In such circumstances (which might be taken to imply the acceptance of the need for a compulsory and comprehensive planning system) it was helpful for the inexperienced and previously rather reluctant authorities involved to share their work with other (possibly more experienced) authorities through regional joint town planning committees.

The organizational basis of the joint committee or standing conference, sometimes reconstituted, also formed a basis for the second generation of regional advisory plans initiated by central government (notably those for Greater London, for South Lancashire-North Cheshire (Manchester and District), for Merseyside and in Scotland and Wales for the Clyde Valley and South Wales). From the early 1940s the undertaking of this second generation of regional plans brought a new range of planning techniques to bear on both doctrines with a basis in fact as well as ideology, expressed most notably in the *Greater London*

Plan, 1944 and the *Clyde Valley Plan*. Elsewhere joint committees survived on a smaller scale until 1948, carrying out with greater or lesser enthusiasm the routines which had brought them into being and helping the planning system adjust to the new demands emerging from the post-war legislative programme and the needs of reconstruction until the establishment of the 1947 Town and Country Planning Act system based on county borough and county councils.

In contrast to the ad hoc, 'bottom up' approach which had developed since 1919, a new form of regional planning structure emerged from the Ministry of Town and Country Planning (established in 1943). As befitted the idea of a new 'central authority' it was based on a systematic, 'top down' comprehensive structure of standard regions. Their tasks were administrative - to supervise local authorities (and joint regional committees, few of which extended to the scale of the Ministry's new regions). With the task of preparing the new Development Plans after 1947 given to county borough and county councils, the job of co-ordinating policies and proposals fell to the Ministry's Regional Offices rather than the local authorities' own regional working. From that time the 'new era' foreseen in 1931 by Adams had come to pass; the 'experimental era' of regional town planning had been accomplished.

Notes

1. Ashworth, W. (1955) *The Genesis of Modern British Town Planning: A Study in Economic and Social History of the Nineteenth and Twentieth Centuries*, London: Routledge and Kegan Paul, p.205.
2. Examples can be found in Cherry, G.E. (1980) 'Interwar Regional Planning Schemes in Britain: an interim review', *Planning History Bulletin 2*, pp.14-16; Cherry, G.E. (ed.) (1981) *Pioneers in British Planning*, London: Architectural Press; Gunby, D. (1983) 'The Scope and Purpose of Town Planning in the 1920s: with Reference to Regional Planning on Teesside'. Paper presented at the Institute of British Geographers' Conference, Edinburgh; Gunby, D. (1987) 'The Scope and Purpose of Town Planning in Britain: The Experience of the Second Town Planning Act, 1919-1932'. Unpublished PhD. thesis. The Open University; Young, K. and Garside, P.L. (1982) *Metropolitan London: Politics and Urban Change 1837-1981*, London: Edward Arnold.
3. Cherry, G.E. (1974) *The Evolution of British Town Planning: A History of Town Planning in the United Kingdom during the Twentieth Century and of the Royal Town Planning Institute, 1914-1974*, Leighton Buzzard: Heath and Reech, p.94.
4. Cherry (1980) 'Interwar Regional Planning Schemes', p.15-16.
5. Sheail, J. (1981) *Rural Conservation in Inter-War Britain*, Oxford: Clarendon, Chapter VIII.
6. Sheail (1981) *Rural Conservation*, p.96.
7. Adams, T. (1932) *Recent Advances in Town Planning*, London: J. and A. Churchill, p.73.
8. see also Cherry (1981) *Pioneers in British Planning*, p.136.
9. Cherry, 'Interwar Regional Planning Schemes', p.16.

10. For a detailed discussion of this point see Gunby (1983) 'Scope and Purpose of Town Planning in the 1920s', pp.27-28, and Gunby (1987) 'Scope and Purpose of Town Planning in Britain'.
11. Gaskell, M. (1979) 'Model Industrial Village in S. Yorkshire / N. Derbyshire and the Early Town Planning Movement' *Town Planning Review* 50, pp.537-558.
12. Adams, T. (1917) *Rural Planning and Development: A Study of Rural Conditions and Problems in Canada*, Ottowa: Commission of Conservation, pp.128-9.
13. Gaskell, (1979) 'Model Industrial Village', p.545.
14. Local Government Board, *Annual Report 1914-15*, London: HMSO p.37.
15. Buchanan, D.M. (1971) *London Road Plans* 1900-1970, London: GLC Intelligence Unit, pp.11-13.
16. The model of the London Arterial Roads Conference formed the basis for a proposal in 1918 that a Joint Advisory Committee should be formed to co-ordinate post-war reconstruction in Greater London. At a specially convened conference attended by 170 delegates from 92 local authorities, it was resolved that the local authorities in London should work as a co-ordinated whole, on the basis of six sectional conferences following the arrangements for the roads conference. For a detailed discussion, see Young and Garside (1982), *Metropolitan London*, pp.147-152.
17. Abercrombie, P. (1924) 'The Preliminary Survey of a Region including the Built-up Areas of its Urban Centres'. *Papers of the International Town Planning Conference*, Amsterdam, pp.36-37.
18. Mellor, H. (1981) 'Patrick Geddes' in Cherry, G. (ed.) *Pioneers in British Planning*, London: Architectural Press, p.57.
19. Mellor, 'Patrick Geddes', p.58.
20. Dix, G. (1981) 'Patrick Abercrombie 1879-1957' in Cherry (1981) *Pioneers in British Planning*, pp.104-8.
21. Cherry (1974) *Evolution of British Town Planning*, p.74.
22. Abercrombie, P. (1918) Contribution to discussion on H.J. Fleure (1918) 'The Regional Survey Preparatory to Town Planning' *Journal of the Town Planning Institute* IV, pp.31.-38.
23. Cherry (1981) *Pioneers in British Planning*, pp.133-137.
24. Fawcett, C.B. (1930) 'Regional Planning in England and Wales' *Report of the Proceedings of the International Geographical Congress Cambridge 1928*, Cambridge: The Executive Committee of the Congress, pp.453-61.
25. Sheail (1979) 'Statutory Planning in Rural Areas'.
26. Dix (1981) 'Patrick Abercrombie', p.126, n.41.
27. Simpson, M. (1985) *Thomas Adams and the Modern Planning Movement: Britain, Canada and the United States 1900-1940*, London: Mansell, pp.171-8.
28. Willatts, E.C. (1987) 'Geographers and their Involvement in Planning' in Steel, R.W. (ed.) (1987) *British Geography 1918-1845*, Cambridge: Cambridge University Press, p.102.
29. Stansfield, K. 'Thomas Sharp 1901-1978' in Cherry (1981) *Pioneers in British Planning*, pp.150-51.
30. Simpson (1985) *Thomas Adams*, p.30.

31. Brownell, B. (1980) 'Urban Planning, the Planning Profession, and the Motor Car in Early Twentieth Century America' in Cherry, G.E. (ed.) (1980) *Shaping an Urban World: Planning in the Twentieth Century*, p.68.

32. Johnson, D.A. (1974) 'The Emergence of Metropolitan Regionalism: An Analysis of the Regional Plan of New York and its Environs,' PhD. thesis, Cornell University, New York, p.544.

33. Abercrombie P. (1924) 'Preliminary Survey of a Region'.

34. Manchester and District Joint Town Planning Advisory Committee (1926) *Report upon the Regional Scheme*, Manchester: The Committee, pp.40-41.

35. Cherry (1980) 'Inter-war Regional Planning Schmes', p.16.

36. L.C.R.O. (Liverpool City Records Office) *Minutes of the South-West Lancashire Joint Town Planning Committee*, 6/4/25 - 21/3/30. (Joint Committees 352/JO1, 16/1).

37. Stephenson, G. (1980), *The Greater London Plans of 1933 and 1944* mimeo (30/4/80). p.5.

38. Stephenson, G. (1980), *The Greater London Plans*, p.3.

39. Young and Garside, *Metropolitan London*, Chapters 5-7.

40. PRO (Public Record Office) HLG 4/3239-42 (Greater London): 4/3241.

41. Unwin, R. (1931) *Interim Report on Decentralization*, London: Greater London Regional Planning Committee.

42. Smith, D.H. (1933) *The Industries of Greater London; being a survey of recent industrialization of the northern and western sectors of Greater London*, London: P.S. King & Co. p.(v).

43. Foley, D.F. (1963) *Controlling London's Growth: Planning the Great Wen 1940-60*. Berkeley: University of California Press, p.15.

44. see Jackson, F. (1985) *Sir Raymond Unwin: Architect, Planner and Visionary*, London: Zwemmer, p.149, for Unwin's conceptual breakthrough from regarding all land as potentially building land (with open space reserved) to a model of building against a background of protected open land.

45. For central government's involvement see Young and Garside (1982) *Metropolitan London*, pp.164-72. For a discussion of the involvement of voluntary bodies and interest groups in regional planning machinery for Greater London, see Garside,P.L. 'Town Planning in London 1930-1961: A Study of Pressures, Interests and Influences Affecting the Formation of Policy', PhD. thesis, University of London, 1979.

46. Young and Garside (1982) *Metropolitan London*, pp.204-218. Jackson, (1963) *Sir Raymond Unwin*, p.154.

47. Young and Garside (1982) *Metropolitan London*, p.218

48. Stephenson (1980) *Greater London Plan*, p.2.

49. Jackson (1985) *Sir Raymond Unwin*, p.52.

5

Regionalism in Interwar Britain: The Role of the Town and Country Planning Association

Dennis Hardy

Introduction

The idea of the region, and its applicability in a policy context, gained ground in the interwar years - moving from largely unexplored territory on the periphery of political and economic debate, to occupy a more focal point of interest in British political life. Particularly by the second half of the 1930s, regional issues were more widely discussed in official circles than at the start of the period, and a lobby was active in pressing for governmental action in this field.

Undoubtedly, the changing fortunes of regionalism and regional planning were bound up with the course of wider events, and, in particular, with the changing fortunes of the regions themselves. But if it was events - or structural processes - which forced the pace, there were also agency factors at work. Politicians and industrialists with an interest in the regions, academics who were attracted by the geographical and economic logic of regional entities, and interest groups who (from a variety of perspectives) were calling for a stronger planning input from government, all responded in their own ways to the consequences of uneven patterns of development. Amongst the interest groups that were active in this way was the then Garden Cities and Town Planning Association (its name being changed in 1941 to the Town and Country Planning Association).

It is argued in this chapter that the GCPTA contributed to the regionalism debate in this period in three ways. For a start, in a theoretical sense, the Association could offer the concept of the 'social city' as a unit in regional planning. Secondly, the Association championed the cause of the statutory town and country planning process as a means to secure, at the very least, sub-regional plans. And finally, in the latter half of the 1930s, events drew the Association into the wider arena of inter-regional planning. It is also argued that it was in the last of these situations - in relation to inter-regional planning - that the Association was able to make its most telling contribution.

The Idea of Social Cities

The origins of the organization in question date from the end of the last century, when, in 1899, the Garden City Association was formed to promote the ideas contained in a book by Ebenezer Howard, *Tomorrow: A Peaceful Path to Real Reform* (published in the previous year).[1] The Association had two initial aims - to promote discussion of Howard's ideas, and to set about putting these ideas into practice through the formation of the first garden city. Within a few years, in 1903, it is interesting to note that the aims of the Association were reformulated in what we would now regard as regional terms, being 'to promote the relief of overcrowded areas and to secure a wider distribution of the population over the land'.[2]

Indeed, at the very heart of the garden city idea is a sense of the need to tackle the social question and the land question on a larger, regional scale. This can be evidenced in two ways. For a start, the basic notion of the garden city is really an example of planned dispersal - a small, self-contained city, initially drawing its population and industry from the metropolis, and, in turn, regenerating the life of the rural area in which the new settlement is located. A second aspect of the regional dimension is that relating to the growth of garden cities, where, instead of allowing unlimited growth, new development would be channelled into surrounding satellite settlements to create what were conceptualized as 'social cities'. Each of these social cities might have a population of as much as a quarter of a million.[3]

The Association was constituted to promote these ideas. From the outset, and in spite of changing aims, it operated as a propagandist body, seeking to disseminate ideas rather than to implement them itself. From an early history that revolved very closely around the fortunes of what became the first garden city, Letchworth (dating from 1903), the Association expanded into a broader campaigning role in connection with the passing of the first Town Planning Act in 1909. From then until the outbreak of the First World War it campaigned not only for town planning, but also for new building in the form of garden suburbs, with Hampstead Garden Suburb as the model to be emulated, where garden cities as such were not attainable. Thus, by 1914, garden suburbs in various forms were becoming quite commonplace, but Letchworth was still the only garden city and Howard's concept of social cities almost a forgotten hope.

And there, one might reflect, the Association might quietly have faded from the scene, like so much else from Edwardian England. Instead, the First World War, and particularly its aftermath, was to breathe new life into the organization, engendering a new sense of urgency and drawing it beyond its original field of interest, not least of all into the realm of regional planning. Under extreme political pressure, towards the end of and immediately after the war, the Coalition Governments led by Lloyd George conceded the promise of rich social rewards to the nation in exchange for political stability. The brightest jewel in the crown of reforms was that of housing. In an enduring phrase (that long outlived the content of what was promised) Lloyd George pledged to the electorate in 1918 that he would secure 'habitations that are fit for the heroes who have won the war'.[4]

Intertwined with this immediate postwar housing campaign, the Association sought to ensure that new houses were discussed within a wider context of garden cities and town planning. Government ministers and officials were approached directly, but also the Association believed that there was still a wider role to be performed in informing public opinion. The general thrust of the Association's message in this period was that it was a time of opportunity, and that official endorsement for the idea of planned towns was within reach. Garden cities, it was argued, made good sense for a nation about to embark on a housebuilding programme of the scale projected.

However, neither the national 'homes for heroes' programme nor the Association's own attempts to secure a place for garden cities lived up to their promise. A second garden city was, in fact, built immediately after the war, at Welwyn, but that was very much a product of private initiative and not part of a wider strategy.

One event, though, signalled a future role for the State, and proved to be the first of a number of tentative steps in this period. In 1919, Neville Chamberlain, newly elected to Parliament, was appointed by the Minister of Health to chair a committee known originally as the Slum Areas Committee, and then, more generally, as the Unhealthy Areas Committee, to look into the whole problem of slum clearance and rebuilding. Its Interim Report in 1920 (confirmed in the Final Report in the following year) included the significant recommendation that 'the development of self-contained garden cities, either round an existing nucleus or on new sites, should be encouraged and hastened by State assistance in the early stages'.[5]

Although it was not immediately acted upon it embodied the principle of planned dispersal that was to become a crucial feature of future planning strategies. For the Association, Neville Chamberlain's personal involvement and commitment to this approach, given his influential political role in the years ahead, proved to be important in itself.[6] In the meantime, the Committee's recommendation for garden cities was seen as a clear endorsement for the Association's policy. There were, indeed, two members of the Association on Chamberlain's Committee, namely R.L. Reiss and G.L. Pepler. The former in particular, as Chairman of the Association's Executive, would have been active in promoting the case for garden cities from his position 'within' government. At the same time, it had to be acknowledged that Chamberlain was already an experienced reformer at the municipal level and 'had no need simply to be the mouthpiece of a propagandist body'.[7]

In propagandist terms, the findings of the Unhealthy Areas Committee were significant for the Association's cause. But as well as operating at a national level, the Association also had some success in lobbying local authorities. At this level, 'their strongest influence appears to have been in London, where Herbert Morrison (as Secretary to the London Labour Party, and a former resident of Letchworth) espoused the cause with especial enthusiasm. Even before the end of the war the Association had submitted a Memorandum to the London local authorities, sowing the seeds of the garden city idea in the great reconstruction programme that was predicted.[8] Then, as part of the *Daily Mail* Ideal Home Exhibition in February 1920, the Association mounted a conference on Satellite Towns for Greater London. The Association Secretary, C. B. Purdom, put the case, explaining that it was because of their belief that 'housing is a much larger question than the size of rooms or heights of ceilings, or even the supply of building trade labour or material' that satellite towns were proposed.[9]

A diagram was produced to show a system of twenty three satellite towns around London (a forerunner of the Greater London Plan of 1944). Morrison responded eloquently to the proposal, asking his colleagues to 'conceive London as the sun with a whole series of planetary towns scattered round it at suitable points in the Home Counties', and urging them 'not to treat this garden city proposal as if it were a hazy idea on the summit of the Welsh mountains'.[10] But if for Purdom and Morrison the idea was already clear enough, for others it was to be another twenty years or more before the haze cleared sufficiently for general progress to be made.

Regionalism and Regional Plans

Garden cities, then, represented one link with the emergence of regional planning - encouraging thoughts of cities in a regional context. And it was housing policy that was the crucial link in this respect.[11] It was, in fact, the Minister of Health with his responsibility for housing who, in February 1920, set up a body, the South Wales Regional Survey Committee, to provide a basis for allocating State expenditure for new housing in the South Wales coalfield. The establishment of the Committee was, in itself, a recognition that housing could not reasonably be left to the individual local authorities, some of which in that region could offer only small pockets of land in steeply-sided valleys.

The Committee examined industrial trends as well as housing needs and concluded that new housing should be located to the south of the valleys on the agricultural plain. Of particular interest to the GCTPA was the proposal that some of this housing should be concentrated in two new dormitory towns. To implement the proposals, four Joint Planning Committees were recommended, together with a Regional Town Planning Board to prepare an overall development plan.[12]

For the GCTPA, campaigning for the rational distribution of new housing, the South Wales example added weight to the Association's call for a coordinated national approach, with plans to be prepared on a regional basis. Prejudging the outcome of such a process, it was confidently predicted that 'this will probably mean the prevention of the continued growth of the largest towns, reasonable proposals for the increase of many smaller towns, and finally, the creation of new towns planned on garden city principles on sites selected for their natural suitability and because of their relation to other portions of the region'.[13] It was fundamental to the Association's belief in garden cities that urban growth should no longer be left to localized initiatives; on that basis, the best to be hoped for might only be garden suburbs, with large cities simply becoming larger. Thus, the Association welcomed signs of growing acceptance and support for a regional approach, and that in turn was dependent on a stronger role for the State.

For a start, the Association was encouraged by the fact that 'almost every Government Department has, for its own purposes, divided England into larger areas',[14] though in most cases these divisions followed existing local government boundaries that were not necessarily appropriate for the particular task in hand. There were, however, three novel schemes between 1919 and 1921 that attracted the Association's interest. One was an idea conceived within the Ministry of Health, suggesting the subdivision of the country into fifteen natural 'regions' (based largely on the lines of watersheds) and fifty nine 'sub-regions'.[15] The other two schemes lacked official standing, but took a broader view of the country's administrative arrangements, and contributed to a growing regional debate in the interwar period. The first of these, that of C.B. Fawcett, was published in 1919 as a book with the title of *Provinces of England*. Advocating a subdivision of the country into twelve provinces, boundaries were carefully drawn on the basis of geographical criteria, and a provincial capital was selected in each case.[16] The other scheme was the work of G.D.H. Cole, *The Future of Local Government,* and in this nine provinces were proposed as a basis for a new system of local government. The determining factor in identifying these provinces was the location of suitable cities to serve as regional centres.[17]

In addition to supporting schemes such as these, and engaging in debate at a national level, the Association also became directly involved in promoting regional solutions to specific metropolitan problems, in the first place for the conurbations of London and Manchester. From as early as 1918 the Association had been calling for a Greater London Town Planning Commission 'to exercise control with regard to housing, industrial and residential development and all means of suburban communication, over the whole region which is in direct and continuous economic dependence upon London'.[18] In the same submission, the Association (anticipating by some twenty six years the Greater London Plan of 1944) made a specific proposal for garden cities to be located between twelve and forty miles from the centre of London, as a way of relieving pressure on the 'insanitary districts'. A Greater London campaign was to be pursued consistently throughout the interwar years. The Association, for instance, took a close interest in the Royal Commission for London Government (which started work in December 1921), urging that the metropolis be conceived as three spheres - London, Greater London and Greatest London. 'In a word', concluded the Association, 'we should be thinking of the Metropolitan Province or Region of London... '.[19] Although the danger of drawing away too many jobs from the capital was noted by critics even at that stage, the case for planned decentralization was considered by the Association, at least, to be overwhelming.[20]

Manchester was also seen to be in need of urgent regional attention. At a conference organized by the Association in May 1920 a proposal (made by Professor Abercrombie, then at the University of Liverpool) for a regional town planning commission for South Lancashire was adopted as a basis for lobbying the Ministry of Health. The South Wales initiative was cited as a suitable model, worth emulating not only in South Lancashire but in other parts of the country too, and the Ministry was congratulated for its policy of encouraging regional studies into 'the relations between housing, industry, communications and recreation in the urban areas of this country'.[21] Whether or not a direct outcome of the conference, the Association could at least take satisfaction in seeing the formation of the Manchester and District Town Planning Advisory Committee.

As we saw in the previous chapter, joint advisory committees of this sort empowered in the 1919 Town Planning Act, became a familiar and important feature of town and regional planning in the 1920s. If they fell short of the Association's hopes for regional planning - 'joint town-planning is not necessarily regional planning'[22] - they nevertheless represented an improvement of sorts on a system based solely on the work of individual authorities. The number of joint committees increased steadily, from seventeen in 1923 to fifty seven by the end of 1928, by which time more than one fifth of the country was covered and the Association felt able to claim that it was its own education work that had contributed to this.[23] Plans produced for these committees were regularly monitored, and the Association took particular interest in those (such as that for East Kent) which proposed garden cities as part of a regional development strategy.[24] As if to explain the connection, the Association was also keen to point out that some of its own members were proving to be prominent in the ranks of this new breed of regional planners.[25]

In its propaganda, regional planning was promoted by the Association as a consensual issue that cut across political boundaries. After the turbulence of the war and immediate postwar years, with strikes and talk of revolution, the Association looked ahead, seeing no reason why 'this refashioning of the physical side of our life should not become of intense interest, and ... the people may learn to turn aside from vague and romantic cries to those questions which, after all, will concern our economic, hygienic and social life much more closely than former generations believed'.[26] In the mid-1920s, regional planning was urged as an issue 'as yet untarnished by party strife'.[27] Moreover, it was now being promoted as an approach that could offer far more than the solution of housing problem alone. 'The talk about coal and power, roads and transport, railway reform and house construction should all lead on to serious thoughts on regional planning... '.[28] Indeed, it was argued from time to time, that regional planning should itself ideally be located within a planning hierarchy, midway between a national and local tier: ' ... just as town-planning called for regional-planning, so regional-planning sees the necessity of national-planning as a logical outcome of its labours'.[29]

The logic of the Association's case is difficult to dispute, but there is also a sense in which its regional campaign was remarkably unfocused. Its initial coherence, where it was argued that regional planning should be seen as part and parcel of a massive programme of housebuilding after 1918, was somehow overtaken by events. Joint committees evolved in an *ad hoc* way, and the Association's tacit support for these gave way in time to a more critical stance. As well as the fact that the committees initially lacked executive powers, R L Reiss drew attention in 1927 to some of the shortcomings in the plans so far produced.[30] He questioned whether the methods and principles adopted had been satisfactory, and whether the plans had succeeded in doing any more than confronting immediate problems as opposed to taking a more synoptic view. Reiss, as Chairman of the Association's Executive Committee, looked outwards to the flimsy apparatus of regional planning for his reasons to explain limited progress to date. Several years later, and with the benefit of his ongoing experience of examining the regional problems of London, Raymond Unwin wondered if the Association's own campaign might also have been lacking. It seemed, suggested Unwin, as if the Association was in danger of keeping its head in the clouds, and losing sight of what was actually happening on the ground. During the 1920s the population of Greater London had grown by a million people, and yet the only new garden city was that of Welwyn. 'As a movement it behoves us to consider how it is that we have worked for thirty years, and have only succeeded in that period in accommodating about 24,000 persons in the two garden cities of Letchworth and Welwyn; whereas during the last ten years that number of available persons have settled in the Greater London area every twelve weeks ... Is it not possible that our movement has exhibited, beyond the date when it was necessary, too much desire to keep the garden city movement a purist movement free from the contamination of town expansion, with the result that we have somewhat lost the influence which we should be exerting in this matter?'[31]

If anyone was in a position to question the role of the Association at this time it was Unwin. Not only had he, himself, a long involvement with the Association, remaining loyal to the idea of the garden city (although, significantly, not to the exclusion of all else), but he had from early 1929 assumed a new role as Technical Adviser to the Greater London Regional Planning Committee. Although this, like many other joint committees, was purely advisory, its work (mainly attributable to Unwin) proved to be something of a landmark in the emergence of regional planning. Its brief was to examine an area within a radius of some twenty five miles from the centre of London, and the Committee was composed of representatives of all the local authorities covered by the survey. From at least the end of the war, there had been an active lobby calling for a comprehensive approach to deal with the development of Greater London.[32] The GCTPA had been active in this lobby, and was understandably pleased when at last something seemed to be happening: 'It has been a great year for us in that we have witnessed the acceptance by the Government of the ideas which we have put forward for many years, the idea of planning, on a large scale, for the future development of Greater London'.[33] In fact, while the Association contributed to the formation of this new body, its own role does not appear to have been instrumental. Instead, on this occasion, it was the Town Planning Institute (representing professional planners) which initiated a petition to the Prime Minister in January 1926, calling for a regional policy for London and the Home Counties.[34]

The GCTPA was a signatory, but so, too, were the London Society, the Royal Institute of British Architects, the Commons and Footpaths Preservation Society, the Institute of Mechanical and Civil Engineers, the National Playing Fields Association, the National Housing and Town Planning Council, the Roads Improvement Association and the Metropolitan Public Gardens Association. The call for regional planning was broadly based, and it was fortunate that the deputation was invited to meet the Minister of Health, Neville Chamberlain - a senior politician already informed and sympathetic to the idea.

Chamberlain's response was to set up the above Committee, with a modest budget of £300 per annum, which at least permitted the appointment of Raymond Unwin from the start of 1929. The Committee produced its First Report at the end of 1929, two Interim Reports (one on Decentralization, and one on Open Spaces) in the following year, and a Second Report in 1933.[35] The reports were not weighty, but between them they offered a coherent statement on what intra-regional planning could achieve. From the perspective of the GCTPA, it was also a powerful endorsement of the whole garden city idea. Amongst the recommendations was the idea of regional open spaces and a 'green girdle' around London (a precursor of the metropolitan Green Belt). The pattern of outward growth could be articulated within successive rings, starting with planned suburbs on the outskirts of London ('as self-contained as practicable') and beyond these, development would be directed to self-contained satellite towns up to twelve miles from the centre of the city, with 'still more complete industrial garden cities' in a ring between twelve and twenty five miles from Charing Cross.[36] To create these new settlements, it was suggested that the Government should play a leading role by providing grants or guarantees.

But neither Government nor local authorities responded to the proposals. With dwindling financial support for the Committee, Unwin personally subsidized the publication of the second and final report in 1933. The recommendations lay dormant, but, with hindsight, one can see how they represented another link in the slowly unwinding chain of regional thinking. It was proving to be a long and frustrating campaign for the GCTPA - and Unwin was probably right in implying that the Association might have been more effective in that period - but at least the garden city enthusiasts could take satisfaction from the fact that their original gospel was still offering a topical message. Indeed, in the face of a relentless outward spread of development around all the major cities, the need for a regional solution seemed stronger than ever.

To give effect to its continuing concern, the Association had already, in 1929 and 1930, issued two policy memoranda. The first (presented in October 1929 in a submission to the then Labour Minister of Health, Arthur Greenwood) called for the establishment of a special body 'with the definite duty of fostering development of Garden Cities, located in accordance with regional plans'.[37] This new body would have powers to acquire land, to raise capital for a basic infrastructure, and to lease areas to public utility companies or local authorities to develop. The Minister warned that he would not be prepared to support a proposal which threatened to interfere so much with the rights and powers of local authorities. As a result, the Association drafted a new statement, this time naming the 'special body' as a Development Board or Commission and stressing that local authorities should be strongly represented on such a Board.[38]

The early 1930s was not, however, a time of bold action, and a similar pattern of hope giving way to frustration can be seen in another regional planning initiative at this time. Responding to the growing number of planning reports produced by joint local authority committees, the Labour Minister of Health in January 1931 set up a Departmental Committee (under the Chairmanship of Lord Chelmsford) to consider what needed to be done to implement some of the proposals.[39] The Committee was particularly asked to look at those proposals that could lead to schemes of work to relieve unemployment. By then there were some sixty Joint Advisory and twenty Joint Executive Committees in England and Wales, involving some 880 local authorities,[40] and their reports were already of keen interest to the Association. Indeed, in a survey of recommendations at about that time, the Association discovered that no less than fifteen of the reports contained proposals for new settlements. It was consequently agreed that 'few adequate regional plans can be made without the establishment of new communities planned according to the garden city principle'.[41]

The Chelmsford Committee included amongst its fourteen members four prominent members of the Association, R L Reiss, Raymond Unwin, T Alwyn Lloyd and W R Davidge.[42] Hopes were expressed that the Committee would 'discover that regional planning, now so well established as an idea, can be brought into action to the general advantage of the country and of the employment of labour'.[43] But the Committee, created while the Labour Government was in power, was to suffer from changing political fortunes and met on only five occasions before producing an Interim Report in July 1931. In it, the Committee expressed its reservations about existing regional reports as a basis for future action. These reports (a product of local authority cooperation) covered only one fifth of England and Wales, they were unable to embrace redevelopment schemes for built-up areas, they were largely advisory and at an interim stage, and they did not address the question of public works as such. The Committee therefore felt unable to offer definite proposals for development. But the garden city lobby secured the important statement that the Committee was 'much attracted by the possibilities offered by the development of satellite towns, with the recommendation that this merited further consideration'.[44]

Thus, in July 1931, the Labour Minister of Health, Arthur Greenwood, (heeding the advice of the Chelmsford Committee), established a new committee, under the Chairmanship of Lord Marley, to review the experience of garden cities to date. More specifically, the Marley Committee was asked to consider 'the steps, if any, which should be taken by the Government or local authorities to extend the practice of such garden cities and villages and satellite towns'.[45] The Committee was asked to pay particular attention to the question of industrial growth, to financial and administrative arrangements and to the possible application of planning of this kind to the extension of existing towns. Amongst the fifteen members were Sir Theodore Chambers (Chairman of the Welwyn development, and a vigorous proponent of garden cities) and the ubiquitous Raymond Unwin.[46]

Politically, with the fall of the Government, the potential of this initiative was blunted before it started, and then overtaken by events, and it was not until 1935 that its findings were finally published (significantly without Ministerial comment). The Association found itself 'cordially in agreement with the substance of the Report'.[47] In a wide-ranging set of recommendations, endorsing garden cities as a key element in town, regional and national planning a proposal was made for a new Planning Board (appointed by the Minister of Health) to provide a basis for land development and redevelopment throughout the country. The Board would not itself undertake development, but would pass on this responsibility to the local authorities. In the opinion of the Committee, there were already sufficient garden city powers under the Planning Acts to enable a start to be made. More than one national newspaper announced the publication of the Report with headlines of 'Garden Cities all over the country', but the Association while welcoming such enthusiasm, was rightly more cautious about the prospects.[48] The Association had, no doubt, learnt through the experience of dealing with a Conservative Government since 1931, in the harsh economic conditions at that time, that there was a world of difference between ideas on paper and a will to commit them to practice. The implementation of a new towns policy in a regional context was still some years away.

North and South

For the first fifteen years or so after the First World War, progress in advancing the cause of regional planning was largely limited to extending an awareness of the possibilities. On the policy-making front little was gained. Particularly during the second half of the 1930s, however, the context of the debate was changed by the gravity of the economic situation with its regional consequences. It is in this context that the Association was drawn from its initial preoccupation with garden cities, and into a wider debate about national policies and governmental planning in general. In the context of regional inequalities that now had a political dimension, the concept of decentralization itself assumed a broader significance.

At a macro level, the Association gained from a gathering consensus for governmental planning that the historian, Arthur Marwick, has termed 'middle opinion'.[49] It is beyond the scope of this paper to follow this route in detail, save to illustrate one view in support of planning, less from any deep ideological motive (which some who attached themselves to this consensus certainly did have), than from a sense of pragmatism in the face of pressing conditions at the time. Thus, the young Harold Macmillan wrote that '"Planning" is forced upon us ... not for idealistic reasons but because the old mechanism which served us when markets were expanding naturally and spontaneously is no longer adequate when the tendency is in the opposite direction'.[50]

As the idea of planning gained acceptance during the 1930s so, too, did its specific application to regional issues. The problems of unemployment in the older industrial areas became a national issue, and it was to that debate that the Association contributed. The first evidence of this comes in an article in March 1929 - on unemployment, transference and decentralization. A coherent strategy had yet to emerge, but the article was, at least, an attempt to relate the Association's longstanding policy of urban decentralization to the new situation of uneven rates of development in different regions, with the consequent shifts in population that were already apparent. The article (an attempt to explain 'our philosophy') reveals as much as anything the conceptual leap that was involved in moving from an intra to inter regional level of explanation, but it concludes with a positive enough suggestion: ' ... of all remedial measures we look to town and country planning to provide a new physico-industrial structure for our country, which shall exhibit, in full power, the principle of Decentralization'.[51] In the following year, the Association produced a book (an edited collection of papers) *Decentralization of Population and Industry* in which evolving ideas on these issues were further developed.[52] Although there is little apparent appreciation of the causes of regional change, a chapter on 'National Planning and Decentralization' signals the beginnings of a shift in thinking towards what was to become a major plank in the Association's policy later on in the 1930s. National planning (it was explained elsewhere) might simply be conceived of as the 'coordination in the elements of the physico-economic structure of the country ... an extension of regional and town-planning structure ...'.53

In spite of the gravity of the national economic crisis in the early 1930s, the clear impression from the records is that any talk of regional and national planning was still largely within a traditional and restricted concern for the physical environment. The drift to the South was simply adding to the perennial problem of metropolitan growth. Although the Chelmsford Committee had a brief to examine ways in which regional planning might contribute to the relief of unemployment, it proved to be a body of meagre influence, overtaken by events. Throughout the first half of the 1930s, the Association's interest and influence on the regional question (which, in effect, economic events had cast as a national question) remained negligible. There is a sense in which the Association's policy was in the hands of 'yesterday's men',54 seemingly incapable of instituting a new approach from within. By way of contrast, in the second half of the 1930s both external and internal factors conspired to restructure what had become jaded and outmoded policies, at variance with changing economic circumstances in the country at large. 1936 marks a real turning point in this respect. Externally, political debate about the differential plight of the regions finally breached the walls of the Association, while, internally, the arrival of Frederic Osborn as Honorary Secretary brought the degree of analytical and campaigning ability that is required to connect traditional priorities with the new situation.55 As an indication of a changing context, an editorial in June 1936 (reporting on a debate in Parliament in March of that year) led with the heading, 'The Location of Industry'. A year in advance of the formation of the Barlow Committee, the Member for East Middlesbrough is reported as calling for a complete survey of the nation's industries to be undertaken without delay: 'It is becoming essential that the Government should take definite action and I am therefore proposing that the Government should appoint a commission ...' There was much in the debate of interest to the Association, though in a letter to *The Times*, the cautious Secretary, A.T. Pike, wondered whether the Government would wish to go quite as far as the Member for East Middlesbrough was suggesting.56 The Association, in distancing itself from a more interventionist approach, was not yet in the vanguard of a regional planning lobby (its own priority remaining the building of more garden cities as a contribution to the problems of growth, if not of decline).

However, in the following year, 1937, events unfolded, and, with Osborn now clearly in control of policy, the Association was in a position to adopt a more affirmative line. It was Osborn's constant contention that the contradiction between decline in some parts of the country and excessive growth in the London region could only be resolved through the introduction of effective planning machinery. The key to any rational change lay in a policy for the siting of industry and that, in turn, depended on 'at least a broad outline of a national plan'.57 The point had been passed where the location of industry could be left to free market forces, although Osborn was not advocating total control either:

'What we stand for .... is the control of the size of towns, and equally the preservation of the countryside from scattered and ribbon building, through the guidance of the location of factories and business premises under a national plan ... Compulsion of particular industries to go to dictated locations is no essential element of this idea. Certain towns and agricultural districts generally would be barred except under special permit. Certain other towns and areas, as well as the new satellite towns and garden cities, would be the subject of support by definite inducement to industrial or business settlement. Between these extremes there could still be many districts among which firms would make their own choice'.[58]

Osborn was thinking ahead of what was then being done in practice. The Special Areas Policy was inherently a one-sided approach, and even though the Commissioner for England and Wales had proposed putting London 'out of bounds' for most new industries, while at the same time offering inducements to locate in the Special Areas, the Association despaired 'for any indication that the Government has as yet grasped the necessity for national planning'.[59]

Within a few months, however, as one of his first acts on succeeding Stanley Baldwin as Prime Minister, Neville Chamberlain, established a Royal Commission to enquire into the location of industry.[60] The Association drew satisfaction from the fact that Chamberlain was retaining a close interest in issues for which they were themselves campaigning, and the the brief was wide enough to embrace all areas (as opposed to confining attention to the Special Areas). It hoped that the 'mere appointment of the Commission is a proof that the days of laisser-faire which have caused the present chaos are numbered'.[61]

Referring to the problem that faced them as the 'greatest of all the problems of modern civilization', the Chairman of the Commission, Sir Montague Barlow, urged on his members that issues of immense national importance were involved.[62] The Royal Commission on the Geographical Distribution of the Industrial Population first sat in October 1937, and proceeded over the coming months to take evidence from a wide range of Government and other bodies. For the Association (and, in particular, through Osborn) this long-awaited sign of political awareness, coupled with the attention given to the work of the Commission in the press, offered an exceptional opportunity for a campaign to arouse public opinion on what the Association now regarded as an overwhelming case for national planning. The 'great and the good' were invited to lend their support to the campaign - not mere ciphers this time, prepared to stamp the Association's efforts with a seal of respectability, but effective politicians who might well play a part in translating the new ideas into official policy. Significantly, as events proved, Clement Attlee led the way with a statement endorsing the work of the Association, and calling for a 'national organization to say where particular industries are to be located, where the land is to be kept free for residential development, and where there are to be parks and open spaces'.[63] He was supported by other prominent Labour politicians, notably Arthur

Greenwood and John Parker, the latter of whom pointed to 'the negative powers of the present regional committees working in isolation and each planning almost competitively for a vast population which should never be allowed to drift into its areas at all ...'.[64]   Liberal politicians, active preservationists, and the old campaigner Seebohm Rowntree added their names to the planning lobby.

The Association was encouraged by what it saw as an awakening of public opinion to these issues, though it warned that much work had yet to be done before the wheels of national planning would effectively begin to turn.[65] Indicative of the work to be done, at two hearings in May and June 1938, the Association submitted its own evidence for planning to the Royal Commission. Contained in a forty three page document (prepared by Osborn) the statement took the form of a closely-argued case, probably the most important document for the movement since Howard's original book on garden cities.[66] Conceptually, the thinking behind it was far in advance of the self-justifying utterances of the 1920s and early 1930s, when Letchworth and Welwyn were cited as arguments in themselves for more garden cities. Any doubts about the role of the State were finally expunged, and the whole thrust of the Association's case was for a new framework of national planning machinery to enable the wholesale changes that were needed.

In its submission, the Association laid the ground with a review of the garden city idea and experience to date. It followed this by setting out the 'facts' of centralization, explaining as well as describing centripetal forces in Britain. Having established the situation as it then was, a detailed argument was presented, enumerating the various disadvantages of concentration. Resultant high densities, a lowering of housing standards, higher costs of housing, long and unnecessary journeys and traffic congestion, a shortage of play space, separation from the countryside, damage to health and other disadvantages including the danger from hostile aircraft (a timely issue that was beginning to attract more attention than some of the more traditional arguments) were all cited as reasons to oppose the continued growth of larger cities. The Association then went on to point to the inadequacy of existing town and country planning legislation to deal with these problems: ' ... local and regional Planning Schemes cannot deal with the problem of agglomeration nor adequately with its converse of scattered development'.[67]

The problem, then, was what to do about it all. Of its recommendations, the first proposal was for the institution of national planning, starting with the formation of a National Planning Board to designate areas which should be 'out of bounds' for fresh housing and industrial development, and areas where growth should be encouraged. It was explained that these extreme categories of designation would form the first elements of a national development plan. In the first place, a National Planning Board might be an offshoot of the Ministry of Health, 'though it may be foreseen that the natural line of evolution is towards a separate Minsitry for Planning'.[68]   A second major proposal was for another central body to be established, this one to be responsible for building garden cities and satellite towns, and for the development of existing small towns. These two major proposals were supplemented by additional recommendations for what was regarded as 'a stiffening of standards' in respect of statutory planning bye-laws,[69] for the administration of housing and other public services to be related to the new national planning bodies, and for a London Regional Authority to deal with the special problems of the capital.

Taken together, it was an important statement, not simply as a sign of the Association's thinking but also (in terms of what was proposed) as a sign of things to come. 'One of the ablest and most devastating political documents of recent years' is how Osborn's work was described by the General Secretary of Political and Economic Planning.[70] Osborn himself was more modest about its qualities, referring to it as 'some scientific-looking evidence',[71] and confessing that the real reason that it had an influence on the findings of the Commission had less to do with the cogency of the arguments as such, and more to do with some behind-the-scenes lobbying. 'I worked very hard on the doorstep and behind the arras of that Commission',[72] Osborn explained, with Abercrombie (a member of the Commission, as well as being a long-standing member of the Association) emerging as a crucial contact. 'For example, when he was a member of the Barlow Commission I redrafted for him some of the key paragraphs of the majority report and drafted some of his own minority report - but it was all very 'hush-hush' ...'.[73] Tellingly, one reason why it was all so 'hush-hush' was that Osborn wanted to keep his regional planning ideas clear of the ring of fanaticism that many people still attached to the garden city movement. The inference is that had it been widely known at the time that Barlow's thinking was being so directly influenced by the Association, the credibility of the whole exercise might have suffered.[74] In fact, Barlow himself publicly acknowledged his interest in the Association's ideas by becoming a member.[75]

It was not until 1940 that the Commission's report was published and the impact this had can best be discussed in relation to the wider setting of wartime planning. At least by 1938, however, the Association had planted the seeds of new ideas on more fertile ground than it had been able to do on successive attempts with various committees in previous years. Its style of campaigning was changing, and, in particular, the 'insider' role of influencing and persuading key figures in the policy-making chain was to characterize some of the Association's most important work in the future. This new role is illustrated by Osborn's observation, on being asked by Lord Reith in 1940 to prepare some notes on regional planning, that he felt 'a certain effrontery in reorganising British local government on paper in a weekend without any consultation'.[76]

Conclusion

The argument has been put that, in addition to contributing the idea of social cities, the GCTPA was drawn into the interwar debate on two fronts. There was, firstly, the involvement that stemmed from its basic interest in promoting garden cities, and the Association's antipathy towards suburban sprawl. This led, in turn, to an interest in the joint regional plans of local authorities and Central Government's response to these. The second front (which proved to be the more significant) was in connection with the regional economic disparities of the 1930s, and in particular, the case presented by the Association to the Barlow Committee.

In terms of a direct output, nothing tangible had been achieved by 1939 to reward the Association's efforts. In certain respects the Association's strategy was found to be lacking. The only garden cities to have been built were a product of private initiative, and were not part of a wider strategy. But it can be argued that what the Association had done (particularly as a result of its efforts in the latter part of the 1930s) was to contribute to a 'climate of opinion' in favour of some form of regional planning. Opinion was undoubtedly more strongly disposed towards regional planning at the end of the interwar period than at the beginning, and the Association might at least (particularly as a result of its activities in the late 1930s) share some of the credit for that. It was by no means the only group promoting the regional cause, but it had at least played an active role.

As Wayne Parsons has shown in his analysis of the emergence of regional policy, it would be a mistake, however, to suppose that what follows in the war years is simply a result of an unbroken progression of event.[77] Postwar regional policies are not simply an inevitable outcome of the work done before the war, but are very much influenced by events during the war itself. At the same time, the fact that so many of the 'building blocks' of regional ideas were already in place by 1939 is certainly not insignificant. Evidence to Barlow, particularly, articulated many of the ideas that were later to enter the statute books.

Development in the 1940s marked a crucial turning point in the acceptance of regional ideas and policies, but there was still a long way to go - especially towards achieving a more integrated approach. As a last word, we can sympathize with Frederic Osborn, who, writing in 1971, lamented the slowness and frustrations in the whole process of trying to achieve rational change. 'What is the lesson for the propagandists? Hope and pray - that is, plead, or press the case - but don't expect! After seventy-three years of continuous advocacy, the urban dispersal, green belts, and new towns policy is still only in its infancy'.[78] Sadly, the evidence since 1971 would only serve to bear out Osborn's message, 'don't expect!'

References and Notes

Abbreviations of journal titles:

> *Garden Cities and Town Planning (GCTP).*
> *Journal of the Town Planning Institute (JTPI)*
> *Town and Country Planning (TCP).*

1. The 1899 version was subsequently revised in minor ways and published in 1902 as *Garden Cities of Tomorrow*, London: Swan Sonnenschein.
2. In addition to establishing garden cities this broad aim was to be achieved by 'encouraging the tendency of manufacturing to remove their works from congested centres to the country; by cooperating or advising with such firms, public bodies and other associations to secure better housing accommodation for work-people near to their place of employment; by taking steps to promote effective legislation with this end in view; and by generally advocating the ordered design and development of towns'.
3. In addition to the original source by Howard, a useful article on this aspect of garden cities is F.J. Osborn, (1971) 'The History of Howard's Social Cities' *TCP*, Vol. 39, No.12, pp.539-545.
4. Cited in M. Swenarton (1981) *Homes Fit for Heroes*, London: Heinemann, p.79, from a speech by Lloyd George reported in *The Times* 13th November 1918.
5. 'Chamberlain Committee' (1920, 1921): *Principles to be followed in dealing with Unhealthy Areas,* London: Ministry of Health.
6. The importance of this link is stressed in F.J. Osborn, 'The Garden City Movement': Reaffirmation of the validity of Ebenezer Howard's Idea', *Landscape Architecture*, Vol. XXXVI, No. 2, January 1946, p.52; and in G.E. Cherry, 'The Place of Neville Chamberlain in British Town Planning', in A. Sutcliffe (ed). (1980), *The Rise of Modern Urban Planning*, London: Mansell.
7. Cherry, op. cit. p.168.
8. '*A Memorandum by the Garden Cities and Town Planning Association for the consideration of the Local Authorities represented at the Greater London Housing Conference called by the London County Council on October 30th 1918'.* The Memorandum was prepared by a sub-committee consisting of W.R. Davidge, H.V. Lanchester, Cuthbert Brown, Warwick Draper and C.B. Purdom.
9. A report of the conference (including Purdom's diagrams of satellite towns around London) is included in *GCTP* Vol. X, No.5, May 1920, pp.93-107.
10. Ibid, pp.101 and 105.
11. Although in the immediate postwar period housing emerged as an important source of regional interest, it should be acknowledged that during the war the production of munitions and proposals under the Electricity Act had been organized on a regional basis.
12. The South Wales Regional Survey Committee was established, with Sir W.H. Seager as Chairman, in February 1920. It reported in September 1920. In fact, as G.E. Cherry shows, a Joint Committee for the South Yorkshire coalfield predates the first major study. See G.E. Cherry (1974): *The Evolution of British Town Planning*, Leighton Buzzard:

Leonard Hill, pp.87-88, and 'A National Housing Policy (III)', *GCTP* Vol. XI, No. 5, May 1921, pp.107-111.

13. *GCTP* Vol XI, No 5, May 1921 p.111.

14. 'The Provincial Government Areas of England', *GCTP* Vol.X, No.9, September 1921, p.214.

15. The Ministry of Health's proposals were published in its own shortlived journal *Housing* (22nd November 1920), and discussed in *GCTP* 'A National Housing Policy (IV)', Vol XI, No 7, July 1921. The Association preferred to refer to the subdivisions as 'regions' and 'sub-regions' rather than the Ministry's terminology 'divisions' for larger areas and 'regions' for the smaller.

16. See C.B. Fawcett (1919) *Provinces of England: A study of some geographical aspects of devolution* , London: Williams and Norgate.

17. See G.D.H. Cole (1921) *The Future of Local Government* , London: Cassell.

18. 'A Memorandum by the Garden Cities and Town Planning Association', submitted to the Greater London Housing Conference called by the London County Council, 30th October 1918.

19. *GCTP* Vol.XII, No.1, January 1922, p.2.

20. *GCTP*, Vol.XIV, No.4, April 1924, p.70 reported a statement by the then Minister of Labour, Tom Shaw, warning that the removal of factories would add to the difficulties of London boys and girls in finding work. In an editorial note, it was argued that a planned process of decentralization would result in gains all round.

21. 'Regional Planning Conference at Manchester', two reports (before and after the conference), in *GCTP* Vol.X, No.5, May 1920, p.116 and No.6, June 1920, p.140.

22. *GCTP* Vol.XVI, No 12, December 1925, p.306. The Association's position on this was expressed in the form of evidence to the Royal Commission on Local Government in 1925. It was pointed out that large cities were experiencing difficulties in building beyond their boundaries, and were precluded from establishing satisfactory garden cities. A small Departmental Committee was recommended to seek a solution.

23. *GCTPA* Annual Report for 1928.

24. See, for instance, 'Regional Planning Reports', a summary of reports to date, in *GCTP* Vol.XVI, No.12, December 1925, pp.306-308.

25. GCTPA Annual Report for 1930. Although names are not mentioned in this particular note, the Association will be referring to the likes of Professor Abercrombie, W.R. Davidge and Professor Adshead, all of whom were active in preparing regional reports.

26. *GCTP* Vol XIII, No 10, October 1923, p.173.

27. In an editorial, addressed to the Labour Government of the day: *GCTP* Vol.XIV, No.9, September 1924, p.185.

28. Ibid

29. 'The Idea of a National Plan', *GCTP* Vol.XIX, No.4, April 1929, p.79.

30. R.L. Reiss, 'Regional Planning in Relation to Garden Cities and Satellite Towns', *GCTP* Vol.XVII, No.6, July 1927, pp.169-171.

31. R. Unwin, 'Garden Cities and Regional Planning', *GCTP* Vol.XXII, No.1, January 1932, pp.7-8.

32. Some references to the direct involvement of the GCTPA in this lobby have already been cited in this section. Neville Chamberlain's role on the Unhealthy Areas Committee (1921) is also significant as a link. So, too, is Unwin's membership and the work of the London Society, including Unwin's contribution of an essay, 'Some Thoughts on the Development of London' in Sir Aston Webb (1921) *London of the Future*, London: Duttons pp.177-192. Another important source of support was the London County Council, which in 1924 resolved to examine whether to move towards the establishment 'of garden cities (alternatively known as satellite towns or new industrial centres) on the general lines of Letchworth and Welwyn garden cities'. (*GCTP* Vol.XVI, No.4, April 1926, p.75).

33. Chamberlain's Address to the Annual General Meeting of the GCTPA, 24th February 1928.

34. Cherry (1974) op.cit. (note 6), p.97, based on a report in the *JTPI*,. Vol.XII, No.6, 1926, pp.147-148.

35. Greater London Regional Planning Committee: *First Report* (1929), *Interim Reports* (1930), *Second Report* (1933), London: Knapp Drewett.

36. Greater London Regional Planning Committee, op.cit.

37. 'Garden Cities in Relation to the National Housing Policy and Regional-Planning', Memorandum from the Council of the GCTPA to the Minister of Health, submitted on 18th October 1929.

38. This Memorandum was first aired at the Annual Conference of the National Housing and Town Planning Council in November 1930, an occasion chosen because of the attendance of a large number of local authority representatives.

39. The full title of the Chelmsford Committee was the Departmental Committee on Regional Development.

40. *GCTP* Vol.XXI, No.2, February 1931, pp.27-28. A distinction is made between advisory and executive committees. A Joint Executive Committee is endowed with the power of itself preparing a joint statutory scheme on behalf of its constituent members, while a Joint Advisory Committee is limited to preparing plans and proposals to be recommended to its consitutent members for their individual adoption. The advantage of joint executive action was seen to be that it increased the prospect of organized arrangements for carrying out the features of a concerted plan of joint rather than local benefit.

41. GCTPA submission to Marley Committee, p.8.

42. The other ten members were Lord Chelmsford (Chairman), Mr H. Alexander, Sir Ernest Clark, Mr A. Dryland, Sir George Etherton, Mr W.J. Hadfield, Mr F.W. Hunt, Mr J. Norval and Mr J.H. Rothwell.

43. *GCTP* Vol.XXI, No.2, February 1931 p.27.

44. Ministry of Health (1931) *Garden Cities and Satellite Towns: Interim Report of Departmental Committee*, London HMSO.

45. From the terms of reference of the Committee in *Garden Cities and Satellitte Towns: Report of Departmental Committee*, Ministry of Health (1935), London: HMSO.

46. Apart from Chambers and Unwin, the rest of the committee were Lord Marley (Chairman), Mr R. Bell, Mr J.C. Burleigh, Sir Ernest Clark, Alderman Rose Davies, Mr J. Chuter

Ede, M.P., Mr C. Gerald Eve, Mr T. Peirson Frank, Alderman W.T.Jackson, Mr J. Noral, Mr P.J. Pybus and Sir William Whyte.

47. *TCP* Vol .II, No.11 June 1930, p.80.

48. Ibid, pp.83-85.

49. A. Marwick 'Middle Opinion in the Thirties: Planning Progress and Political Agreement', *English Historical Review*, Vol.LXXIX, No.311, August 1964, pp.285-298.

50. Harold Macmillan, quoted in Marwick op.cit., p.287.

51. 'Unemployment, Transference and Decentralization', *GCTP* Vol.XIX, No.3 March 1929, pp.49-51.

52. Warren, H. and Davidge, W. R. (1930) *Decentralization of Population and Industry: A New Principle in Town Planning*, London, King.

53. 'The Idea of a National Plan', an editorial in *GCTP* Vol.XIX No.4, April 1929. This editorial has the hand of Davidge (who wrote the chapter on national planning in his book with Herbert Warren, op.cit.).

54. The Association's book of 1930 was written largely by members who had been active before 1914. Warren and Davidge were the editors, with chapters contributed, for instance, by Unwin, Pepler, Loftus Hare, Parker and Adams. The fact that members had been active over a long period is not in itself an indictment, but there is certainly little evidence of fresh ideas to match a new situation.

55. As early as 1932, Osborn had addressed town planners on the importance of the location of industry, and the further development of his ideas was published in a leaflet for the New Fabian Research Bureau in 1934, *'Transport, Town Development and Territorial Planning of Industry'*. In the latter, the importance that Osborn is consistently to attach to getting the right machinery for planning is reflected in his proposal for a National Industrial and Commercial Siting Board, charged with the duty of guiding the location of new manufacturing businesses and industrial and commercial developments throughout the country.

56. Letter to *The Times*, reprinted in 'The Location of Industry', *TCP* Vol .5, June 1936, pp.79-81.

57. From an important statement of the Association's new approach: F J Osborn, 'Planning is Possible: The Missing Link in National Policy', *TCP* Vol.V, No.18, March 1937, pp.39-42.

58. Ibid. In this context, Osborn goes on to propose the establishment of a National Industrial Siting Board.

59. 'A Critical Commentary', *TCP* Vol.V, No.18, March 1937, p.62.

60. The full terms of reference of the Royal Commission were threefold:

    'To enquire into the causes which have influenced the present geographical distribution of the industrial population of Great Britain and the probable direction of any change in that distribution in the future; to consider what social, economic or strategical disadvantages arise from the concentration of industries or of the industrial population in large towns or in particular areas of the country; and to report what remedial measures if any should be taken in the national interest'

61. 'The Royal Commission', *TCP* Vol.V, No.20 September 1937, p.115.

62. As reported in *TCP* Vol.VI, No.21, December 1937, p.3.

63. From a symposium of views, in *TCP* Vol VI, No 23, March 1938, pp.25-30.

64. Ibid

65. 'Public Opinion and Planning', *TCP* Vol.VI, No.23, July-September 1938, p.89.

66. The evidence for the Association was prepared by Osborn and submitted by Cecil Harmsworth (as chairman of the Council) on 5th May and 15th June 1938. See Garden Cities and Town Planning Association (1938): *Evidence of the Garden Cities and Town Planning Association to the Royal Commission on the Geographical Distribution of the Industrial Population*, London.

67. GCTPA (1938) op.cit. p.31.

68. Ibid, p.36.

69. Ibid, pp.40-41. This 'stiffening of standards' included proposals for compensation and betterment.

70. The Association's evidence was reviewed by Max Nicholson, General Secretary of PEP (Political and Economic Planning) in *TCP* Vol.VI, No.23, July-September 1938, pp.92-93. There was, in fact, mutual appreciation between the two organizations, both of which were campaigning for more planning. Thus, in *TCP* Vol.VII, No.27, July-September 1939, pp.103-105, Osborn wrote a favourable review of PEP's own publication (1939) on the need for planning, *Report on the Location of Industry*.

71. Osborn, in Hughes, M.(ed.) (1971) *The Letters of Lewis Mumford and Frederic Osborn: a transatlantic dialogue, 1938-1970*, Bath, Adams and Dart.

72. Ibid, p.17.

73. Ibid, p.271. Osborn also acknowledged the support of another member of the Commission, Mrs W.L. Hichens, who kept both Osborn and Abercrombie 'hard at this underground work'.

74. Ibid, p.17.

75. Letter to Osborn, 28th July 1939 (Osborn Papers, Welwyn).

76. PRO File HLG/86/16, Letter from Osborn to Reith, 17th November 1940.

77. Parsons, W. (1986) *The Political Economy of British Regional Policy*, London: Croom Helm.

78. Osborn, F. J. (1971) 'The History of Howard's Social Cities', *TCP* Vol.39, No.12, p.545.

6

The Failure of Regionalism in 1940s Britain:
A Reexamination of Regional Plans,
the Regional Idea and
the Structure of Government

Patricia Garside

Introduction

At the outbreak of the Second World War, Britain seemed poised to accept a fundamental reappraisal of the function and organization of government at central, regional and local level. Sir Ernest Simon was one of many who understood how radical such changes might be. In an article 'Town Planning: Moscow or Manchester', published in 1937 he said:

> 'We need economic reform; the whole question of town planning is crushed under the burden of compensation to private interests. We need political reform; both central authorities and local authorities are wrongly constituted and have inadequate powers. We need spiritual reform; we need a new enthusiasm and determination to build fine and beautiful cities'.[1]

The extent of the changes required for a rationally planned, economically sound and spiritually satisfying post-war society was spelled out in a series of reports published immediately before and during the war. The Scott, Uthwatt and Barlow reports showed in their various ways how the Gordian knots of land ownership, private interests and the vested interests of local authorities could be overcome in post-war reconstruction.[2] During the 1930s the rational planning of a wide range of services and activities had become a rallying point for moderate politicians of all parties and professional experts, not least in town planning, were eager to present Ministers with the necessary schemes and programmes.[3] Furthermore, the strategic necessities of total war which threatened aerial bombardment of vulnerable urban centres only underlined the necessity for regional dispersal and reorganization.

Calls for a fundamental reorganization of Britain's economic and physical structure generated a flurry of activity in the early years of the war, not least the preparation of a series of ambitious reconstruction plans for major cities which strikingly conveyed the message that dirty, muddled streets and dreary suburban sprawl were symptoms of a social disorder that required institutional as much as architectural treatment. Yet the plans failed to generate the expected momentum for reform of local government. This failure is usually explained by the powerful resistence of existing local authorities to changes in their boundaries and functions. Their hostility was indeed intense, but in explaining why the prospect of planning was insufficient to overcome it, we must look also at the nature of support for planning itself.

My argument will be that because the parties concerned at local and national level did not will the end, (the comprehensive planning of land-use) they therefore failed to will the means (the reform of the area, power and responsibilities of local authorities). In other words, because planned use of land was so insecurely established as a legitimate sphere for government throughout the 1930s and even as late as 1945, then the reform of local government to enhance and promote planning was unlikely to proceed, given the political upheaval and conflict that was anticipated. I shall aim to show how fragile government's commitment was to planning both at local and national level, and how the preparation of wartime advisory plans such as those for Greater London and the London County Council (LCC) in fact hindered rather than facilitated the reform of local government on regional lines.

The Importance of London and the London Plans

By 1945 it was clear the reform of local government necessary to achieve social, physical and economic reconstruction was to be shelved. Though the existing structure of local government had been shown to be obsolescent, yet it remained intractable and immutable, most particularly in terms of areas. Given this intractability, the outcome was that many functions previously performed by local authorities, for example in health and public utilities, were transferred to central government departments or to single function quangos[4]. Shorn of many of their pre-war functions, local authorities were forced onto the defensive. The significance to them of their remaining functions and especially those of housing and planning were heightened because of the loss of others. By 1950 planning, which had hitherto been most closely identified with the movement for regional reform in local government, had become one of the greatest barriers to it. London planning and the structure of London government played a major part in this reversal. The drive to regionalize local government foundered on London's reputation as metropolis and imperial capital which overrode 'rational' plans to disperse its functions, influence and administration, and on the reemergence of pre-war political realities based on alliances and bargains between local politicians, their officers and London's industrial and commercial interests.

The focus of this chapter will therefore be on London because the future of the capital was central to discussions of post-war reconstruction and regional planning, and because the London experience was crucial in forcing the regional idea off the political agenda in the post-war decade. The chapter begins by outlining the character of London and especially LCC government as it developed in the 1930s with particular reference to town planning. The impact of war on these established patterns will then be assessed with particular reference to the role of Professor Patrick Abercrombie and the *County of London Plan (1943)* and *Greater London Plan (1945)*. The reemergence and reinforcement of prewar patterns of acting and thinking will be described in the light of the responses to these plans of Ministers, local politicians, local authority officers and a range of 'London' interests. It will be argued that, in essence, the regional idea had faded as early as 1943-4 because it seemed both feasible and desireable to achieve post-war reconstruction within the existing political and economic framework, without recourse to fundamental changes in the structure of local government. The incoming Labour Government of 1945, therefore, found pre-war patterns already re-establishing themselves and sought ways to circumvent and modify them rather than reform them.

Depression, Regional Planning and 'Municipal Progress'

One effect of the economic and political crisis of 1931 was to focus critical attention on the activities of local authorities. It seemed likely that, 'For the first time in modern English history, the institutions of local government were threatened with a fundamental subordination to national policies on public expenditure, both in terms of service costs and staff salaries'.[6] A revival of the Anti-Waste Campaign of the early 1920s seemed likely, supported both by the sweeping recommendations of the Committee on Local Expenditure (the Ray Committee) and by the political force of the ratepayer movement[7]. Conservative county councils fell to the task and

> 'with shirt-fronts bursting with patriotic fervour, councillors and aldermen filled their fountain pens and prepared to slaughter the local estimates'.[8]

The counter-attack took shape only slowly, led initially by NALGO and interested academics. Sir Hilton Young, Chamberlain's replacement at the Ministry of Health, himself underlined the value of local authority services and the need to make judgements in other than narrow financial terms. 'The development of the assets of the nation', he said, 'are not measureable in money'.[9] Local authority services were steadily reestablished as vital to national well-being and the 'centenary of municipal progress' in 1935 provided a 'heaven sent focus' for the celebration of the achievement of existing local authorities.[10] The publication in 1935 of *A Century of Municipal Progress* broadened the claims of local government to the furthest temporal and spatial realms. For the average British citizen, it was claimed, 'progress to the old Greek style of "beautiful goodness" depends on his local government more than on any other factor in his environment'.[11] Similarly, local government was said to be an essential element in the imperial expression of British civilization. Such breathless claims reached even dizzier heights with the growing recognition of the realities of Fascism in Europe. The virtues of local freedom and initiative, of local responsibility and opportunity were sharply focused by the rise of the dictators, enhancing the rhetoric and ideology of localism in Britain.

London, of course, experienced the ebb and flow of opinion about exis'ing local authorities particularly keenly in the mid-1930s. With the expansion oî the metropolitan built-up areas increasingly being seen as both a regional and national problem, the adequacy of the existing local authorities was a matter of recurrent debate. In particular, the causal links being propounded between unemployment and industrial decline in the 'Special Areas' and the economic bouyancy and physical expansion of London led to calls for national planning to deal with imbalances both within the metropolitan region itself and between that and the other less fortunate conurbations. Even here, however, Ministers hesitated to act in the face of local authority opposition to reorganization while local authorities themselves and especially the LCC seized the initiative and identified their own activities with urban improvement and progress.

After the Labour victory in the 1934 LCC elections, their leader, Herbert Morrison, set his previous enthusiasm for regional reform aside. Instead, he sought to capture the new spirit of 'civic pride' and, by focusing it on the LCC itself, to reestablish the political fortunes of the Labour Party so bruised by the events of 1931. Practical and theoretical support for regional initiatives was withdrawn, embryonic schemes for promoting broad involvement in drawing up a regional plan for London were abandoned, and the LCC itself took centre stage. Using radio to address the widest possible audience, Herbert Morrison set out his major objectives portraying the LCC as the body to whom Londoners could look for vision, hope and democratic values.

'London is to be planned. For the first time in its history it is possible to guide the future development of London by a central coordinating force and the body to whom this has been entrusted is the London County Council. London has never been planned: it has just grown. We cannot now rebuild London on virgin soil. We have not even the opportunity that followed the Great Fire of 1666. But we can lay down a plan for the future of London, and we can control development as and when it takes place. In its plan for London, the Council will lay down lines of progress designed to create, in the course of time, a new London, in which the good things we have now will be preserved, and the bad replaced by the good. In this we hope to receive the cooperation of all landowners, and that they will be fired with the enthusiasm for order and fine conceptions which has distinguished the most enlightened of their predecessors.   After all, town planning is merely good estate management on a grand scale'.[12]

Implied in Morrison's vision, was a gradualist 'non-doctrinaire' approach to planning, far removed from the grandiose, even authoritarian schemes of professional town planning experts.   Respect for the status quo, and for established interests was intrinsic to London planning under Morrison and the ultimate effect was to undermine the support for regional planning and to enhance the standing of the LCC.

Morrison, nevertheless, needed concrete achievements to reestablish the Labour Party's right to govern, and his modus operandi secured this through conceptually simple and organizationally powerful aims which emphasized maximum effort in areas of policy and in locations which aroused minimum confrontation with opposing political and economic interests.   Regional planning was reduced to town planning, town planning to good estate management and good estate management to slum clearance schemes.   The manifesto slogan *Down with the Slums and Up with the Houses* epitomized Labour's objectives for London and the LCC.

This narrowing of the LCCs planning focus and their identification of it with the authorities' own activities may be illustrated by comparing the activities of Municipal Reformers prior to 1934 with those of the Labour Party after 1934. Municipal Reformers had rejected the possibility of preparing a plan for the County of London but had accepted the need for a regional London Plan: they had even explored the possibility of involving conservation and planning groups with the LCC, the Greater London Regional Planning Committee and other local authorities in the preparation of a regional plan.[13]   Under Labour, the regional dimension was largely abandoned and Municipal Reformers schemes for LCC involvement in a regional planning body were never reconsidered.

Withdrawing from the regional framework, with the exception of the Green Belt schemes which Morrison captured and identified with the LCC itself, the Labour majority committed itself to preparing a plan for the whole of its area, the Administrative County of London.   At its first meeting after the elections of 1934, the Town Planning Committee established new terms of reference for the Plan for London Sub-committee which was to be made up solely of Council members including Herbert Morrison in person.   No representatives from any outside groups were to be included - instead, specific groups and in particular representatives of metropolitan borough councils, statutory undertakings and London's commercial and industrial interests were to be invited to comment on planning proposals as they were drawn up.   This access, however, was not to be direct to councillors, but indirectly via certain officers.   The insulation of LCC members from direct contact with outside groups, together with strict adherence to party discipline, reflected Herbert Morrison's aim to avoid all taint of corruption in London's tenure of power on the LCC.[14] The effect was to turn the attention of members and officials alike away from outside sources of information and ideas, and towards internal objectives and channels of information. With the passing of control to Labour in 1934, the planning of London's built-up areas received considerable impetus, members and officers became partners in a joint enterprise, new rules of access were established for outside groups, and the kind of group admitted to participation was altered to give more scope to borough councils and commercial interests, and less to town planning pressure groups and professional associations. The opposition of property owners to the 1932 Town and Country Planning Act had ensured maximum protection in the legislation for established interests and the status quo: the LCC's desire for tangible achievements under Labour reinforced this protection even further. The Council's guiding objective in planning was 'to frame its schemes so far as possible so as not to give rise to claims to compensation'[15] and where opposition occurred, therefore, the policy was largely one of non-interference, despite the public activity of drawing up planning schemes and development standards. The LCC's response to property owners was, in fact, twofold - with those owners who were willing to concede that the LCC had a duty to measure individual projects against some abstract 'London interest' or 'town planning point of view', the LCC established a modus vivendi: in these cases compromise and bargaining over particular proposals took place largely on an ad hoc basis. Developers were encouraged not to regard the Council's official planning standards on such things as building height and plot-ratio 'as cast iron maxima' but as a starting point for negotiations.[16] Much of the LCC's planning in the late 1930s had this private character where a series of essentially tentative proposals were presented 'subject to such modifications as may be found desirable to meet the views or remove the opposition of estate owners'.[17]

Generally, it seems that the LCC was able to proceed by such piecemeal compromises, but there was one case where the LCC's right to intervene in development was challenged on a more fundamental basis, and here the private bargaining machinery could not operate. This challenge came from the Duke of Westminster whose estates in Mayfair and Belgravia amounted to 350 acres of London's most valuable property. The Duke's agents did not base their criticism on the LCC's involvement in town planning, rather they denied the utility of planning altogether. The public interest, they argued, was best served by the free play of market forces, and any intervention by the LCC was bound to be injurious. In London, they argued, the usual economic limiting factors of food supply and sewage disposal were absent and it was neither necessary nor desirable to limit the size and distribution of population. So complete and overt a reliance on market forces precluded any recognition of the LCC's right to intervene and the LCC's officers concluded that there was little hope of agreement between the two parties.[18] The outcome was to effectively block any progress towards a planning scheme for the West End and this area was given the lowest priority in the LCC's order of work, while the Architect turned with considerable relief to simpler, less contentious areas.[19]

In the 1930s, the character, scale and scope of LCC planning was determined by the possibilist strategy of Morrison, and the response of the countervailing political and property owning agencies in London. These agents were the metropolitan borough councils and the owners of industrial and commercial property, especially where they were concentrated on large estates. The consequences were that the LCC did not *enforce* planning standards, based on the Ministry of Health's strict model clauses, but established them to use as bargaining counters with owners in respect of individual schemes. The need to avoid claims for compensation from owners was, moreover, paramount . The LCC's orientation to planning in the 1930s had three major elements -

(1) to abandon policies and areas where there was fundamental opposition and where no bargaining framework could be established (these were chiefly in the West End and may be termed the LCC's *uncontestable* areas); (2) to formulate plans and standards for those areas where a bargaining framework could be established, but to enforce these only weakly (such places may be termed the LCC's *contested* areas); and (3) to direct the major thrust of policy making and enforcement towards those areas which were not contested either by private owners or by metropolitan borough councils (these were the LCC's *uncontested* areas within the East End and the South Bank).

There is no doubt that the 1930s saw contradictory tendencies at work in the sphere of regional government, and in particular responsibility for regional planning. The simultaneous publication of Gibbon & Bell's *History of the London County Council 1889-1939* and Robson's *Government and Misgovernment of London* highlighted the contradictory tendencies at work. The former, 'suffused with the Jubilee Spirit' dwelt upon what the authors saw as the excellence of the services provided, as well as the value of the working links built up between the LCC, the metropolitan borough councils and ad hoc bodies in Greater London. Robson, on the other hand, inveighed against the 'present makeshift muddle' which he asserted resulted from the separate administration of services in the region.[20] Rhetoric aside, it seems clear that by the end of the 1930s, the LCC had laid down the foundations of a planning machinery that were to be maintained even after the upheaval of the war. As Labour's poliical ascendency on the LCC and the metropolitan boroughs was established, priorities became entrenched, access by outside groups was further limited and controlled, and decision-making on planning matters was internalized with members and officers, and especially Labour party leaders and chief officers, accepting the major responsibility for the formulation of policy. Even Lord Reith's attempt to break the mould of London planning through Abercrombie's war-time plans for London was only temporarily and marginally successful. The LCC's reconstruction priorities were in many important respects to follow the patterns established in the 1930s - especially the predilection for large-scale projects in the 'uncontested areas' of the East End and South Bank, and the relative neglect even into the late 1950s, of the 'uncontestable areas' of the West End.

How regional ideas faded despite the wartime plethora of regional plans and the myriad proposals for the reform of local government will now be explored.

War, Reconstruction and Local Government Reform

I have traced in detail elsewhere the debate which raged both inside and outside Government in the early years of the war about London's physical and administrative future.[21] I need only summarize here the arguments put forward in *Metropolitan London* - that once the Blitz had proved less devastating than the total annihilation bombing that had been feared, London's survival and dogged persistence become rallying cries for the 'free world's' resistance to dictatorship and Fascism. Propaganda films such as *London Can Take It* and the broadcasts of *London Calling: London Calling* identified the resistance of the capital with the defence of freedom and democracy. By 1943, London no longer represented the national and strategic disaster of a few years before, but symbolized national pride and ultimate victory. Despite the continuous reviews and committees of 1940-43 on the issues of local and regional government reform, the time for action never seemed to present itself. Initially, the need to organize to win the war predominated, and later the priority was to anticipate and prepare for the return to a peace-time economy. Neither set of circumstances seemed appropriate for a general reorganization of local and central government. As Sir William Jowett, the Solicitor General, concluded in a report to the Cabinet Committee on Reconstruction Priorities:-

'If we were living in an age of universal peace, such a general reorganization (of local government) might be a practical possibility. I am convinced that it is not a practical possibility in the middle of a major war or in the stress of events which will follow hard upon the conclusion of peace. Plainly, it would be fantastic to ask local authorities at the moment, with depleted staffs and greatly enhanced responsibilities, to face an upheaval of the first magnitude'.[22]

Indeed, no scheme for the reform of local government did emerge from these debates at national level. Nevertheless, it is surprising that the preparation of war-time advisory plans for the reconstruction of major cities and their regions could not keep the issue alive, most notably through the publication of the *County of London Plan (1943)* and *Greater London Plan (1945)*. I propose to examine how and why these plans failed to sustain the impetus for local government reform on regional lines, and I will argue that the failure is to be explained by the ambivalent and equivocal involvement of the LCC, various political and economic interests, and successive Ministries in the preparation and promotion of the London Plans which undermined rather than enhanced the case for reform.

Despite the rhetoric of reconstruction, the context in which the wartime London Plans were drawn up was a continued Government reluctance to envisage radical interference with existing land use and most especially land ownership. Although the County of London plan is said to have been prepared at the request of Lord Reith when he was Minister of Works, 'to assist the Ministry in considering the methods and machinery for the planning and ... reconstruction of Town and Country',[23] the LCC received only limited support from central government with the Ministry advising caution. In discussing the nature of the proposed plan, the LCC was advised not to contemplate long-term schemes and to postpone any plans involving compulsory purchase.[24] Nevertheless, it was agreed that a 'provisional plan' for immediate post-war work could be drawn up, and it was this which Lord Reith formally asked the LCC to prepare in March 1941.[25] Lord Reith stressed again the limitations of planning in wartime, but expressed the hope that the plan for London could eventually become 'part of a more comprehensive plan on broader lines which it may be possible to envisage after the war'. There was no mention of employing an outside consultant, and Lord Reith's mandate to the LCC was clearly a very limited one indeed.

The LCC, however, used Lord Reith's request as the starting point in a campaign for new planning powers which lasted throughout the War. Professor Patrick Abercrombie was retained as consultant, ostensibly to assist the Council's own architect on general questions and to defend the plan vis a vis the Ministries and others concerned.[26] Abercrombie was chosen because of his established reputation in planning. He had been one planning's earliest advocates, a founder member of the Town Planning Institute, and he had maintained and broadened his commitment to planning during the 1930s despite the general hostility to it. He published his handbook *Town and Country Planning* in 1933 and was responsible, it is said, for more than 80 per cent of the regional planning reports published during the decade.[27] He had held chairs in civic design and town planning at the University of Liverpool and at University College, London. Using Lord Reith's limited proposal, Abercrombie and the LCC's own architect 'conceived our instructions in the widest terms, assuming that the new legislation and financial assistance would be forthcoming'.[28] The *County of London Plan*, published in 1943, was not at all the kind of limited provisional plan which Lord Reith had anticipated.

The tactics adopted by the LCC suggest not a close relationship with a committed and supportive Ministry, but the mounting of a campaign for new legislation and financial aid, so that the LCC could pursue *its own* planning aims more effectively, especially in those 'uncontested' areas revealed by planning negotiations in the 1930s. The LCC's appointment of Patrick Abercrombie represented an opportunistic attempt to take the initiative as part of a campaign to secure new legislation and financial aid for its own purposes in the post-war period.

There was indeed little evidence to suggest that the Coalition Government intended to make concerted efforts to overcome the political, financial and organizational problems associated with comprehensive planning, nor that the fierce opposition of property interests had been suspended. The caution of the Government and the problematic future of planning at the urban and regional scale seemed to be confirmed by the nature of the planning legislation introduced by the Coalition Government between 1943 and 1945, and by the reaction to these measures from groups inside and outside Parliament. The 1943 Town and Country Planning (Interim Development) Act did no more than extend to all local authorities the negative power of requiring developers to seek planning consent. Local authorities were not, however, required to prepare planning schemes to guide them and Arthur Greenwood described the progress achieved by the Bill as 'microscopic'.[29] There was no statement of government planning objectives, nor anything about financial aid, powers of compulsory acquisition for local authorities, compensation, betterment, or land nationalization.[30] Despite its limited nature, the Bill provoked the hostility of property owning groups, who attempted to have amendments introduced at the Committee stage.[31] Sir Francis Fremantle, Conservative M.P. for St Albans and a veteran of the 1932 Planning Bill battle, agreed that 'proper planning' was necessary, but attacked any inference with 'the rights of private property'.[32]

With the publication of the Coalition Government's major piece of planning legislation in June 1944, the misgivings of the LCC leaders about Ministerial commitment to large-scale planning seemed confirmed. The new Town and Country Planning Bill was not concerned with planning on anything but a highly localized and temporary basis. Its major objective was to give to local authorities the necessary finance and powers of land acqusition so that they could tackle what the Minister, W.S. Morrison, called 'the novel and formidable problem' of the bombed city.[33] It became obvious, however, that what the Government had in mind was a narrow once and for all solution to a particularly urgent problem, without any commitment to long-term planning or to extensive intervention by local authorities in redevelopment. Had Britain experienced the total urban devastation that was to be inflicted upon Hamburg or Dresden, this attitude would scarcely have been feasible: in 1944, however, it was possible to separate 'blitzed areas' from other urban land and to advocate special treatment for them. In the bombed areas, local authorities were to receive greater powers of acquisition and more generous financial aid from central government than ever before, but they were not encouraged to regard action in blitzed areas as part of a comprehensive plan for the whole city.[34] While with hindsight it may seem that the 1944 Act represented a 'fundamental breakthrough' and that the 'beginnings of comprehensive urban planning date from this time', there was no confidence at the time that 'one logical step would lead to another'.[35]

The Bill distinguished between three categories of land - firstly, areas which were completely bombed; secondly, areas where there was less than total damage; and, thirdly, areas suffering from 'bad lay-out' and the 'tooth of time'.[36] Financial and administrative provisions in the Act made it clear that it was the acquisition of totally bombed areas which were to have priority. Even in these areas, powers of compulsory acquisition were limited to a five year period, though loan charges to cover the costs of acqusition could be waived for up to ten years.[37] Costs of development, however, were to be borne by the local authority and if private enterprise was willing to redevelop, the local authority was to be excluded. At the other extreme, local authorities were empowered to acquire 'blighted', obsolete areas which had not been bombed, but no Exchequer assistance was offered, and the powers of acquisition were to lapse after two years.[38] The Minister justified these distinctions by saying that a 'bombed area is dead, and needs resuscitation; blighted land is still alive, though squalid', and must wait.[39]

Local authorities and professional bodies such as the Royal Institute of British Architects and the Town Planning Institute criticized the new Bill for falling short of what was needed. Indeed, they expressed the view that the Act would actually prejudice the prospects for comprehensive planning. The RIBA emphasized that 'unless such immediate acqusition of land for various urgent purposes arising from the consequences of war is also related to needs beyond this temporary emergency, any attempt at creating a rational, constant and continuous development in respect of the use of land will be irretrievably lost'.[40] The LCC joined with the Association of Municipal Corporations and other local government associations, in opposing the bill. In the House of Commons, opposition was led by Lewis Silkin, Chairman of the LCC's Town Planning Committee. He forced a division on the Second Reading and a debate on the principles of planning ensued.

The debates on the Bill demonstrated a polarization of political views between Labour and Conservative M.P.s which suggested that planning had become a more, rather than a less, contentious issue by 1944. There is little evidence that planning had established itself as an accepted part of political life, and the prospect for creating planning machinery and planning powers on a regional scale seemed distant indeed.

Most Labour M.P.s were said to be opposed to the Bill, but some were constrained by the fact that a Coalition Government was promoting it.[41] Besides criticizing the exclusion of 'blighted' areas from the most generous clauses in the Bill, leading Labour members opposed it as fundamentally unsound. 'Our only standard on this side of the House', said Arthur Greenwood, 'in judging a plan dealing with national development, is that it must be based upon the national ownership of land'.[42] Whereas in the 1930s, land nationalization had been advocated only by a small group on the left of the Labour Party, it was now regarded by Party leaders as 'the inescapable solution' and 'an important part of Labour policy'.[43]

On the Conservative side, the doctrinaire 'Whig' group of the 1930s was still intact, and beyond an acceptance of the fact that 'these are the most exceptional times and therefore property owners should, and generally did, recognize the necessity for some degree of control over the use of land', their opposition to the idea of constant, continuous control remained. While members of the moderate Tory Reform Committee were said to be the strongest supporters of the Bill, a small group of right-wing Conservatives attacked it as a threat to the rights and freedoms of the people, and as 'another step in the direction of National Socialism'.[45] Robert Tasker, Lieutenant-Commander Dower and Dr Russell Thomas refused to support the Second Reading and brought forward a series of amendments in Committee designed to further reduce the scope and impact of the Bill.[46]

Dower and Russell were both Vice-Presidents of the National Federation of Property Owners and acted as links between property owners and 'Whigs'. Close contact between these M.P.s and the Federation's Parliamentary Agents was maintained during the Committee stage. As the Minister accepted a series of amendments which delayed and complicated acqusition procedure Silkin accused him of giving in to sectional pressures and remarked that the Minister 'had changed since the beginning of Committee', and had altered things which had been 'the basis of all discussions between the Minister and the local authorities'.[47]

The effect of the 1944 Town and Country Planning Act was to permit local authorities to undertake merely 'piecemeal, parochial planning', in severely bombed areas for a limited period.[48] Private property in land was preserved except in bombed areas, and in most cases planners still had to consider 'who owns the land and what is the price of it, as well as is the land suitable for my purpose'?[49] Henry Guest, M.P. for North Islington concluded that nothing in the Act was 'big enough to cope with the emergency which faces the country' and that the government was not seriously interested in 'big planning proposals'.[50] Ernest Bevan accused Conservative members of the Cabinet of dealing with the narrow issue of bombed cities with the deliberate intention of blunting public agitation and 'indefinitely postponing the powers to reconstruct the rest of the cities and towns'.[51] Such views were not confined to Labour Party politicians, and *The Times* accused the Government of 'continuing to behave as though the Uthwatt Committee had never reported, and as if they had forgotten the existence of the Ministry of Town and Country Planning'.[52]

The message that local authorities were receiving from the Coalition Government's planning legislation was that the future of planning was fragile - the new powers were to be limited and shortlived; decisions about compensation and betterment and about local government reform were continually being postponed because of the conflicts and difficulties that could be foreseen. Advisory plans like those for the County of London, and for Greater London were the products therefore of uncertainty rather than confidence that in post-war Britain it would be possible to plan and redevelop land in a 'rational, constant and continuous manner'. Once it was possible to distinguish between bombed and blighted areas, the apocalyptic vision of new cities rising from the ashes of the old no longer had power to overcome distaste for state direction and regard for private property. A respect for established patterns of ownership, for continuity and for democratic principles re-emerged. The war, far from annihilating Britain, actually seemed to vindicate the 'good, old British style' of non-dogmatic pragmatism. The need for a programme of public ownership and control ceased to seem inevitable from the summer of 1941 when the heavy bombardment of Britain's cities ended. The Government saw no need for a master plan, nor for any statement of long-term aims except of a most general kind.

In 1944 the case for the comprehensive planning of built-up areas had still not been fully accepted: property owners' groups continued to be a well organized opposition inside and outside Parliament, and the political gulf between right and left appeared to be widening. In such a situation, it seemed extremely unlikely that the Coalition Government would add to the controversy and risk the wrath of existing local authorities by bringing forward proposals for the reform of local government to provide a framework for planning on a regional scale. Neither the *County of London Plan* nor the *Greater London Plan*, therefore, should be seen as part of a Government strategy to promote comprehensive planning. Rather they owed their origin to the Government's need to show token support for post-war reconstruction at a time of particular military threat, and to the LCC's use of them in pursuit of its own tactical ends.

Despite, or even because of, the issues which the London Plans raised in relation to planning law, the finance of reconstruction and the powers and functions of local government authorities, it was clear that the Coalition Government regarded fundamental changes in these areas as politically impossible. For their part, the LCC saw no reason to use the Plans to campaign for regional reform. In many respects, the *County of London Plan* was an embarrassment to the LCC - its recommendations were largely Professor Abercrombie's own and did not represent agreed policy. Relations between the LCC members and officers and their consultant were often strained because of Abercrombie's cavalier, even arrogant, approach to policy making.[53] Despite the fanfare of publicity with which the County of London Plan was launched, the LCC leaders had subsequently to renegotiate the Plan's proposals through its regular internal political channels and external consultation procedures. Significant modifications were required, and of particular significance was the reduced commitment to the policy of decentralization which was crucial to Abercrombie's regional strategy for London.[54] Robson's hope that the County of London and the Greater London plans would 'possibly be found to mark a turning point in our social and political history ... may well form the watershed between the unplanned world of yesterday and the planned Britain of tomorrow' was shortlived. Neither at central nor at local level did the plans provide the impetus to drive the regional reform of government forward.

Indeed, in the post-war period the prospect retreated even further as the newly-elected Labour Government pursued a national framework for most major services, and employed ad hoc single purpose bodies under Ministerial direction to deal with planning issues which cut across existing local authority boundaries such as the National Parks and the New Towns. Local authorities emerged from the war with their functions much reduced. Leaving aside their ambiguous responsibility for education, housing and local planning had emerged as their major spheres of influence, yet they held these functions in isolation, divorced from most other crucial urban elements, in particular the utilities, transport and production which remained in other hands. Yet despite their truncated and isolated powers, local authorities were still the focus of rhetoric lauding civic pride and local democracy. The emphasis was on demonstrating the vitality and drive of local government, and a commitment to lofty ideals backed by concrete results was what authorities needed in order to demonstrate their continued worth.

By continuing to play lipservice to the grand schemes embodied in Abercrombie's plans while pursuing most vigorously only those elements which coincided with the 'spheres of influence' identified through the experience of the 1930s, the LCC retrieved its position and reestablished itself as the London authority. The LCC's concentration of effort on comprehensive redevelopment on the South Bank and in the East End, and the lack of enthusiasm for decentralization underline the reemergence of pre-war priorities. Both the LCC and the Ministry of Town and Country Planning were happy to adopt those parts of Abercrombie's plans that matched their own priorities while ignoring many others. Furthermore, the existence of the Plans enabled the semblance of regional planning to be maintained at the expense of the substance.[55] In particular, the very existence of the Greater London Plan pre-empted further moves to regional reform - since the Plan already existed, it was argued, there was no need to create regional planning authorities to devise one, and the job of coordination and implementation could be left to central government departments and existing local authorities.[56]

Conclusion

This paper has addressed the issue of why planning failed to break the mould of local government in the 1930s and 1940s despite the recognition that existing structures were inadequate to devise and implement appropriate strategies. The need for planning policies at the regional scale was emphasized in many quarters in the 1930s and 1940s, but reform of local government was rejected despite almost continual consideration of the issue in Government commissions and committees. The reasons for this, it has been argued, were the continued resistance to planning itself among Conservative politicians and property groups at local and national level, and the opportunistic tactics adopted by local authorities like the LCC in response to this continued uncertainty. In the changed circumstances of the post-war period, both central and local government preferred the semblance of regional planning to the reality and in this respect, war-time regional plans such as Abercrombie's served to postpone rather than accelerate moves to regionalize planning and the structure of government.

Notes and References

1. Simon, E. (1937) 'Town Planning: Moscow or Manchester?', *Journal of the Town Planning Institute* (JTPI), 23, pp.381-389.
2. Royal Commission on the Distribution of the Industrial Population, *Report*, Cmnd 6153 London: HMSO, 1940 (known as the Barlow Report). Ministry of Works and Planning, Expert Committee on Compensation and Betterment, *Final Report*, Cmd 6386 London: HMSO, 1942 (known as the Uthwatt Report). Ministry of Works and Planning, Committee on Land Utilization in Rural Areas, *Report*, Cmd 6378 London: HMSO, 1942 (known as the Scott Report).
3. Ward, S.V. (1974) 'The Town and Country Planning Act 1932', *The Planner* 60 (5), pp.685-689.
4. Electricity and gas were taken over from local authorities by public corporations in 1947 and 1948. Local hospitals were taken over by the national health service in 1947, and central government assumed responsibility for trunk roads in 1936 and 1946.
5. Loughlin, M., Gelfand M. David and Young, K. (1985) *Half a Century of Municipal Decline* 1935-1985, London: George Allen & Unwin.
6. ibid, pp.5-7.
7. Sir William Ray (Chairman) Report of the Committee on Local Expenditure, Cmd 4200 London: HMSO, 1932.
8. Robson, W.A. (Jan-March 1933) 'The Central Domination of Local Government', *Political Quarterly*, p.87.
9. Sir Hilton Young, quoted in Ministry of Health, (1933) *Fourteenth Report of Ministry of Health*, Cmd 4372 London: HMSO, 1933.
10. Spoor, A. (1967) *White Collar Union: Sixty Years of NALGO*, London: Heinemann, p.136.
11. Graham Wallace, cited in Loughlin, Gelfand & Young, *Municipal Decline*, p.2.
12. Morrison, H.S. (1935) 'Planning London', *The Listener*, XIII, p.987.
13. For a description of this episode see Garside, P.L. *Town Planning in London 1930-1961: A Study of Pressures, Interests and Influences Affecting the Formation of Policy*, Unpublished PhD Thesis, University of London, 1980.
14. Jones, G. 'How Herbert Morrison Governed London', *Local Government Studies*, 5, 1973, p.5.
15. London County Council (LCC), Minutes of Meetings, 10 July 1934, Report of the Town Planning Committee.
16. *City Press*, 20 March 1936.
17. LCC, London Development Sub-Committee Minutes, 3 May 1936, Joint Report, Architect and Valuer.
18. Greater London County Record Office (GLCRO) C/C/704/3/22A Area I, representations of owners of property, The Grosvenor Estate.

19. The six divisions of the County were:

West	Chelsea, Fulham, Hammersmith, Kensington, Paddington, Westminster
North	Finsbury, Hampstead, Holborn, Islington, St. Marylebone, St. Pancras, Stoke Newington
East	Bethnal Green, Hackney, Shoreditch, Stepney
South West	Battersea, Wandsworth
South	Bermondsey, Camberwell, Lambeth, Southwark
South East	Deptford, Greenwich, Lewisham, Woolwich.

20. Gibbon, Sir G. and Bell, R.W. (1939) *History of the London County Council* 1889-1939, London: Macmillan, 1939; Robson, W.A. (1939) *The Government and Misgovernment of London* , London: Allen & Unwin. For a comparison of these two works, see Stocks, M. (1939) 'London Government', *Political Quarterly*, 10, pp.365-74.

21. Young, K. and Garside, P.L. (1982) *Metropolitan London: Politics and Urban Change 1837-1981*, London: Edward Arnold, 1982, Studies in Urban History, 6, Chapter 8, pp.234-43.

22. Quoted in Cullingworth, J. B. (1975) *Environmental Planning*, Vol.1: *Reconstruction and Land Use Planning* 1939-1947, London: HMSO, 1975 p.50.

23. Forshaw, J.H. and Abercrombie, P. (1943) *County of London Plan*, London: Macmillan, p.(v)

24. GLRCO, C/C/705/1/8. Notes on 'Planning of London Conference', 13-14 January 1940, held at the Ministry of Works.

25. ibid., letter to the LCC Clerk signed by Lord Reith, March 1941.

26. ibid., letter to Abercrombie signed by the LCC Clerk, 26 March 1941.

27. *Journal of the Royal Institute of British Architects* (1952) 59, p.160.

28. Forshaw and Abercrombie, *London Plan*, p.5.

29. *Commons Debates*, Vol.386, col.512.

30. ibid., col.519.

31. Opposition in Committee was led by Lieutenant-Colonel Dower, member of the Property Owners Protection Association.

32. *Commons Debates*, Vol.386, cols.527-8.

33. *Commons Debates*, Vol.401, col.1592.

34. ibid., col.1681.

35. Cherry, G. (1964) *The Evolution of British Town Planning*, Leighton Buzzard: Leonard Hill, pp.124-5.

36. *Commons Debates*, Vol.401, 1594.

37. ibid., cols.1599, 1608-10.

38. ibid., col.1611.

39. ibid., col.1600.

40. ibid., Vol.403, cols.797-8.

41. ibid., Vol.401, col.1663. The Bill's sponsors included Clement Attlee, then leader of the Labour Party.

42. ibid., col.1616.

43. ibid., col .747

44. Lord Chesham (President of the National Federation of Property Owners) speaking in the House of Lords Debates, 27-8 September 1944), quoted in the National Federation of Property Owners, *Gazette*, November 1944, p.133.

45. *Commons Debates*, Col.401, col.1832.

46. ibid., Vol.403, cols.2410-2666.

47. ibid., cols.2419, 2425-2426.

48. ibid., col .650.

49. ibid., col .673.

50. ibid., cols.1641-1643.

51. ibid., Vol.403, col.809.

52. *The Times*, leading article, 15 May 1945.

53. Lewis Silkin said of Abercrombie: 'Once having got an idea, he was more concerned to defend it, than to discuss it.' See Garside, *Town Planning in London*, pp.270, 278-9, and 288-9.

54. For the publicity surrounding the publication of the County of London Plan, see Garside, *Town Planning in London*, p.275, and for the shift in the LCC's position on decentralization to what F. J. Osborn termed a 'token' commitment after 1945, pp.331-33.

55. Young and Garside, *Metropolitan London*, pp.245-6.

56. ibid., pp.261-262.

7

The Origins of the Regional Studies Association

Michael Wise

Antecedents

The first volume of *Regional Studies*, which appeared in 1967, opens with a note by the late Andrew Sharman, the then Honorary Secretary, on 'The Regional Studies Association: Origins and Opportunities'.[1] Sharman stated that the need for the Association had existed for 'for at least the last 12 years'. During that period, large numbers of people from many professions, economists, engineers, geographers, agronomists, architects and planners had come together for discussion about regional planning. The meetings, he suggested, though somewhat lacking in continuity of purpose, had been fruitful. Existing organizations had not fostered or provided for the inter-professional approaches which had drawn forth vigorous discussion at the meetings. The need had been shown for an organization to provide for continuity and communication. So, the Regional Studies Association had been born in 1964 and with the aid of a grant from the Rowntree Memorial Trust took formal shape in 1965. Sharman also provided a brief chronology of events from 1955, the date of origin of the International Centre for Regional Planning and Development (ICRPD). This chapter enlarges upon that chronology.

But the origins, in terms both of ideas and of individuals, may be traced back to earlier years than 1955. There is a helpful note in the *Report of the Proceedings of the Bedford College Conference 28 September - 2 October 1955* published by the Provisional Committee of the ICRPD from Brussels. The Conference owed its origin to an initiative taken by some members of the ex-students' association of the School of Planning and Research for Regional Development which had been founded in 1934 by the Architectural Association as an off-shoot of its School of Architecture. Percy Johnson-Marshall was

Chairman, and Leslie Ginsburg Secretary, of the former students' organization, the School of Planning Club. Under the influence of E.A.A. Rowse, its principal from 1935, the School, rebelling against the limitations of statutory planning, 'inspired its students with the comprehensive outlook, taking the ideas of Le Play, Geddes and Mumford, and trying to apply them to the development problems of this present era'.[2] The Report of the Conference indeed paid special tribute to Rowse, describing him as 'our Honorary Founder Member', though Rowse at that time was abroad, engaged in regional planning in Burma on a United Nations assignment.

The School of Planning generated great enthusiasm and strong loyalties. It was never strongly based financially. The School advocated positive planning, not just zoning land for different uses, covering a large geographical region such as a river basin: the Tennessee Valley Authority had been much studied. It believed that planning should be carried on by teams composed from the relevant professions. It was interested in training persons for work in planning departments in the British Commonwealth.[3] During the 1939-45 war its work was carried on under the aegis of the Association for Planning and Regional Reconstruction (APRR) a body chaired by Lord Forrester and including Rowse as a member of its Board. The Association, while undertaking specific investigations, served as a centre for research, on regionalization among other things.[4] It urged that planning and reconstruction after the war must be accepted by local and regional bodies in Britain, as well as by Whitehall. Planning and associated research should be accomplished by well balanced groups of some 15 to 20 persons. Planning should be locally and regionally based with only broad outlines and practical standards laid down by the centre.[5] Planning was defined as 'the intelligent use by a free community of its environment for the common good of its neighbours, its successors and itself and with the object of developing human life and society as organic and not as mechanical units'.[6] The Association published regular reports, broadsheets and maps. In 1945, *Maps for the National Plan* appeared, to provide a broad national context, clearly revealing the hand of Professor E.G.R. Taylor, geographer of Birkbeck College, London and a member of the Board. This volume also reflected work that was vigorously in progress amongst geographers notably in the group directed by Dr. E. Christie Willatts in the Ministry of Town and Country Planning.

The Association was proud of the fact that it had 'the full advantage of the experience gained by the School of Planning and Research for National Development during the six years before the war; a new body incorporated as a company limited by guarantee had been formed to carry on the School's work'.[7] A curriculum for a correspondence course suitable for those serving in the forces or prisoners of war was compiled which brought in some 1600 enrolments. Wherever possible, students also took a practical three months completion course at 34 Gordon Square from where Jacqueline Tyrwhitt, the Association's Director of Research, exercised her considerable influence. The one-year course was developed. Hebbert writes of Tyrwhitt that 'her contributions' (to the

Association's teaching texts) 'capture perhaps better than any other the bracing sense of what could be achieved by a scientific regional planning which tackled land use and social and economic problems not piecemeal but holistically as elements of a single community design'.[8]

The School of Planning closed for financial reasons in 1952. Lord Forrester, one of the principal supporters, had died in an accident in Portugal and Rowse's attempts to enlist support from official quarters did not succeed. Planning departments had by then been established in universities and overseas students were being trained in their own countries. But with the recommendation of the Schuster Report (1950) on the training of planners in mind, especially the idea of a planning staff college and centre for planning research, former students of the School, together with a few other interested persons, banded together to find ways of carrying forward the ideas and spirit of the School. One idea which was floated was that of a Commonwealth School for research and teaching in connection with the planning and development of the Commonwealth countries.[9] Percy Johnson-Marshall, Otto Koenigsberger, lately Adviser on Housing to the Government of India, George Atkinson, Adviser to the Ministry of Overseas Department and others organized, in March 1953, an influential conference on Tropical Architecture at University College, London, attended by over 200 people from a variety of countries. Leslie Ginsburg and Otto Koenigsberger were leading instigators and Otto then developed the work in Tropical Architecture at the Architectural Association. Later in the year, the School of Planning Club organized a symposium at the Imperial Institute, held in collaboration with Community Development Projects Limited, which brought together about 100 people. A Preparatory Committee was elected to investigate the possibility of establishing a Centre for research and education and to provide an information service. Widespread advice was sought from existing organizations: nearly one thousand individuals from many countries expressed support, and the Committee was encouraged to organize the Bedford College Conference.

In view of the influence exerted by the members of the School of Planning Club and by individual supporters of the Association for Planning and Regional Reconstruction it may be worthwhile to recall the names of the first members of the Preparatory Committee. They were W.H. Beckett, John Bolton, Leslie Ginsburg, Norman J. Hart (Executive Director of Community Development Projects Limited), Otto Koenigsberger, Arthur Ling, Max Lock, John Logan (U.S.A.), Percy Johnson-Marshall, Robert Gardner-Medwin (Conference Chairman), John Phillips, Ralph Rookwood, G.P. Wibberley, Ian Aitken. Professor J.E.S. Allen, F.J.C. Amos, E.C. Gordon-England and S. Brassey-Edwards were co-opted. Bolton withdrew on appointment to the International Bank in Washington and pressure of work forced Aitken (who represented the Association of Consulting Engineers) to withdraw.

The Bedford College Conference 1955

No conference which I have ever attended opened in such an electric atmosphere as the First International Conference on Regional Planning and Development at Bedford College, London on 28 September 1955. This was in part a product of the international and inter-professional character of the membership. About 420 registrations were received from at least 44 countries (though about 60 subsequently withdrew). There was also the expectation of hearing from a number of internationally distinguished speakers, among them Dr. Edward Ackerman on the Tennessee Valley Authority, under the Presidency of Madame Pandit, then High Commissioner for India in the U.K. An exciting new venture in the international organization of regional planning research was in prospect. But the electric charge had been produced by the intervention by the British Foreign and Home Offices which became evident on 23 September. It had become clear that the Foreign and Colonial Offices had advised some governments not to send representatives. The Home Office had communicated to civil servants known to have received invitations in an official capacity that they were expected not to attend.

The view had been taken officially that the organization of the Conference was, in some measure, under Communist influence. Vigorous representations were made by the Chairman of the Preparatory Committee, Professor Gardner-Medwin and members of the Preparatory Committee directly to the Foreign Office, through a letter to *The Times* (28 September 1955) and a press conference, and through the help of friends in the political world of whom Mr. Austen Albu deserved special mention. To no immediate avail. Madame Pandit was spared political embarrassment and released from her commitment. The situation, revealed openly in the press, was known to the members as they assembled and the buzz of coversation may be easily imagined. To their credit a number of civil servants and officials who had been advised not to attend disregarded the advice.

Throughout the argument the Preparatory Committee stressed the professional and entirely non-political approach which had been adopted to the organization. There had been no political screening of the members of the Committee. Later a full set of the correspondence and documents was issued by the Committee. The matter was raised in the House of Commons on 31 October and debated in the House on 7 November when the conference organizers received support from both sides of the Chamber. The Joint Under-Secretary of State for the Home Office made a statement absolving those people of eminence in their own professions whose interest was confined to the declared object, but making no apology.

The full story of the evidence and reasoning which lay behind the government's decision to intervene has not yet been told and, no doubt, will one day make an interesting paper. It was, and is, apparent that a gross mis-judgement had been made. Perhaps the matter may be left with the remark by

Mr. Kenneth Younger, M.P., in a response to the Minister's statement: 'A most unsatisfactory reply. I hope the Government are thoroughly ashamed.'

Putting the political issues on one side, the Conference went on to a series of vigorous discussions. The content of the programme reflected the originating influences derived from the School of Planning as well as the interest of the time in multi-purpose regional planning projects. Four such projects were studied and discussed: the TVA, the Volta River Project, the Indian Community Development Project, and the Ivrea sub-region, Piedmont, plan. There were subsidiary papers on planning problems in the Middle East, the reclamation of the Zuiderzee, village community problems in Jamaica, shifting cultivation in Tropical Africa, to mention only some. Walter Isard spoke on "The Value of the Regional Approach." Regional planning was much more than physical planning: it was deeply concerned with social and economic well-being. It required contributions from many professions: it needed an international framework of reference, reporting and research. It was as concerned with problems of development in poor areas and poor countries as with the rich.[10] 'Plans,' Andre Philip remarked in his concluding address, 'had to be conceived with the people and by the people: it must not be only a plan of the technicians for the people.'

Against this background the resolution to establish an International Centre for Regional Planning and Development was warmly received and approved. Its activities were to include 'the setting up of a documentation service; the undertaking of research and field surveys; the investigation of problems concerning the availability of suitable experts, education, training, personnel; and the establishment of a meeting place' (Interim Report of the Congress). The establishment of a widely representative Provisional Committee was approved. G.E. Janson-Smith (U.K.) was Chairman, E.C. Gordon-England (U.K.) and J.L. Servais (Belgium) were Vice-Chairmen, L. Turin (France) was General Secretary, Norman J. Hart (U.K.), Deputy General Secretary and H.O.E. Wohl (Netherlands) became Treasurer. The organization was thus heavily European in domination, the more so for, despite four members from Africa, two from the Middle East, four from Asia, one from Australia and two from the Americas, there were six other members from Western Europe and eight others from Britain. The British Committee members were Professor J.S. Allen, Mrs. G.M. Culwick, Professor Robert Gardner-Medwin, Leslie Ginsburg, Professor Charles Madge, Percy Johnson-Marshall, Ralph Rookwood and Dr. G.P. Wibberley.

The British Group of the International Centre for Regional Planning and Development

In the year following the Bedford College Conference discussions took place on future activities in Britain and it was decided to form a British Group. An inaugural meeting was held at the Architectural Press, 9 Queen Anne's Gate,

SW1 on 22 January 1957 attended by about 60 persons. The discussion was opened by Sir Patrick Abercrombie and Dr. (later Sir) Dudley Stamp and a business meeting followed. Robert Gardner-Medwin became Chairman and a committee of 18 was appointed. In addition to the British members of the International Centre committee it included F.J.C. Amos (who became Honorary Secretary), Richard Bailey (PEP), S. Brassey Edwards, Dr. S.F. Collins (Edinburgh), John Madge (then Secretary of the British Sociological Association), G.B. Masefield (Institute of Agricultural Economics, Oxford), Miss Solomans (Housing Centre), P.A. Scott and three members of different disciplines from the London School of Economics, P.J.O. Self, Paul Stirling and myself. Leslie Ginsburg prepared a paper on 'The Meaning of Region' and ideas from this paper were included in the published Statement of Aims. Lewis Mumford's definition of regional planning was adopted '...the conscious direction and collective integration of all those activities which rest upon the use of earth as site, as resource and as theatre.' There was a look back to Geddes and a reference to Abercrombie and the kind of teamwork which had been established by him and others in the post-war regional planning surveys and plans. There was a holistic basis to the document; thinking in regional terms of human welfare was the essence, the region being a scale appropriate to the time. Having played a small part in the 'simultaneous thinking' process of the West Midland Group on Post-War Reconstruction and Planning and having had the entrée to Abercrombie's seminars at the time when he and Herbert Jackson were preparing the West Midland Plan, I was attracted to the work of the Group.

In addition to the general aims of furthering the understanding of the value of regional planning there were practical tasks to be accomplished. These included an Information and Documentation service, a register of experts, the development of educational facilities, the improvement of techniques, the establishment of a meeting place. A research sub-committee was established (Stirling, Wibberley, Johnson-Marshall, Amos, Wise) and I recall discussion on a comparative evaluation of multi-purpose river valley projects, amongst other topics. There was also a documentation sub-committee, though eventually these two committees were combined.

Further sub-committees on the Programme of Activities and on the Constitution were set up. At the First Annual General Meeting held at the Royal Empire (now the Royal Commonwealth) Society on 19 October 1957 much time, perhaps inevitably, was taken up by constitutional matters: should there be different categories of membership? Should the title British Group remain as such or should it become the British Association for Regional Planning and Development? The documentation and research committee, for whom Paul Stirling spoke, saw the need for funds to develop the library and documentation centre as well as for research assistance not only for the River Valleys project but also to assist with preparation of a paper for the forthcoming United Nations Department of Social Affairs conference in Tokyo.

The afternoon session was mainly devoted to a discussion on 'The Translation of Economic Planning into Physical Planning' with a paper by M.J. Wise and a vigorous discussion opened by Otto Koenigsberger with contributions, among others, from G.P. Wibberley, L.D. Stamp, Percy Johnson-Marshall, G.B. Masefield and Andrew Sharman. Plans for the formation of a Scottish Branch were put forward and approved. This proposal had been initiated by Sir Robert Matthew, its first Chairman, Professor J. Wreford Watson, Frank Tindall (a former member of the School of Planning) and others. Sir Robert was succeeded as Chairman by Percy Johnson-Marshall, who had gone to Edinburgh University to set up a new post-graduate Department of Urban Design and Regional Planning. The Scottish Group, as it was known, was to become very active and develop a vigorous programme.

That first annual general meeting in October 1957 also heard a report by Jim Amos and Leslie Ginsburg on the seminar sponsored by the International Centre and held at the Hague July 1 - 6, 1957 on 'Methods and Problems of Regional Planning and Development for the Benefit of Man' at which Dudley Stamp had spoken on planning in Britain. It was said that the gaps between disciplines much in evidence at the start of the Seminar were considerably diminished by its end.

By this time the International Centre had become established in Brussels with aid from the Belgian government and J.L. Servais had become its Secretary General. Relations with Brussels were the subject of frequent discussion. Should space be taken for a display on regional planning at the Brussels Exhibition in 1958? How did the work of ICRPD relate to the International Federation of Housing and Town Planning and was there a case for affiliation?

Meanwhile, a paper had been prepared by Otto Koenigsberger and Leslie Ginsburg as a background paper for the United Nations Asian Regional Planning Conference in Tokyo 1958 on the subject of "Regional Planning in Relation to Social and Economic Development". A series of lectures and discussions was held in London. In March 1958 Dudley Stamp spoke on "What is a Region". The April meeting brought George Berthoin, Acting Head of the High Authority of the European Coal and Steel Community to discuss 'The Common Market, an example of Regional Planning' while, in June, Paul Brenikov and J.F.Q. Switzer opened a discussion on the training of planners.

Meetings and Activities 1959-63

In reviewing the work of the Group in these years, the voluntary character of its activities must be remembered. All those who gave their time were busy engineers, architects, planners, university teachers, fired with the desire to advance regional studies based on a higher degree of inter-professional and inter-disciplinary collaboration. Robert Gardner-Medwin was a staunch Chairman. Leslie Ginsburg stimulated colleagues with his zeal for the regional idea; Percy

Johnson-Marshall fired the Group with enthusiasm; Otto Koenigsberger's experience and concern for inter-disciplinarity was extraordinarily valuable. I mention these four only, and hope to be forgiven by others, to bring out the importance of the personal element in the Group's work.

Much work was accomplished by a sub-committee convened by Arthur Edwards on the preparation of evidence for the Royal Commission on Local Government in Greater London (the Herbert Commission). The document stressed the regional character of London's problems, criticizing the narrow definition of the Commission's area of reference, and advocated the establishment of a Regional Authority and a two-tier structure with a second tier of city districts for areas of between a quarter and half a million in population.

The Group was represented in discussions at the Hague in September 1959 on the possible organization of a graduate course on Comprehensive Planning to begin in September 1960 bringing together theory and experience in the economic, physical and institutional aspects of planning. Leslie Ginsburg was much involved in this activity, which was to bear fruit in the regional planning courses for developing countries taught to this day at the Institute for Social Studies in the Hague.[11]

Much work was put into the organization of a series of Study Days. The first of these took place at the London School of Economics on 7 March 1959, on 'The Gap Between Social and Physical Planning' when the principal papers were given by Dr. Ruth Glass and Mr. W.L. Waide. On 21 November over 130 persons were present for a discussion of "Economic Forces Leading to Urban Concentration" with a team of speakers under my chairmanship including Professor P. Sargant Florence, A.G. Powell, Bryan Anstey, J.H. Westergaard, G.R. Allen, Peter Self and Professor Colin Clark. The series continued into 1960 with "Urbanization in the Tropics - Causes and Methods of Control" as the subject on 30 April and A.D. Knox, Professor R.W. Steel and A.T.A. Learmouth, Anne Martin, Paul Stirling, Otto Koenigsberger and M.J. Wise speaking. About 80 attended. I have no papers of the 4th study day: the 5th on June 3rd 1961, at the Architectural Association, considered "The Ideal Metropolitan Region" and papers by Marius Reynolds, Arthur Edwards, Andrew Sharman, Leslie Ginsburg, Colin Buchanan, John Madge and Robert Grieve were discussed.

It was a lively series and much work went into organizing programmes, arranging discussion leaders and printing and distributing the substantial reports. The Scottish Group arranged its own Study Days: alas, I do not have a full programme though I recall travelling to Glasgow to speak on 9 May 1959 on "Industrial Location" with J.A. Donachy of the Scottish Council giving the afternoon paper.

Council and its sub-committee met regularly. By February 1960 with a subscription of £2.2.0 (50% of this remitted to the Scottish Branch in respect of their members) the Group had £490 in the bank. It was agreed to transfer the Group's Library of 1080 books which had been purchased for £100 from the

School of Planning, to the University of Edinburgh, with access to members. Many of these books are now in the Patrick Geddes Centre for Planning Studies in the Outlook Tower Edinburgh, a Centre which is directed by Percy Johnson-Marshall. There was concern about the perceived inactivity of the International Centre in Brussels: discussions between it and the IFHTP had come to nought and IFHTP representatives were keen to enter into direct discussions with the British Group. However, a Canadian group of the ICRPD had begun activities in 1958 as the Regional Planning Committee of the Town Planning Institute of Canada.

By October 1960, new Honorary Secretaries, David Oakley and Emrys Jones, had been appointed to replace Otto Koenigsberger (ill) and R.R. Symonds (abroad). Paul Brenikov had agreed to undertake a study for the UN of physical planning of industrial estates in the U.K., the Netherlands, Italy and Africa. On the report of a sub-committee comprising John Madge, Andrew Sharman, Emrys Jones and M.J. Wise, a proposal for a series of international seminars was considered. The first seminar was to be held in September 1961 on the subject of new and extended towns. The Ford Foundation was approached for funds ($20,000) though the negotiations were unsuccessful.

In January 1961 Leslie Ginsburg attended the meeting of the Council of the International Centre in Brussels. His full report revealed doubts about the organizational efficiency of the headquarters though some work was in prospect, notably a survey of European institutions which carried out training in regional planning, to be supported by the European Economic Community. Ginsburg also reported on the aforementioned course in comprehensive regional planning at the Institute for Social Studies in The Hague with which he and Koenigsberger had been involved. In August 1961 a review of activities was undertaken by the British Group: further study days were proposed and new developments were to include a twice yearly information bulletin on regional planning in Britain and abroad.

Discussion of future activities continued in 1962. Questions began to be asked about the continued need for the Group in view of the gradual acceptance of regional planning ideas by other bodies. A reviewing sub-committee (Ginsburg, Sharman, Wise and Jones) advised that the relationship with Brussels had become nebulous and should be severed. The group should develop as the "Association for Regional Planning and Development". It could still make a distinct contribution as an interdisciplinary body with a focus on regional problems. A regular publication was necessary and the idea of 'Regional Planning Abstracts' was put forward. Progress was also needed in establishing a graduate course in regional planning. The proposals were received sympathetically by the Council in March where Koenigsberger advised that a course on regional planning in under-developed countries was being planned at the Architectural Association. Further work was done on the content of the publication, to be entitled "Regional Planning: Current Theory and Practice" and possible editors were identified: John Holliday of the Birmingham School of

Planning agreed to undertake the editing though, sadly, he was later to report negatively on success in obtaining suitable material. The possibility of a European symposium on methods and problems of regional planning was also under discussion.

Relationships with the International Centre in Brussels came to a head in May 1962. The General Secretary had, without adequate consultation with the British Group and others, arranged to hold a conference in Rhodes in spring 1963. The Group's Council disassociated itself from the arrangements and proposed that the conference should not take place. A statement was issued indicating the Council's view of the inadequacy of arrangements 'which can do nothing but harm to the cause of the International Centre'. It was proposed instead that an international seminar of high standard be arranged at a European university centre in 1964 and that at the same time the International Centre should review its organization and prepare realistically for its future. But in practice the link with the International Centre had collapsed and much of the steam had gone out of the British Group's energy. Sporadic activities continued in 1963 and discussion on the future took place but there were no more Study Days and little progress was made.

The Dissolution of the British Group and the Formation of the Regional Studies Association

By the beginning of 1964 the earlier doubts about the continued usefulness of the British Group had become serious. Regional planning had become respectable again in government and political circles. The international centre in Brussels was regarded as inactive: the British Group, while hoping that international links could be continued, had disassociated itself from Brussels. There had been substantial research progress in the contributing disciplines. The Regional Science movement had gathered strength in the United States and its influence was spreading. Other bodies, including the Town Planning Institute, were extending their interests into regional planning. The Group had not been able to establish a permanent secretariat or a publication. There was also a limit to what could be achieved by voluntary effort given the history of the Group's origin and the particular formulation of its aims.

A sub-committee of Council was established to consider the future: it began work in February 1964. Its first thoughts were that there was still a need for an organization to develop knowledge on regional planning and that the Group should continue, though in a reconstituted form. A more formal organization was needed. There should be an Annual Conference and a permanent secretariat was necessary. It might be renamed the Regional Planning Centre. Views were sought from members of Council. A minority were in favour of discontinuation: the majority, though their views were almost all qualified, were in favour of continuing. The suggestion (from Leslie Ginsburg among others) that there should be an exploration of the possibility of amalgamating with another body was seriously received. In Britain, the Town Planning Institute, the Town and Country Planning Association and Political and Economic Planning were thought about. There were also the International Federation of Housing and Planning and the Regional Science Association. The position was summarized in a paper to Council in May 1964. A period of exploration was in progress in which Emrys Jones, Joint Honorary Secretary of the Group, and Leslie Ginsburg were active. Hopes had been raised (only eventually to be dashed) by the moves of those in the TPI who were keen to widen its membership and to open up the Institute for members of relevant disciplines.[12] Contacts between Emrys Jones and John Madge (then Deputy Director of PEP) were, however, encouraging.

A fresh strand must now be brought into the story. The Regional Science Association had been founded as an international organization for the advancement of regional analysis and related spatial and areal studies by Professor Walter Isard of the Department of Regional Science in the Wharton School of Finance and Commerce, University of Pennsylvania, at Philadelphia in 1954. It had gathered over 800 members in its first three years. Isard's own work, as well as that of Britton Harris, Mel Webber, Harvey Perloff and others, aroused widespread interest, as may be judged from the report by H.W.E. Davies on the Second European Congress of the Regional Science Association held in Zurich, September 1962.[13] By 1963 about 25 British planners and academics had become members of the RSA while many others were interesting themselves actively in the new ideas and methods that were being disseminated. During 1963, G.P. Hirsch, L.S. Jay and Nathaniel Lichfield undertook exploration into the possibilities of founding a properly constituted British branch of the Association and it was agreed that Hirsch should ascertain Walter Isard's views on the proposal. On a visit to Professor Isard in the United States Hirsch found him enthusiastic and encouraging.

After sounding out many people in planning and in related fields, Hirsch, Jay and Lichfield took the initiative of arranging a meeting to which over 100 persons were invited at the London School of Economics, on July 11 1964, at which Walter Isard spoke on "The International Situation in Regional Science". There was a vigorous discussion on the possibility of forming a British section of the Regional Science Association.

One of the problems raised was that the constitution of the International Regional Science Association contained a prohibition on, among other things, activities attempting to influence legislation. This was seem as too limiting at a time when, in the U.K., regional policy was very much under discussion. There was broad agreement that the new body should have a strongly intellectual orientation and should focus on the inter-disciplinary nature of regional studies.

In the words of Dr. Hirsch, 'the meeting endorsed the suggestion that a society should be set up in Britain to promote regional research and development but a large number of those present expressed a preference for the establishment of an independent British association'. A Steering Committee was appointed to explore ways and means. This meeting was a decisive step in the eventual foundation of the Regional Studies Association. It brought into the discussion many who had not been active or interested in the British Group including many young economists, geographers, planners and others whose ideas and methods ranged well beyond those which had inspired the founders of the British Group. It also opened up the possibility of developing an Association which had a central interest in the application to regional problems of new developments in the contributing academic disciplines. In the U.K. at this time, political interest in the development of regional policies was strong in both government and opposition and the opportunities for applied studies were seen to be great.[14]

The Steering Committee consisted of 14 members (T.W. Arnold, H.W.E. Davies, R.T. Eddison, P.G. Hall, G.P. Hirsch, L.S. Jay, Otto Koenigsberger, N. Lichfield, John Madge, D.J. Robertson, Andrew Sharman, R.J. Smeed, L.T. Sweetman, M.J. Wise). Madge became its Chairman. Five or six held, or had held, leading responsibilities at one time or another in the running of the British Group so that an appropriate overlap existed. At a meeting on October 6th 1964 at the offices of Political and Economic Planning, a sub-committee consisting of John Madge, Peter Hall, N. Lichfield and G.P. Hirsch (who became secretary) was appointed to work out detailed questions of name, constitution etc. The full Steering Committee met on three occasions and the sub-committee twice. It was at first suggested that the title should be "Association for Regional Research and Development" but at the Steering Committee meeting on January 19th 1965 the title "Regional Studies Association" was decided upon. It was agreed that the Steering Committee should invite the British Group for Regional Planning and Development to a joint meeting. Informal contacts had continued between officers.

The Inaugural Meeting of the new Association was held at LSE on 9th April 1965. Mr. William Rodgers, M.P., Parliamentary Under-Secretary of State in the Department of Economic Affairs, addressed the meeting on the significance of regional planning and its role in government policy. He said that his Department took a benevolent interest in regional studies such as those to be undertaken by the proposed Association which embraced both economic and land use considerations.

The formation of the Regional Studies Association was unanimously agreed and a Provisional Committee was set up. John Madge became Chairman and Emrys Jones Vice Chairman. G.P. Hirsch found it necessary to withdraw from the Honorary Secretaryship because of commitments abroad and Andrew Sharman took this post. The other members were R.T. Eddison (Hon. Treasurer), T.W. Arnold, H.W.E. Davies, P.G. Hall, G.P. Hirsch, L.S. Jay, Otto Koenigsberger, N. Lichfield, P.J.O. Self, R.J. Smeed, L.T. Sweetman and M.J. Wise. The Provisional Committee prepared the final version of the Cosntitution which was adopted at the first General Meeting of the Association held at LSE on October 9th, 1965.

Meanwhile, appropriate steps had been taken to wind up the British Group as an independent organistion. By 16th March 1965 Emrys Jones and his colleagues on the Group's sub-committee felt able to recommend to an open meeting of the Group, to be held on 9th April, that its work could be carried on successfully within the proposed new organization. There were then about 103 members of the Group. The open meeting on April 9th agreed that the Group's work could be subsumed in the new Association and that the Group should be dissolved. Appropriate action was put in hand. On 18th May 1965, Andrew Sharman, as Honorary Secretary of the Regional Studies Association, wrote formally to Emrys Jones welcoming the British Group into the new Association and giving assurances, which had been sought, that the identity of the Scottish Group for Regional Planning and Development (formed in 1957) could be continued under the new Association. The Council of the Group took the necessary steps: the Group was formally dissolved and its assets (c. £630) were handed over to the Regional Studies Association. Members of the Group were informed on 4th August 1965 and were recommended to join the new Association.

The amalgamation, as it may be called, was well handled. The older organization had lost its way: new vigorous, intellectual stimulus was provided by the Hirsch-Jay-Lichfield initiative. There was suitable overlap of individuals enabling some continuity between the membership of the British Group and that of the new Association. But the proposal for organizational change with new ideas and objectives was a timely response to changed intellectual and practical contexts. The Association prospered. In February 1966 a secretariat was established to provide the continuity and support whose absence had been fatal to earlier efforts. A series of duplicated Newsletters was begun in 1966 and the first conference on "Regional Planning and Forecasting" was convened by G.P. Hirsch, Chairman of the Conference Sub-Committee, in March/April 1966 at the University of Sussex. By January 1967 there were 350 individual and 31 corporate members: groups or branches were at work in Scotland, Yorkshire and Humberside, East Anglia and the East Midlands. A programme of study days and conferences had been arranged. With the appearance of *Regional Studies* in May 1967, under the editorship of Peter Hall, the success of the new Association was assured.

Acknowledgements

In preparing this paper I have relied upon my own collection of papers acquired as a member of the British Group of the ICRPD. I am also much indebted to Professor Emrys Jones, Honorary Secretary of the Group 1960-1965 who has given me access to the papers and correspondence in his possession, and for his advice and discussion.

I am greatly indebted to those who have provided me with comments on an early draft of this paper. They include Mr. Leslie Ginsburg, Professor Percy Johnson-Marshall and Professor Nathaniel Lichfield and the editors of this book. Dr. G.P. Hirsch and Professor H.W.E. Davies have been especially helpful on the growth of interest in regional science and on the movement to found a new organization in 1963/4. I have drawn substantially upon the material which they provided and I am grateful to them both. The paper remains a mainly chronological sketch based very much on personal participation.

Notes

1. Sharman, F. Andrew (1967) 'The Regional Studies Association: Origins and Opportunities', *Regional Studies*, 1, pp.1-2.
2. International Centre for Regional Planning and Development, (n.d.) *Report of the proceedings of the Conference held at Bedford College, London 28 September - 2 October 1955*, Brussels, p.3.
3. International Centre, *Report of Conference Bedford College London* 1955, p.13.
4. See the two Broadsheeets, Association for Planning and Regional Reconstruction (1942 reprinted 1943) *The Delimitation of Regions for Planning Purposes: The Concept of a Functional Region* (1943, reprinted 1946) *Regional Boundaries of England and Wales: An Examination of Existing and Suggested Boundaries.*
5. Association for Planning and Regional Reconstruction (1945) *Maps for the National Plan*, London: Lund Humphreys.
6. Osborn, F.J. (ed.) (1943) *Planning and Reconstruction Year Book*, Tudor Publishing Co, London, pp.305-7, see also issue for 1946, p.393. The fullest statements and applications of the Association's philosophy of planning are to be found in Tyrwhitt J. (ed.) (1950) *Town and County Planning Textbook* London: Association for Planning and Regional Reconstruction.
7. See entries in the annual Planning and Reconstruction Year Book. Some of the prewar experience is conveyed in Rowse, E.A.A. (1939) 'The Planning of a City', *Journal of the Town Planning Institute* 25, pp.167-171.
8   Hebbert, M. (1983) The Daring Experiment: social scientists and land-use planning in 1940s Britain, *Environment and Planning B: Planning and Design*, 10, pp.3-17.
9. Gurney, W. (1952) *Synopsis of a proposed survey of the existing facilities in Great Britain and elsewhere for research and teaching in relation to administrative, social, economic and land-use planning*, mimeographed.
10. Isard, W. (1956) Regional Science: the Concept of Region and Regional Structure, *Papers and Proceedings of the Regional Science Association*, 2, pp.1-11.
11. The regional philosophy of the Institute for Social Studies course was later set out in a text by one of its teachers, a former civil servant with Silkin's Ministry of Town and County Planning: F.B. Gillie (1967) *Basic Thinking in Regional Planning* London: Mouton & Co.
12. Lichfield, N. (1966) Research for Planning, *Journal of the Town Planning Institute*, 52, pp.115-119, and 'Objectives for Planners', *JTPI*, 52, pp.309-313. The story of the TPI membership is told in Cherry G.E. (1974) *The Evolution of British Town Planning* London: Leonard Hill.
13. Davies, H.W.E. (1962) 'Regional Science and Planning in Britain', *Journal of the Town Planning Institute*, 48, 10, pp.315-6.
14. Lane, L.W. (1964) Presidential Address, *Journal of the Town Planning Institute* 50, pp.422-431. See also Ginsburg, L.B. (1965) 'A Plea for Regional Thinking', *Journal of the Town Planning Institute* 50/51, pp.432-3.

8

The Yorkshire and Humberside
Economic Planning Council 1965-1979

Diana C. Pearce

(This paper conveys the personal views of the author and does not in any way purport to be an account of Government policy)

Introduction

The eight Economic Planning Councils for the English regions were disbanded in 1979 but their departure from the scene did not seem to lead to any great change in the flow of economic assistance to the regions or to any reordering of investment priorities. Now, with the benefit of almost a decade's hindsight it seems timely to query what was to show for the time and energy which went into one specific council.[1]

In this paper I do not intend to recount a straight history of the Yorkshire and Humberside Economic Planning Council. That has already been very well done by Peter Lindley, formerly of the Civil Service College.[2] I intend to look at three basic questions - who, how and what - and then attempt to draw out lessons for any future attempt there may be to coordinate the regional voice. However, before we look in detail at the Council some background on the status of Regional Economic Planning Councils and the Yorkshire and Humberside Region will help to set the scene (Figure 8.1).

The Economic Planning Councils were created in 1965 to advise the Economic Planning Boards, groupings of senior representatives of Government Departments in the regions chaired by the senior official from the regional office of the newly-created Department of Economic Affairs. Initially it was the Economic Planning Boards who were given the task of preparing draft plans for the regions, as well as co-ordinating the work of government departments in implementing those plans, but in March 1966 the responsibility for preparing the draft regional plans was transferred from the Boards to the Economic Planning Councils.

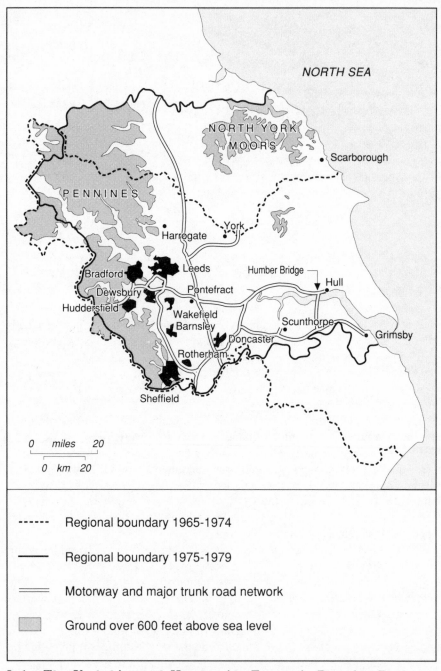

NORTH SEA

NORTH YORK
MOORS

Scarborough

P E N N I N E S

York

Harrogate

Bradford   Leeds   Humber Bridge

Dewsbury   Pontefract   Hull

Huddersfield

Wakefield   Scunthorpe

Barnsley

Doncaster   Grimsby

Rotherham

Sheffield

0   miles   20

0   km   20

------ Regional boundary 1965-1974

―――― Regional boundary 1975-1979

═══ Motorway and major trunk road network

Ground over 600 feet above sea level

8.1   The Yorkshire and Humberside Economic Planning Region

They retained this responsibility, and a wider advisory role, after the Department of Economic Affairs was abolished in 1969 and in the following ten years before their own demise each developed along different lines. The Yorkshire and Humberside Economic Planning Council tended to be less critical of the national government of the day than some of the other Councils and its more pragmatic line perhaps enabled it to claim Ministers' ears more effectively, on some occasions.

The development of a pragmatic attitude may, however, have owed much to the inevitable compromises that had to be made by members who were drawn from an exceptionally diverse and widespread region.

'Yorkshire and Humberside' is, like all the standard regions, an artificial entity. In essence it is a 'Greater Yorkshire', extending that province to the historically quite distinct parts of Lincolnshire to the south of the River Humber. As standard regions go, it is reasonably well accepted as a territorial division by government departments but little used by quangoes such as water authorities, tourist boards and transport utilities. Hogwood and Lindley show that Yorkshire and Humberside appears in the administrative map of just 26 of the 60 bodies covered in their analysis of regional boundaries used by government.[3] Unfortunately, and perhaps instructively, the Royal Commission on the Constitution in its major survey of regional identification chose to treat it as two regions, separated by the Humber. Even in Yorkshire, which they treated as a natural region in its own right, the commission's researchers encountered only a limited interest in regional self-government, less than in the North West and East Midlands, though more than in East Anglia, the South East or Greater London.[4]

The Yorkshire and Humberside Region, then, is a large area stretching from the Pennines to the North Sea coast and containing a wide diversity of identity, landscape and industry. As the regional boundaries were chosen to coincide with county boundaries, the 1974 local government reorganization which created new counties had a significant impact on the definition of the region. Prior to 1974 it had contained the ancient counties of the West Riding of Yorkshire and the East Riding of Yorkshire, together with the County Borough of York and the County of Lincolnshire (parts of Lindsey) which excluded Lincoln County Borough. Thus it extended from the Pennine uplands through the textile areas of the West Riding (Bradford and Leeds, Halifax and Huddersfield) and the coal and steel areas of the Yorkshire coalfield (Wakefield, Sheffield, Barnsley and Rotherham) across the flat and fertile agricultural lands of the East Riding and Lincolnshire to the steelworking town of Scunthorpe and beyond to the Humber estuary, with the isolated ports of Kingston-upon-Hull on its north bank and Grimsby on its south. After 1974 the region gained the new county of North Yorkshire (which contained much of the old North Riding) and lost the southern rural part of Lincolnshire which was not contained within the new County of Humberside, but the boundaries of the new counties of South and West Yorkshire were fairly close to those of the old West Riding. Consequently the city of York found itself geographically central to a region which now stretched northwards almost as far as the Tees basin and had gained two large, attractive upland areas containing National Parks - the Yorkshire Dales and the North York Moors - as well as the rich agricultural land of the vales of York and Pickering and the seaside and fishing towns of Bridlington, Scarborough and Whitby.

The wide diversity of interests spanned by the region's boundaries, and the legendary independence of the Yorkshire character, posed a great challenge for anybody purporting to speak for the region as a whole, but one which the Economic Planning Council endeavoured to meet.

The Council membership

The Yorkshire and Humberside Economic Planning Council, like the other seven throughout the country, was set up with a membership designed to draw on a wide range of experience and interests within the region. There were 30 members under a Chairman chosen directly by the Secretary of State for Economic Affairs, initially George Brown. Both members and chairman were appointed for a fixed term of three years but they could and did stand for further terms.

These members were drawn approximately one-third from local government, one-third from industry - both the employers' and employees' sides - and one-third had no specific allegiance but were those people who could contribute special regional knowledge or experience. The first group included officers and members from both tiers of local government, county councils and borough or district councils; the second included a wide range of nominees from the local Confederation of British Industry (CBI), the Trades Union Congress (TUC) and Chambers of Commerce such as company directors and union organizers, including an accredited Communist; while the third group included distinguished local academics, a member of the Country Landowners' Assocation and the Regional Administrator of the Womens' Royal Voluntary Service.

Although chosen from these specific backgrounds, members of the Economic Planning Council were not expected to act as representatives of any particular interest. They were nominated or asked to serve by virtue of their individual qualities, reflecting George Brown's original aspiration to give the councils a personality of their own, 'not only consultative bodies but also embryos of something that could become a new form of regional government'.[4]

As with any organization there were slight changes in the composition of the Council year by year, with larger changes occurring in 1968, 1970, 1971, 1972 and 1974 when between 7 and 12 seats changed hands. Individual length of service on the Council ranged from 1 month to the full 14 years of the Council's existence, but among the 105 people who were members at some time the most frequent lengths of service were one year (9 members), three years (15 members) or five years (13 members). The first chairman, the late Sir Roger Stevens, an ex-diplomat, served for 5 years and the second chairman, Bernard Cotton, the chairman of a Sheffield steel firm, continued in the post until the Council was wound up.

Administration and relationships with other bodies

The Economic Planning Council met monthly, although it was rare for all 30 members to be present. An average attendance was closer to 17. It had a small part-time secretariat of two to three civil servants from the sponsoring Department - initially the Department of Economic Affairs, subsequently the Department of the Environment - and also had access to other civil service resources through the Economic Planning Board. All its meetings were held in Leeds, the seat of the regional offices of Government Departments and most other regionwide organizations.

Detailed discussions on particular topics were carried out in sub-groups of the Council. The Coordinating Group considered policy matters and recommendations on items referred to the Council by outside bodies; the Environment Group housing and health, as well as land and land use; the Industry Group looked at the locational and manpower impacts of industry and the changes within industry; and the Communications Group considered road, rail and air links to and from the region. These groups met at monthly intervals, in between the monthly meetings of the main Council. It was rare for a member to belong to more than one sub-group but even so the calls on their time for these meetings were not inconsiderable.

The findings of the Economic Planning Council were fed through to the national government via the Economic Planning Board, a formal grouping of the senior civil servants in the region, the heads of the regional offices of those Departments concerned with employment, trade and industry, housing and local government, transport, agriculture, education etc. The Board was serviced by a small but high-powered research group who carried out studies commissioned by the Board, or the Council through the Board. On occasions too the Council chairman commissioned work directly from the research group.

Perhaps because it already contained a wide diversity of regional interests the Economic Planning Council did not have formalized linkages with any other regional bodies. It corresponded with and occasionally met groups such as the regional CBI and TUC, the West Riding Clean Air Council and the Yorkshire Council of Social Services. It held regular briefing meetings with local groups of both Conservative and Labour Members of Parliament and occasionally met neighbouring Economic Planning Councils when cross-boundary topics or problems demanded. The Chairman had a specific right to be able to write directly to the Secretary of State and to receive a substantive reply. This privilege was regularly taken up and in addition the Secretary of State and various Ministers met the Council from time to time.

The Standing Conference of Local Planning Authorities, a pre-1974 Committee representing all the local planning authorities in the region, had been set up as a rival regional planning body. Both it and its two post-1974 successors, the Strategic Conference of County Councils in Yorkshire and the grouping of districts which retained the name of Standing Conference of Local Planning Authorities (and claimed the name of Economic Planning Council after the original one was wound up) resented the fact that the Economic Planning Council was putting forward a strategy for the region which it was powerless to implement. The local authorities had the statutory development control and plan-making powers, yet their plans were expected to conform to a regional strategy prepared by a non-elected body. From 1972, the Department of the Environment had a general policy of encouraging its nominated regional councils to collaborate with local authority associations and central government in preparing 'tripartite' strategies for their regions. Such strategies were achieved in East Anglia, the Northern Region, the North-East, South-East and West Midlands, but never in Yorkshire and Humberside.[5]

What did the Council produce?

The Economic Planning Councils and Economic Planning Boards were set up to prepare comprehensive plans for each region within the framework of the national plan. But as the idea of a national plan faded away, and with the winding-up of the Department of Economic Affairs in 1969, the role of the Council changed. The first few years of its existence were occupied with the preparation of the Regional Review.[6] This document was initially drafted by the research group and incorporated the views of the Economic Planning Board before Council members got to consider it. This they did by setting up the sub-groups for Industry, Environment, Communications and Development, which continued to exist in one form or another through the life of the Council. The final version of the Review was published in 1966. It included not only a statistical inventory of available data but also a wide-ranging analysis of the region's major assets and problems and a number of preliminary suggestions for future action. Prominent among these were the need for new housing to stem outmigration and consequent labour shortages; a programme of new industrial building and investment in labour saving production methods; geographical concentration of industrial development in specific areas with clear advantages for growth; that top priority in major road improvements should be given to a new motorway network to Humberside, followed by routes across the Pennines; that the Humber Bridge be constructed as early as possible; and that eventually a major intercontinental airport would be required east of the Pennines. These proposals reflected the quietly optimistic tone of the Review, which assumed increasing rates of economic growth and saw the region's main problem as an over-tight labour supply because of outmigration.

The region's bid for investment fell upon receptive ears. Because of its proximity to the North Sea gas field, Government had already identified Humberside as a major growth area. Harold Wilson and his cabinet saw it as a showcase for planned economic expansion. The Cabinet Committee on Environmental Planning (set up to bring transport, physical planning and the Department of Economic Affairs together) decided in June 1966 that 'Humberside should now take priority over everything else'.[7] This followed commitments made by Barbara Castle, Minister of Transport, in speeches that helped to swing a crucial by-election at Hull North, to build a new road bridge across the Humber notwithstanding the reservations of her department.[8] 'I agree with Wedgie[9] that a country cannot live by economic return alone', she wrote in her diary. 'We need vision, an 'act of faith' occasionally as well'.[10]

Following the production of the Review, the main task for the Council was the formulation of a long-term regional strategy. For this, the issues raised in the Review had to be explored in greater detail. Such was Government commitment to major population growth on Humberside that this aspect of the region's development was planned from London by an ad hoc interdepartmental team of civil servants, the Central Unit for Environmental Planning. *Humberside, a Feasibility Study* (1969) foresaw the settlement of a third to threequarters of a million population around the mouth of the river by the year 2000.[11] Meanwhile the regional body's attention shifted westwards. In-depth studies of the declining West Yorkshire industrial areas at the foot of the Pennines based on Halifax,[12] and Huddersfield,[13] and of a potential growth area - Doncaster[14] - were undertaken by the research group and published during 1968 and 1969.

An impetus to the further development of the Council's proposals for growth areas came with the 1967 White Paper on Fuel Policy which predicted decline in home demand for coal.[15] The very high estimates of the number of jobs likely to be lost in West Yorkshire prompted two members to put a paper to the Council suggesting it should put strong pressure on the Government to introduce special measures of assistance. Opportunely, the Secretary of State for Economic Affairs had initiated a committee of inquiry under the chairmanship of Sir Joseph Hunt into the problems of the grey or 'intermediate' areas, which did not qualify for the regional assistance given to Scotland, Wales, Cornwall and Northern England, but nevertheless had below-average rates of growth.[16] The Regional Council pressed home its anxieties that Yorkshire and Humberside was being leapfrogged by industrial investors who sought the employment premiums, capital grants and other benefits available in the adjacent Northern Development area. Worse, it was shown that in the period 1945 to 1965, some 27,000 new jobs had been created in the Northern Region from projects originating in Yorkshire and Humberside, fully a third of all new employment created by 'moves' into the North.[17] Following the Hunt Committee's recommendations, the Yorkshire coalfield and North Humberside were designated for assistance as Intermediate Areas in 1969.

There was concern that the region's diffuse, polycentric settlement structure might deter investors. In February 1968, following an urgent assessment of employment prospects in the coalfields, the Council endorsed the Board's conclusions that efforts to provide replacement employment should be concentrated in selected focal points, rather than in every existing mining community. With the Council setting the criteria and local authorities identifying particular locations, an agreed list of focal points was produced in October 1968. These were Doncaster, Rotherham, Barnsley, South Elmsall and the Five Towns (Pontefract, Castleford, Knottingley, Normanton and Featherstone), all well served by the developing motorway network.

A second round of unpublished area studies covering West Yorkshire, Humberside, Sheffield and York completed the background work necessary for the preparation of the *Regional Strategy*,[18] which looked forward ten years. Initially drafted by the Board and subsequently edited by a small working party of Council and Board members, it was endorsed by the full Council in July 1970 and published in October that year.

The Strategy emerged in a different climate from the Council's 1966 *Review of Yorkshire and Humberside.* Unemployment in the region had now nudged above the national average for the first time. The priority was to achieve diversification with growth. The document envisaged a need for new job opportunities which could best be met by expanding the service sector and science-based industry. Future development would follow the broad pattern of existing settlement. In contrast to the central planners' schemes for Humberside, the regional body felt that no new towns would be needed. There was a new environmental emphasis: towns in the region could only develop their full potential when they were attractive and convenient places in which to live. This fairly pragmatic tone seemed to find favour with the Government as in its response, delivered in July 1971, it asked the Council to carry forward the strategy by producing area studies on a longer term basis jointly with local planning authorities. It also suggested, unsuccessfully, that this ten-year strategy should be developed into a longer term one by the joint efforts of the Council, the Standing Conference of Local Planning Authorities and Central Government. In recognition of the region's growing economic difficulties, intermediate area status was extended throughout Yorkshire and Humberside in 1972.

A number of studies sprang from the Strategy and the Government Response: a survey of service industries and their prospects in the region;[19] an evaluation of the effect on the region of Britain's entry into the EEC;[20] and a survey of growth industries in the region.[21] One of the recommendations in this last report was the creation of a region-wide Industrial Development body with full-time professional staff. This idea was aired at a conference in Leeds in September 1972 and was received with enthusiasm by local authority and other representatives. A draft constitution was endorsed at a further conference in January 1973 after which the Yorkshire and Humberside Development

Association was formally established with the Council chairman as President and the backing of all the region's major local authorities, the regional CBI, TUC and Chambers of Commerce. This successful regional promotion body still functions, attracting inward investment and working closely with Chambers of Commerce, Trade and Industry on export missions.

In response to the Government's requests for joint working, the Council carried out an area study of Bradford jointly with the West Riding County Council and the City of Bradford.[22] but the pressures of preparing for local government reorganization prevented the local authorities from being able to participate more fully in the other follow-up initiatives, area studies of Sheffield and Rotherham[23] and a review of the Yorkshire Green Belt.[24]

Following the formation of the new County Councils and District Councils in 1974 one of the first tasks for the County Councils was to prepare Structure Plans, to set the strategic land-use planning framework which the District Councils could translate into specific map-based plans and proposals in their own local plans. This two-tier system for land-use planning had been introduced in the 1968 Town and Country Planning Act, but many local authorities had found the task of preparing the new style plans impossible for them to carry out quickly, and many others had simply postponed the task pending the large-scale reorganization of 1974. Only the Doncaster area, of all the Yorkshire and Humberside Region, had started work on a new-style structure plan by the date of reorganization but it had not reached formal approval stage. The Government asked the council to review the Regional Strategy as quickly as possible so that it could act as the framework for the new structure plans, and the Strategy Review *The Next Ten Years* appeared in April 1976.[25] It confirmed the Council's priorities for the region as being the encouragement of industrial development in all sectors; the completion of the basic motorway infrastructure particularly the main east/west road network on both banks of the Humber and the Humber Bridge; and improvements in the environment of the region including housing, water and air quality and derelict land. The document was couched in a style of studied moderation, repeatedly acknowledging the need to limit regional aspirations in the light of the difficult national economic situation. With the Humber Bridge under construction and major investment programmes by the British Steel Corporation and National Coal Board in progress, the Council went out of its way to avoid the lobbying manner of some of its counterparts:

'No merit is seen in attempting to make extensive comparisons between the circumstances of the Yorkshire and Humberside Region and of other English regions, as has been attempted, with little apparent impact, in other areas.... Except in some environmental fields, the available statistics suggest that the region as a whole is not markedly worse off than other regions'.[26]

In later years local authorities in Yorkshire and Humberside were openly critical of the self-abnegating stance of the regional body.[27]

The Government response, published in May 1977, broadly endorsed the Strategy Review and once again encouraged the Council to collaborate more formally with local authorities in future work.[28] In 1978 and 1979 two reports elaborating the Strategy Review were published: *Population Movements Across County Boundaries*,[29] produced by a joint working party of the research group and officers of the County planning departments; and the *Annual Report 1978*,[30] which was intended to be the first in an annual series monitoring the Regional Strategy as a whole.

Two final reports were produced in July 1979 by Council sub-groups. The economic scene now seemed appreciably bleaker. The major expansion in steel, for which prospects had appeared so good in the early seventies, was being curtailed and would be abandoned in 1980. Textile, wool and clothing were rapidly contracting (45% of jobs would be lost in 1973-1981). Engineering and metal-using industries were also experiencing above-average decline. Major rounds of pit closures were imminent. The Council's final publications concentrated on labour market problems. *Employment in Tomorrow's World* [31] identified broad trends in the existing regional industries and recommended planning in education and training to produce manpower qualified in the new skills which would be required in the future. *Preparing for Tomorrow's World* [32] faced up to the probability that Yorkshire and Humberside would experience high long-term unemployment. It recommended that more emphasis be given to job creation in regional assistance. It also called for a national scheme for youth service in the community, and an expanded role for education and training to enable all age groups to adapt to the changing skill requirements and expanded leisure opportunities. It was a far cry from the Council's original preoccupation with manpower shortages in Yorkshire and Humberside.

What did the Council achieve?

Since August 1979 when the Economic Planning Councils were wound up, they have passed into the administrative history of the region. Now, with the benefit of almost a decade of hindsight, it is difficult to single out developments which were directly attributable to the existence of the Yorkshire and Humberside Economic Planning Council, with the one exception of the creation of the Yorkshire and Humberside Development Association.

From the Humberside viewpoint the rapid improvements in road communications to Hull and Scunthorpe which took place during the 1970s owed a great deal to the emphasis placed on this by the Council in their dealings with Government.[33] The 1966 Regional Review had pressed for an early start to the construction of the Humber Bridge, and following consultations on the 1970 Regional Strategy the Council Chairman wrote to the Secretary of State for the Environment asking for an announcement on the starting and completion dates for the bridge. This announcement was made in May 1971.

In South Yorkshire the Council's focal points strategy lived on through central government action. The Secretary of State's modifications to the Structure Plan, approved in December 1979, which emphasized that Barnsley, Doncaster and Rotherham should be growth areas, were a direct link back to the Council's recommendations, as was the choice of South Elmsall for an Enterprise Zone, designated in October 1981.

In other respects, however, while the Council's reports, studies and strategies contributed greatly to the knowledge of decision-makers within and outside the region, it is chiefly remembered for its influence rather than its achievements.[34] The Council enjoyed cordial relations with the Board and perhaps for this reason the strategies it proposed were generally well received by Central Government. Ultimately, however, it had no executive powers and no budget, and without these real levers of implementation it could achieve very little directly.

Lessons for the future

From this necessarily brief and partial overview of the workings and activities of the Yorkshire and Humberside Economic Planning Council, what lessons can be learned for future experiments with regional bodies?

The most obvious point is that without a statutory basis and executive functions and powers, a regional body will be able to do little on the ground. It may be able to exert influence but ultimately the decisions on economic and social developments will be out of its hands.

Other, more detailed observations concern the membership, and the organization of any future regional body. Firstly, membership. Although the Council did attract a very high calibre of members it was by no means democratic. Members were invited to serve, having come to the notice of regional civil servants on the Board or of the chairman or members of the Council in a variety of informal ways. It has been described as 'the best club in Yorkshire'[35] and through the independence of the membership it generally succeeded in making recommendations that were truly in the region's interest, not just favouring one faction. One of the Council's strengths was the wide variety of interests represented by its members, but if in future a regional body with real powers is to be set up then it can be argued that it needs to combine this aspect with some form of democratic framework - if only because of the geographical scale of its operations which could influence the living and working environment of almost 5 million people.

Secondly, organization. I have already mentioned the close linkages between the Council, Board and research group. In practice the Council often received papers which were already the 'distillation of wisdom'[36] from civil servants within the relevant departments. In reading back through Council papers and Peter Lindley's account, it is very difficult to disentangle the actions of these three groups. While this made for smooth communications and a willingness by

Central Government to accept Council recommendations, it does beg the question of how independent the Council really was. Any future body should, in all fairness, be demonstrably independent within the administrative structure devised around it, and it should employ its own staff.

In the final analysis a regional body will only succeed if it has a clearly set task, and functions within an organizational framework which allows it definite powers and responsibilities. The Yorkshire and Humberside Economic Planning Council lacked such power and although it was a well respected body and influence in the region, it must represent a blind alley along the long and slow route towards 'regionalism'.

Notes

1. The author observed the transisition at first hand, working for the Yorkshire and Humberside Regional Office of DoE in the period 1976 to 1986

2. Lindley, P. (n.d.) *Regional Planning in Yorkshire and Humberside 1965-80,* Civil Service College internal research paper, unpublished. For the councils in general see Lindley, P. The Framework of Regional Planning 1964-80, in Hogwood, B. and Keating, M. (eds.) (1982), *Regional Government in England,* Oxford: Clarendon Press, Ch. 8.

3. Hogwood, B. and Lindley, P. (1980) *Which English Regions - An Analysis of Regional Boundaries used by Government,* Strathclyde, Centre for the Study of Public Policy, Studies in Public Policy No. 50. Social and Community Planning Research (1973) *Devolution and other Aspects of Government - an attitudes survey,* Royal Commission on the Constitution, Research Paper No.7.

4. Brown, G. (1971) *In My Way,* London: Gollancz, p.108.

5. Lindley (1982) 'Framework of Regional Planning'.

6. Yorkshire and Humberside Economic Planning Council (1966), *A Review of Yorkshire and Humberside,* London, HMSO.

7. See Crossman, R. (1975) *The Diaries of a Cabinet Minister,* London: Hamish Hamilton, p.542.

8. Crossman, R. (1975) Diaries, pp.391-445, especially 394.

9. Anthony Wedgwood Benn, now Tony Benn.

10. Castle, B. (1984) *The Castle Diaries* 1964-1970 London: Weidenfeld, p.151, the full speeches are recorded on p.95.

11. Central Unit for Environmental Planning (1969) *Humberside - A Feasibility Stuudy,* London, HMSO.

12. Yorkshire and Humberside Economic Planning Council and Board (1968), *Halifax and Calder Valley: An Area Study,* London, HMSO 1968.

13. Yorkshire and Humberside Economic Planning Council and Board (1969), *Huddersfield and Colne Valley: An Area Study,* London, HMSO.

14. Yorkshire and Humberside Economic Planning Council and Board, West Riding Council and County Borough of Doncaster (1969) *Doncaster: An Area Study,* London, HMSO 1969.

15. Ministry of Power (1969), *Fuel Policy*, Cmnd 3438, London, HMSO 1969.

16. *The Intermediate Areas. Report of a Committee under the Chairmanship of Sir Joseph Hunt*, Cmnd 3998 (1969), London, HMSO.

17. ibid. pp.55-66.

18. Yorkshire and Humberside Economic Planning Council (1970), *Yorkshire and Humberside, Regional Strategy*, London, HMSO

19. Research Groups, Yorkshire and Humberside Economic Planning Council and Board (1972), *The Service Industries: Prospects in Yorkshire and Humberside*, City House, Leeds.

20. Report of a Working Party (1972), *Implications of UK entry into the Common Market for the Yorkshire and Humberside Region*, Leeds.

21. Yorkshire and Humberside Economic Planning Council (1972), *Growth Industries in the Region: A Study by the Council*, Leeds.

22. Yorkshire and Humberside Economic Planning Council Board Research Group, West Riding County Council and County Borough of Bradford (1973), *Bradford Area Joint Study*, Leeds.

23. Yorkshire and Humberside Economic Planning Council (1974), *Sheffield and Rotherham Industrial Study*, Leeds.

24. Yorkshire and Humberside Economic Planning Council (1975), *Joint Green Belt Study*, London, HMSO.

25. Yorkshire and Humberside Economic Planning Council (1976), *Yorkshire and Humberside Regional Strategy Review 1975 - The Next Ten Years*, London, HMSO.

26. Yorkshire and Humberside Economic Planning Council, *The Next Ten Years*. p.viii

27. Yorkshire and Humberside County Councils Association (1983) *A New Deal for Yorkshire and Humberside - Regional Strategy Review*, Wakefield, p.1.

28. Department of the Environment, (1977) *Government Response to the Yorkshire and Humberside Regional Strategy Review 1975 - The Next Ten Years*, London, HMSO.

29. Yorkshire and Humberside Economic Planning Board (1978), *Population Movements Across County Boundaries, Report of a Joint Working Party*, Leeds.

30. Yorkshire and Humberside Economic Planning Council (1979), *Annual Report 1978*, Leeds, 1979.

31. Yorkshire and Humberside Economic Planning Council, (1979) *Employment in Tomorrow's World. A View for Yorkshire and Humberside*, Leeds.

32. Yorkshire and Humberside Economic Planning Council (1979), *Preparing for Tomorrow's World. A Look at the Economic and Social Consequences of Advanced Technology*, Leeds.

33. Author's interview with Councillor Alex Clarke, Council member 1974-1979, June 1987.

34. Author's interview with Bernard Cotton, Council Chairman 1970-1979, June 1987

35. ibid.

36. ibid.

9

The Planning Case for Regions and the Evolution of Strathclyde

Urlan Wannop

When delivered at the Salford Conference, the paper upon which this chapter is based was presented as 'The Planning Case for Regions and its Vindication in Strathclyde', a title chosen by the organizers and not me. I initially thought it presumptious for a paper recording the 50 years of cumulative exprience of regional planning in the West of Scotland, culminating in the creation of regional local government in 1975. I knew that I could not pretend to make a comprehensive evaluation of Strathclyde Regional Council. Nonetheless, the onus of such an assertive title suggested a more creative approach to the topic than I might have adopted unaided. It suggested that the modern history of regional planning and administration in the West of Scotland might be analysed not primarily to vindicate the Regional Council, but rather to consider the case for regional planning and administration elsewhere in the United Kingdom.

Accordingly, I record the progressive redefinition of the concepts of regional planning and of the 'region' itself. Both redefinitions are almost certainly relevant for all the metropolitan regions of the United Kingdom. I then introduce the review of strategic and regional planning by a working party of the Royal Town Planning Institute (1986), which evaluated post-war experience of regional planning in Britain as a basis for proposing reform of both regional planning and administration.

Although my instinct is that Strathclyde Regional Council has been vindicated as the nearest to a true, major regional local authority ever experienced in the United Kingdom, I am going to argue only that it was probably the best response for the region and its planning problems for a particular period of social, economic and political history. I will show that the Council significantly differs from the kind of authority which the Clyde Valley Plan of 1946 thought necessary to the conditions of that early post-war period. The region currently

142

administered is also significantly larger than the region for planning and administration defined in the Clyde Valley Plan. Far from being a criticism of that great Plan, I will suggest that this vindicates the Plan's conclusion that because regional planning must be a continuous task, its own proposals were not 'final'.[1] I will go on to suggest that events since the creation of Strathclyde Regional Council are again redefining the area of the region to which its core of the Clydeside Conurbation relates.

Accordingly, three themes underlie the chapter: Firstly, the Strathclyde Regional Council is a conception of regional administration far beyond the models for England and Wales advanced through the Redcliffe-Maud Royal Commission on Local Government in the late 1960s which, of course, went much beyond the model actually introduced to England in 1974. Secondly, the Regional Council has nonetheless been less dominant in its regional planning role than the Wheatley Report on Scottish Local Government envisaged in its recommendations of 1969. The Council has come to share the field of regional and strategic planning with a range of agencies - notably the Scottish Development Agency - which were unforeseen by Wheatley. The conception and implementation of key strategic elements of regional development occurs through several agencies, rather than by the exclusive lead of the Council or of its structure plan. Thirdly, these circumstances reflect the progressive redefinition of the West of Scotland region centred on Clydeside, and of the priorities of regional planning and action. Changing economic, social and political circumstances over the course of almost 50 years have progressively altered the planning case for the region, and have enlarged its scale. For the purpose of strategic planning and action, the region is no longer the river valley system of Patrick Geddes and the Clyde Valley Plan, and certainly not the metropolitan core for which the Plan considered a regional authority to be appropriate. It may no longer even be the area of Strathclyde Regional Council, 200 miles as it may stretch from north to south by ferry and tortuous lochside roads, from Iona in the inner Hebrides to nearly Gretna Green and the English Border.

The Developing Idea of a Region in the West of Scotland: The Clyde Valley to Strathclyde

The Clyde Valley Plan was the first significant stage and is perhaps still the most important event in the West of Scotland's unique contribution to the history of regional planning in the United Kingdom. At the heart of the Plan and still 40 years later central to debate on strategic issues in the region was Robert Grieve, the most distinguished of all regionalists in the British experience. Halted in his car at traffic lights at Carntyne on the Edinburgh Road in Glasgow, he once pointed out to me the carefully chamfered angles by which the fronting terraces of council houses turned at the four corners at the crossroads. That, he said, had been done by the work of the small co-operative regional planning team established by the local authorities in the 1930s. Within less than ten years, a much wider scope for regional planning had been accepted when Sir Patrick Abercrombie drew Grieve into the staff preparing the Clyde Valley Plan.

The Plan, initiated in 1944 by Tom Johnston, an outstanding Secretary of State for Scotland, was not the first recognition of the conurbation's intermingled physical, social and economic problems, nor of the necessity for extraordinary action to counter them. In the nineteenth century, rapid expansion of trade with the U.S.A. and the expansion of coalmining together with associated industrial developments along the Clyde, combined to make Glasgow the hub and focus of a vast urban agglomeration. Cotton manufacture, mining, iron and steel production, port operations and shipbuilding provided a major concentration of employment. Geographical and employment barriers limited the suburban expansion of many towns particularly Glasgow itself while low wages and casual insecure employment combined to create very acute housing problems, particularly overcrowding and congestion. The Glasgow Housing Improvement Trust had taken faltering steps to clear and replace slum housing in the later 19th century. Bad housing conditions and landlords' opportunism centrally contributed to Clydeside's labour unrest of the period during and following the First World War. Through the 1920s and into the 1930s, the difficulties of adapting an economy and labour force rooted in Victorian industries to the new markets and processes of the mid-twentieth century had already brought the launch of new industrial trading estates, built by central government around Glasgow's outskirts. The housing projects of Glasgow City Corporation in the 1920s and 1930s matched neither the scale nor always the immediate needs of the worst housed slum-dwellers, packed in the decaying Victorian tenements at densities and in squalor unmatched in the United Kingdom and scarcely so elsewhere in Europe.

The scale of the problem is illustrated by the fact that in 1938, Glasgow itself housed a population of about 1,130,000 out of a grand Clyde Basin total of 1,800,000. In the rest of the Clyde Valley Region, the population amounted only to 400,000. For the authors of the Clyde Valley Plan, it was this 'combination of great numbers and great density' in Glasgow that represented the Region's outstanding problem.

The Clyde Valley Plan was accordingly assembled in the context of long criticism of the inadequacy of the boundaries and the scope of local government to solve Glasgow's problems - and those of neighbouring towns like Paisley, Motherwell, Coatbridge or Clydebank. The Scottish Town and Country Planning Association had for several years argued for new towns divorced from the built-up area of the conurbation. The tide of planning thought was towards regional planning, and Government ran with it. The commissioning of the Plan was placed in the hands of the Clyde Valley Regional Planning Advisory Committee, comprising seventeen of the region's local authorities but under the dominating influence of the Scottish Office (Figure 9.1).[2]

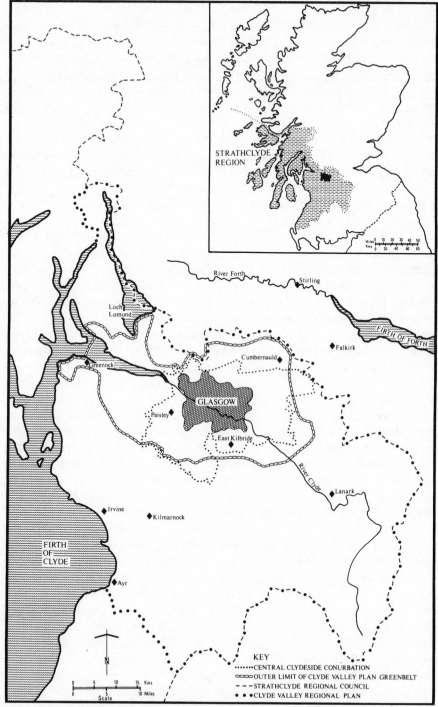

9.1 The Evolution of Regions in the West of Scotland

The area of the Clyde Valley Plan embraced additional river valley systems in Ayrshire, and was not confined to the counties of the West of Scotland within the watershed of the Clyde and to the conurbation straddling the lower reaches of the river. Yet, while the Plan came to confirm that the water-tight compartments of the then system of local government areas were inadequate for the best development of the Clyde Valley, it narrowed the region for its proposed Regional Authority to the immediate area of the conurbation. The area of the Regional Authority was to be contained within the outer line of the Green Belt proposed to embrace Glasgow, the industrial parts of the counties of Dunbarton, Lanark and Renfrew, and a small part of Lanarkshire as well as all four of the Plan's proposed new towns. It was rather larger than the Clydeside Conurbation as defined by the Registrar-General, but substantially smaller than the Clyde Valley or the later Strathclyde Region.

The Plan's case for a confined regional administration rested first on the compactness of the industrial, economic, commercial and cultural ties of the Conurbation and their coherence under Glasgow's domination. The reasoning was that 'a reasonable line must be drawn to include only such areas as have outstandingly common interests and problems. It appears to us that the compact integration and great population of the Clyde Basin form the really convincing argument for treating it as a Regional Administrative Unit.' Secondly, it rested on the geographical separation of the rural counties and on the national concerns which their coastal and recreational issues were thought to be. In contradistinction to the Clyde Basin and its 'great congested area where the threat of complete fusion and close development are imminent,' the Plan posed the situation of Ayrshire, 'geographically separate from the Conurbation,' and the coastal holiday aspect 'which is being more and more looked upon as a national concern rather than as a local or even a regional one.' Implicitly, the Plan anticipated the responsibilities of the Countryside Commission for Scotland and the Scottish National Planning Guidelines which, 30 years later, would be amongst the array of strategic agencies and interventions amongst which the new Strathclyde Regional Council would have to establish its own role in regional planning and development.

Different also to the later conception of the Regional Council, the Regional Authority for which the Plan argued would have been representative, not directly elected. Nonetheless, it would have had major tasks to execute. It would have acquired and controlled land required for the conurbation's green belt; it would have developed regional parks and conserved water resources; it would have established new towns for an overspill population of some 300,000; it would have advised on local planning, sustained the regional plan and advised on the distribution and location of industry within the conurbation. As the Authority would have no political mandate in its own right, however, these major powers were envisaged as being 'shared' by all the local authorities, rather than as being 'ceded' by them to an executive regional body.

National legislation and regulation under the Labour Government of 1945-51 obviated the need for local action on some of the Plan's principal proposals, for example, new towns, while others were accepted only belatedly. In the preamble to the Clyde Valley Plan, it was acknowledged that a number of local authorities had drawn up their own schemes ahead of the Regional Plan: this would have been at best illogical, but the special character of the two planning reports prepared for Glasgow Corporation by the City Engineer presented problems of a higher order. There was 'a fundamental divergence' between the Regional and the Corporation policy which had arisen because 'in the Glasgow Report ... primary regard has been had to the maintenance of the population of the city within the present municipal boundary.' The Clyde Valley Plan flatly condemned this as a policy 'completely incompatible with Regional Planning' which 'not only will not work, but will render their problem wellnigh insoluble' and 'will be detrimental to the best interests of Glasgow.' The Corporation maintained its intense opposition to any decentralization policy into the post-war years. Glasgow drew up its own plan prior to the 1947 Town and Country Planning Act which reaffirmed its policy of absorbing *all* the existing population through high-density schemes within the city's own boundaries. Pressure from the Secretary of State for Scotland, however, secured the development of one New Town at East Kilbride, and in the early 1950s the Glasgow city fathers revised their plan: they also joined with other local authorities to revive the regional advisory committee which recommended the establishment of a second new town. It was also being imphasized that the open space problem, so severe on an urban basis, could be relatively easily solved on a regional basis since 'a bus ride of under an hour leads into some of the finest loch and mountain scenery.' By the mid-1950s, the problems of the Clyde Valley Region were being linked to those of the neglected rural areas throughout the West of Scotland - the former densely developed and overcrowded and the latter underdeveloped and depopulated. By tackling the two sets of problems together, the deficiencies of each might be remedied.

Though the Clyde Valley Plan's proposals were only slowly implemented between 1946 and the early 1960s, they were then fulfilled in quantity. By 1976, 11 of the Plan's 15 key proposals had been implemented, as had 39 of 61 other recommendations of lesser significance.[3] This was a tribute to the Plan's depth and foresight, both in terms of substantive policies and on the need for institutional structures to carry them through. In the 1960s, when the Wheatley Commission (counterpart of the Redcliffe-Maud Commission in England) began to examine Scotland's local government system, the influence of the Plan could still be seen not just on the physical development of the West of Scotland, but on the face of Scottish public administration . However, the context for regional planning had now significantly altered, as the Plan had foreseen.

The Wheatley Commission came after a sustained outflow of people from Glasgow had brought the City's population far below the peak reached at the time of the Clyde Valley Plan. The conurbation system had overrun its statistical boundaries, and effectively reached to the new towns at Irvine and Livingston; a further new town with even stronger intended links to Glasgow was in the offing at Stonehouse. The evolving networks of motor and expressways and of the electrified commuter rail system extended the social and economic ties of the conurbation. Industrial restructuring and the reorganization of retailing further reduced local control, and much reduced the degree to which even the conurbation could be regarded as water-tight, let alone its constituent local authorities. Clydeside could no longer be fairly described as a city-region centred on Glasgow. A regional city was developing. It was dominated by the still intensely built-up core of Glasgow, but the old conurbation had now much strengthened connections to areas beyond it. And this regional city was fragmented between five shire counties, the City of Glasgow, and nearly twenty large and small boroughs in the county area.

Against this much altered and extended pattern of industrial, economic, commercial, educational, recreational and cultural ties, Wheatley proposed a more considerable system of regional administration than the Clyde Valley Plan thought appropriate to its time. Almost all the witnesses who gave evidence to the Royal Commission called for wider planning areas. Driven by a strong conception of regional planning as a central necessity in local government, Wheatley was led to recommend directly elected regional authorities with extensive responsibilities for personal services and infrastructure, covering regions much larger than the scale of county administration in Scotland hitherto. This contrasted with the less radical proposals of Redcliffe-Maud for England and Wales. The Scottish commissioners wrote explicitly that 'We are in no doubt ... that the lack of a single unit for the entire Clyde Valley area is one of the greatest impediments to the economic and social regeneration of the West of Scotland today'.[4] As adopted by Government, the reorganization for Strathclyde was particularly radical by comparison with that for the relatively narrowly-drawn metropolitan areas of England. Although some had populations larger than Strathclyde's, the combined administrative areas of Greater London and all six English metropolitan county councils was less than the area of Strathclyde.

Whether by sleight of hand or misunderstanding, the Wheatley Report explicitly adduced the arguments of the Clyde Valley Plan (1949) for a conurbation region in favour of its own case for a much more extensive Strathclyde Region, embracing the entire river basin of the Clyde Valley as a unified area for regional administration. The careful distinction made by Abercrombie's team between the wider Clyde Valley and the narrower Conurbation was ignored. For the Royal Commission twenty years later, the issue was not whether to limit the region to the Glasgow conurbation - this they ruled out of hand - but whether to extend the Glasgow-centred region even further still to embrace Dumfries and Galloway to the South and the Stirling - Falkirk area to the East. In the event, the Commissioners recommended that this huge tract be divided into three, giving the present division into Central Region, Dumfries and Galloway, and Strathclyde itself. The Wheatley view, as we may now recall with a certain sense of irony, was that too big a region might suffer from administrative overload and so be vulnerable to interference from the centre.

On balance we may say that Wheatley helped introduce a Regional Council for Strathclyde which was appropriate to the form and circumstances of the region at the time of the Commission. But having reported in 1969, Wheatley was already six years behind events at the creation of Strathclyde in 1975. Just as the West of Scotland region had been redefined between 1946 and 1969, it was already being redefined by altering circumstances in the mid-1970s. In the late 1980s, we are as far ahead of Wheatley as he was of the Clyde Valley Plan.

Pluralist Regional Planning: The Scottish Development Agency, Westminster and the Regional Planning Councils

Even at the inception of the Regional Council in 1975, Wheatley's concept of regional planning which had driven his proposals for Strathclyde had already been modified. The creation of the Scottish Development Agency (SDA) occurred only six months after the Council took office. It presaged a progressively increased central government presence in the strategic planning and development of Strathclyde, particularly from about 1980. Although the Agency's investment in urban renewal, environmental improvement and in local economic development did not grow to be more than a small part of the total public sector effort in the region, it was profoundly strategic in its influence. It was innovative in the ways in which it was spent; it levered extra expenditure from local authorities on Agency priorities; it was directed to central Government priorities. The Agency clearly viewed the statutory Structure Plans by which the Scottish Regional Councils most publicly represented their planning role as insignificant to its key concerns : urban regeneration, area projects, environmental recovery, the revival of Glasgow's City Centre, the Glasgow Garden Festival, the development of the Greenock and Dundee waterfronts, the Clydebank Enterprise Zone and the multiplicity of other initiatives by which the Agency strategically intervened in Scottish development.

In its first five years, the new Regional Council did have an almost clear run in strategic planning. Its *Regional Report* , published in 1976, asserted a strategy for the Council's twin objectives of attacking the economic weaknesses of the conurbation, and the social deprivation transferred from the Victorian slums to post-war housing estates. The Report dwelt on the very high unemployment levels in the Region, and the declining opportunities for employment, especially for men. Its strategy was cast in the mould of the *West Central Scotland Plan* of 1974, which had been prepared by a steering committee of Scottish Office and local government representatives over a period of four years immediately prior to the Regional Council's inception. This document was as influential in the short term as the Clyde Valley Regional Plan of almost thirty years before had been in the long. Unlike its predecessor, the *West Central Scotland Plan* found immediate machinery whereby it could be directly implemented. For reasons elaborated by Michael Keating in his chapter below, political conditions in the mid-seventies were favourable to the launch of the Scottish Development Agency, which broadly resembled the economic development agency for the West of Scotland proposed in the Plan. Similarly, the thinking of the new Strathclyde Regional Council was shaped by a new awareness amongst policy-makers that the greatest challenge lay not in the traditional field of housing policy but in the decline of the basic economy of Clydeside.[5]

Although not formally adopted either by its joint steering committee or by the Regional Council, the themes of the *West Central Scotland Plan* matched the instincts of the leading politicians in the new Strathclyde, and helped the new Council assert itself as a force for co-ordination of regional planning and development. The Council made it a special early priority to persuade Government to abandon its proposed new town at Stonehouse, supporting a strategic proposal of the 1974 joint Plan. Pursuing the abandonment of Stonehouse marked the intention of the new Regional Council to supercede the Scottish Office in regional planning. [6] The area of the new Strathclyde housed new towns at East Kilbride, Irvine and Cumbernauld, all already well-established. In regional conditions wherein both jobs and population were dwindling, and in which claims to rehabilitate and renew infrastructure and services in the older areas limited the resources available for urban expansion, a further new town was argued by Strathclyde to be unnecessary and wasteful. Having not only the areas of the new towns within its boundaries, but also additional responsibilities for water, sewerage, social work and education, Strathclyde Regional Council enjoyed powers to influence strategic regional planning lacking to the Greater London and English metropolitan county councils. The Scottish Office agreed to Stonehouse's termination in 1976, but simultaneously announced its Glasgow Eastern Area Renewal (GEAR) Project.

The launch of GEAR under the co-ordination of the new Scottish Development Agency was not followed immediately by other strategic initiatives, but by 1980 a variety of other local interventions through Task Forces and Project Teams had begun to emerge under the direction or patronage of the SDA.[7] The Agency thereby became a de facto regional planning authority for Scotland alongside the local authorities, sometimes picking up and implementing projects conceived by the authorities and at other times conceiving of its own. The situation which had developed in Scotland by 1980 was of pluralist regional planning, and this was so in even the most significant of British experiments in regional planning and administration - Strathclyde.

In the late 1980s, central government was advancing further into local government responsibilities. The community charge and the national business rate were about to further reduce local financial discretion. The intended break up of the very large role of district councils in Scottish housing was to be achieved through a new government agency - Scottish Homes - which would considerably displace local authority management of selected housing estates in Glasgow and other areas. Scottish Homes is to absorb both the Scottish Special Housing Association and the Housing Corporation for Scotland and be given new responsibilities for urban regeneration, including economic as well as housing action. Although Scottish Homes is aimed at directly displacing a district rather than a regional council responsibility, the context for regional councils' allied responsibilities will nonetheless become more dominated by Government policy and influence.

Redefining the Region:
The West of Scotland in the 1990s

On the eve of the 1990s, even by the same socio-economic principles as underlay the Clyde Valley Plan and Wheatley there would accordingly have been some redefinition of the West of Scotland region, let alone through political change in local-central government relationships running for the previous decade or more. Indeed, in the case of the West of Scotland we might identify at least four dimensions to contemporary regionalism.•

First, significant features of the old metropolitan regions remain. Although no longer recognized for Census tabulations, the old Clydeside Conurbation still constitutes Scotlands's most intense and extensive urban area with a metropolitan range and level of social, cultural and administrative functions. It has still the most concentrated mass of physical, social and economic problems in Scotland, just as it had 40 - or 100 - years ago. However, because of suburbanization, the dispersal of manufacturing and distributive industries, and the shift of middle and higher income households to new towns and areas beyond the Conurbation, it had become progressively less able to generate the revenues required to rebuild and maintain itself. From 1989, of course, the introduction of the community charge to replace the Scottish rating system will generate from within the conurbation a higher share of its public sector running costs. Accordingly, by this otherwise regressive change in the local tax system the case for metropolitan administration will be strengthened - although not necessarily made convincingly.

Second, Strathclyde Regional Council survives after the dissolution of the Greater London Council and of the English Metropolitan Counties. Even prior to 1986, it was the only experiment in area-wide administration for a metropolitan region and its rural hinterland ever attempted in the United Kingdom. It has been a regional and not merely a metropolitan authority because more live in its remote rural areas than in the whole of the Highland Region. For its first twelve years of life, the Regional Council had suffered relatively little public criticism by either Government or press - certainly not of the kind which assaulted the Greater London and English Metropolitan County Councils in the early and mid-1980s. Although radical attitudes in Lothian Regional Council had drawn fire during its periods of Labour control, the Conservative government and its Secretaries of State for Scotland appeared to prefer the Regional Councils to a return to all-purpose City Councils on the pre-1975 model. Indeed, Government had explicitly favoured the continuation of the Regional Councils when instructing the todart Committee (1981) to report on anomalies in the two-tier system [8] In 1988 however, strong pressures surfaced in the Scottish Conservative Party to have the regional tier of local government removed

While widely recognized as innovative in redistributing resources, in taking economic initiatives, and in more nearly equalizing opportunities in education, public transport and social services, the Council has been less significant than Wheatley expected in strategic planning.[9] Following its initial success in persuading Government to terminate the new town at Stonehouse, the Council has found the pace and many of the priorities of strategic planning and action being set by Government. New local, financial or organizational initiatives have frequently been introduced through the Scottish Development Agency. The field of strategic planning has become crowded with players in precisely the manner the Wheatley Commission, with its clear conception of the vertical division of labour between central, regional and local governments, sought to avoid when it recommended reorganization into large areal units.[10]

Third, the Scottish Office entered its second century in 1985. However, after the general election of 1987 had reduced Conservative representation to only 1 in 6 of Scottish parliamentary seats, the Scottish Office was more open than for many years to criticism that it was returning to its initial role as a quasi-colonial arm of parliament dominated by English political interests. Certainly, having failed in the Devolution Referendum of 1979 to vote sufficiently for the degree of administrative autonomy offered, Scotland had slipped within a decade to being more nearly than for 50 years an administrative region of the United Kingdom. Within that region, Government was reinforcing its role in executing as well as shaping policy for regional development. Through its battery of agencies for economic, housing, countryside and infrastructural development, Government was progressively displacing local government for the internal regions of Scotland by regional agencies for the whole of Scotland. The responsibilities of both districts and regions had become increasingly entangled with Government's political objectives. The same trend was reflected by Urban Development Corporations and other encroachments on traditional local government functions in England and Wales.

Fourthly, and overlapping the dimension of the Scottish Office, came the revival of political regionalism, or of nationalism as supported by about a quarter of Scots in the later 1980s. After its rebuff in the 1979 referendum, nationalism's force was reduced both by disappointment and the disregard of a centralized government with little sympathy for any kind of regionalism. Meanwhile at Westminster the Scottish collective of cross party and cross-sectional interests which had powerfully lobbied favours from all governments of the previous 30 years, often acting as a third arm of the Scottish Office, found itself without leverage.

After electoral setbacks early in the eighties, the nationalist vote began to recover in regional elections in 1986 and local in 1988. More importantly, members of the Scottish Nationalist Party, the Democrats, and the Scottish Labour Party were being encouraged to work together against the common enemy of Thatcherism. The Campaign for a Scottish Assembly, founded in 1983 to strive for 'the creation of a directly elected legislative assembly or parliament for Scotland with such powers as may be desired by the people of Scotland,' developed a broader base of support than had been achieved for the devolution proposals of the previous decade, embracing the unions and local government interests, and (according to polls) a 77 percent majority of the population. The increasing credibility of an assembly added to the uncertainty over the regions. The Scottish Nationalist Party had always argued that, with the establishment of a national assembly, local government should be organized into a single tier of unitary authorities and the regions abolished. Interestingly, this position is also accepted by the leadership of the ruling Labour group on the Strathclyde Regional Council as an inevitable consequence of a Labour government's institution of a Scottish Assembly. Strathclyde Region may be fortunate to reach its twentieth birthday in 1995.

The Contemporary Condition of Regional Planning and its Future in the United Kingdom

From this account of the development of the regional idea in the West of Scotland it is time to turn to the British context.

In 1986 a Royal Town Planning Institute working party looked back at British experience of strategic and regional planning to assess its successes and weaknesses. The group had a wide membership and included a political scientist and an administrator from a local education authority alongside professional town and regional planners. The report came to the conclusion that far from being 'a fashion of the 1960s' as asserted by Government in its 1983 White Paper proposing the abolition of the GLC and the Metropolitan Counties, regional planning has had a long history in Britain, sufficiently diverse and tested to fairly evaluate. More, it has had very significant and influential successes, of which the Clyde Valley Plan, the West Central Scotland Plan and Strathclyde Regional Council are three examples from only one, small part of Britain. Its less successful cases have sometimes - as in the case of the 1970 Strategy for the South-East - been allied to shortcomings in the technical method of preparing plans. More usually, they have been due to lack of the means to effectively translate plans into action. The political and administrative arm of regional planning has customarily been missing, or broken at best. Notably, the 1974 reorganization of local government in England and Wales failed to observe the principles of effective strategic administration; more so the 1986 abolition of the GLC and the Metropolitan Counties. From the RTPI's perspective discontinuous regional planning can be argued to have exacerbated some of our contemporary problems, notably that of inner city decline, whether this is seen as a socio-economic problem as by the radical left or seen largely as a problem of land and property as by the radical right. Furthermore, the role of local government in strategic and regional planning has been progressively diminished, as central government has become more extensively involved in local intervention with strategic implications. However, national strategic intervention has itself often been disjointed and not obviously co-ordinated; major policy differences between the Environment and Industry Departments in England have persisted for much of the post-war period. In sum, the RTPI's verdict was that circumstances in the late 1980s and in the 1990s are likely to strengthen general acceptance of the case for effective regional strategic planning.[11]

By this analysis, the working party came to the view that the 54 counties of England and Wales created in 1974 should be reorganized into 11 or so regional local authorities, sufficiently resourced to ensure an effective partnership with central government in regional development. Government should also revive and extend its contribution to effective regional planning, including the creation of a national Regional Development Council, chaired by the Prime Minister and comprising key Ministers and representatives of each regional authority. There should be supporting Planning and Development Boards in Ministries' regional offices, and also development agencies for the English regions on the model of the Scottish and Welsh Development Agencies.[12]

These proposals were not a mere revival of regional planning and administration from the mould of the 1940s, or even that of the nearer and supposedly fashionable 1960s. They were cast from a new mould, shaped to expectations of future economic and political circumstances. They recognized that central government would take a permanent and major role in intra-regional planning and development. They recognized that the United Kingdom is both a national region of Europe and also the shelter for a number of internal regions being shaped by economic restructuring: new English regions may be emerging along the M4 corridor from Reading to Bristol and around the landfall of the Channel Tunnel.

Perhaps Regions Outgrow Even Successful Regional Planning?

Combining my interpretation of the Strathclyde experience with the conclusions of the working party of the Royal Town Planning Institute, the threads of the planning case for regions can be drawn together.

Strathclyde's experience shows regional, local administration to be administratively viable, and to be justified by its potential to plan for and redistribute priorities for a wide range of services. Regional planning in the primarily physical tradition of Britain is no longer the dominant justification for regional administration. Strathclyde's case also confirms that the English

Metropolitan Counties and the Greater London Council were unsatisfactory in combining restricted areas with restricted responsibilities; they were too close to their lower tier of districts and boroughs in scale, and too far from central government in their strategic capacities.

Strathclyde's size has not been too big for effective local administration in services as personal as schooling, social services and consumer services, as well as for more traditional strategic services like highways, water and sewerage or policing. It has been neither too large in its volume of administration nor in the area over which it provides services; nor could any other local government in the United Kingdom be designed to be more fragmented into islands, archipelagos and remote communities.

Accordingly, we need not fear the administrative impracticability of reorganizing English county local government at a much larger scale than that of the present counties. The fear of political remoteness in regional local government is similarly much exaggerated; the 1988 experience of local influence upon Strathclyde's region-wide proposals for school closures shows the continuing importance of local politics, even within a strategic region.

Nonetheless, despite the successful case of Strathclyde and widespread dissatisfaction with the institutional structure for planning in England, which the Flowers Committee reported to the Nuffield Foundation in 1986, regional local government throughout the United Kingdom is not an early political objective.[13] Nor is it assured of a long life in Scotland. The local government system is highly unstable, but there is no common political support for the comprehensive regional local authorities which the Royal Town Planning Institute adopted as policy in 1988. Although the working party suggested that a regional level of local government was almost inevitable before the 1990s were out, the conditions for its creation had yet to come in sight in the late 1980s.

The advancing role of central government and its agencies will persist. The growing displacement of previously unchallenged roles of major English local authorities has occurred even in Strathclyde, despite the Council's unique potential to act efficiently in regional issues. Indeed, government agencies are probably more active in Strathclyde than anywhere else in Britain. Just as new towns became a regional issue demanding national resources and intervention in the 1940s, so issues of urban regeneration had in the 1980s come to be not just local or regional issues, but national ones also.

It is proper and necessary that Westminster should retain a stake in and directly fund key elements of regional development. This is not merely the mark of the centralist Conservative government of the 1980s; it reflects the high profile which inner city and local employment issues in particular are likely to hold in national politics for the rest of the century.

Where inner city and employment issues with strong local impact are treated by action by central government and its array of new agencies, it clearly denies the argument that regional local government must be too remote, unresponsive and unaccountable to be acceptable to local electorates for similar action.

Centralism in the 1980s has increasingly substituted Whitehall for council chambers in the shires and districts. It cannot reasonably be argued that local electorates are likely to find a Regional Council Office more remote than a Whitehall Ministry or the headquarters of a government agency; a regional councillor would expect to have more influence on local action than a Member of Parliament. Lack of regional local government accordingly largely removes regional planning and action from local hands and electors.

The most significant of early developments in the progressively changing environment for regional planning is probably the introduction of the Community Charge, and the consequences of it for local discretion in raising and redistributing revenues. The impacts of the new charge and its replacement of local rates will be large within the traditional conurbation areas of the United Kingdom. A much larger share of the cost of maintaining, servicing and renewing these areas will fall on the local residents; commuters and others enjoying the facilities of the conurbations will pay less for their use. The effect of the community charge will be largely regressive. Local authorities will have less scope to geographically redistribute resources, as there will be a significant fall in revenues raised from areas of higher-income households.

It might be argued that this forthcoming restriction on local authority scope to redistribute local revenues undercuts the case for regional local government. It undoubtedly alters the case, but does not destroy it in England and Wales at least. Nor does it really do so in Scotland, even if Strathclyde - the model for the Royal Town Planning Institute's policy for English regional local authorities - may be overtaken by particularly Scottish events. The altered status of the Scottish Office, the changes in local government financing and the consolidation of government agencies in strategic planning and development in Scotland, have together rendered Strathclyde's boundaries obsolete. The case for a Clydeside metropolitan authority closer to the model of the Clyde Valley Plan has been strengthened; not because regional issues in Scotland have shrunk, but because they have increased to more closely correspond to a national scale. The levels of the regional issues analysed by Wheatley in 1969 have shifted; for some, Scotland and not Strathclyde has become the most appropriate administrative scale. For others which were packaged at the Strathclyde level for mere administrative convenience, the scale of metropolitan Clydeside may now be best. In which case, to reverse the old planning adage, the region might be a *smaller* area than the one which last failed to solve our problems. Such shifting untis of administration were foreshadowed by the Royal Commissioners under Lord Wheatley's chairmanship, who to a remarkable degree reflected the ethos of the adaptive sixties in the provisional view they took of their proposed structure of regions, which should, they emphasized, be kept under permanent review.[14]

So, regional planning remains vigorous. What changes are its appropriate scales. Strathclyde has been proof of its feasibility and of its potential - a successful case overtaken by changing regional geography and evolving national politics.

Notes

1. Abercrombie, P. and Matthew, R M. (1949) *The Clyde Valley Plan 1946*, Edinburgh: HMSO, p.16.
2. Smith, R. and Wannop, U. (1985) *Strategic Planning in Action*, Aldershot: Gower, p.221.
3. Smith and Wannop (1985) *Strategic Planning*, pp.210-212.
4. Royal Commission (1969) *Report of the Royal Commission on Local Government in Scotland 1966-1969* (The Wheatley Commission) Cmnd 4150, Edinburgh: HMSO para 759.
5. Strathclyde Regional Council (1976) *Strathclyde Regional Report*, Glasgow: Strathclyde Regional Council.
6. West Central Scotland Plan Team (1974) *Consultative Draft Report*, West Central Scotland Plan.
7. The development of urban policy in Scotland is best traced in Keating, M. and Boyle, R. (1986), *Remaking Urban Scotland*. Edinburgh: Edinburgh University Press.
8. Stodart, J.A. (1981) *Report of the Committee of Inquiry into Local Government in Scotland*, Cmnd 8115, Edinburgh: HMSO.
9. Wannop, U. (1986) 'Regional Fulfillment: Planning into Administration in the Clyde Valley 1944-84', *Planning Perspectives* 1 (3).
10. See Wheatley Report, op.cit., 'The Roles of Central and Local Government in Planning', pp.61-63.
11. Royal Town Planning Institute (1986) *Strategic Planning for Regional Potential* .
12. The Working Party's views are set out more fully in Wannop, U. (1988) 'Do We Need Regional Local Government and is the Scottish Model Relevant?' *Regional Studies*, 22, 417-428.
13. Flowers Committee (1986) *Town and Country Planning*, The Report of a Committee of Inquiry, Nuffield Foundation, London, p.731.
14. ibid. paras 771, 1122-25.

10

Regionalism, Devolution and the State, 1969-1989

Michael Keating

Introduction

The 1960s and 1970s saw a flurry of proposals for regional government, advanced in the context of regional planning, local government reform, democratization and responses to Scottish and Welsh nationalism. Yet in 1989 not a single constitutional reform is in place as a result. In this chapter, I outline the bases of the unitary/centralist tradition in British politics, look at the pressures on this, examine the proposals for regional reform and account for the resilience of the old ways.

The Basis of the Unitary State

At one level, the explanation of Britain's unitary tradition is simple. The principle of parliamentary sovereignty allows for no diminution in the authority of the centre, though providing unlimited scope for changing administrative arrangements. This, admittedly, does not get us far unless we examine the political basis on which this rests and why the principle has survived over the years. Yet the principle itself remains important for on it is built the whole 'Westminster regime' with its procedures and conventions which, based in the idea of parliamentary sovereignty, in turn provide vested interests for its maintenance. Cabinet government, with collective responsibility, allows a further concentration of power and provides a theoretical justification in terms of the accountability of government to Parliament. The unitary civil service, in turn, can be justified by the needs of unitary government, yet it also allows the maintenance of an elitist, homogeneous administrative corps in which new recruits are rapidly socialized into the prevailing norms. Together with the myth of ministerial responsibility, it also obscures the source of decisions and the real distribution of power.

The two party system is another key element of the Westminster regime, since it normally produces parliamentary majorities and so sustains Cabinet government. The two party system itself is, of course, underpinned by the electoral system which, under our constitution, can only be changed by Parliament. The resulting vested interests against constitutional change are bolstered by the nature of the two parties which have dominated British politics for the last fifty years. Conservatives claim attachment to the constitution as part of received tradition and have been its most consistent beneficiaries, regularly enjoying majority government because of the division of the centre-left. Certainly, this has not prevented them countenancing defiance of Parliament when other interests were at stake (as in 1912-14 or, in some cases, following the Rhodesian rebellion of 1965) but they have never become the anti-centre party of peripheral protest found among some of their European counterparts. In the twentieth century, attachment to the unitary state has been strengthened by their fear of municipal and regional socialism.

Labour, after a brief flirtation in the early twentieth century with peripheral protest, has similarly supported the Westminster regime for a combination of absolute and instrumental motives.[1] A deeply entrenched respect for constitutionalism and parliamentary tradition has long characterized the British left and its relatively smooth entry into the parliamentary game reinforced this; an almost mystical respect for the doctrine of parliamentary sovereignty was visible in all wings of the party during the EEC and devolution debates of the 1970s. At the same time, Labour has seen the concentration of authority provided by parliamentary/cabinet government as providing ideal levers of power, to be pulled by whoever can win a parliamentary majority. This, it is commonly assumed, is all that will be required to put through a radical programme of economic and social change. With the adoption of economic planning as a major plank in Labour's platform from the 1930s, the centralist bias was increased. In both major parties, the dominance of the parliamentary leadership has led to an emphasis on Parliament and a disdain for territorial politics.

The Liberals came nearest to being a territorial party in the early part of the twentieth century but, as with Labour, the prospects of office in London led them to downplay their commitments to the periphery. Their eclipse in the 1920s was to remove one force pressing for decentralization, though the Liberal decentralist tradition survived (along with some of the personalities) as an element in the Labour coalition, especially in Wales. The balance of the two party system since the 1930s has also been critical in sustaining the Westminster regime. At least until the early 1980s, each party had a good prospect of winning a majority and a suspicion of anything which could prejudice this or hamper such a majority won. Alternation in power became, for some forty years, a substitute for the dispersal of power, allowing both parties a share in the fruits of office while not diminishing central authority.

Britain's municipal tradition developed as the counterpart of this. Under a sovereign parliament, there is no limit to the administrative delegation which can take place without conceding a loss of power and authority. Indeed, parliamentary elites have long seen administrative delegation as means of sustaining their authority by insulating themselves from local pressures and burdensome detail.[2] Again, partisan structures have helped. Linkages between national and municipal parties are weak[3] and there is virtually no accumulation of local and national mandates. So territorial pressures on the centre could be minimized. For their part, municipal elites were given an important role in the development and growth of public services and urban planning but economic and industrial matters were reserved strictly for the centre, with local government having at best a facilitative role. The functional structure of Whitehall has prevented the emergence, outside Scotland and Wales, of a Ministry of the Interior with a lead role in territorial governance. Central-local relations have tended to be compartmentalized in a series of functional policy networks, rather than taking the form of political dialogue.

The Westminster model of alternating responsible party government, of course, has been criticized as an unreal portrayal of the British policy process. Attention should, it is argued, focus on the network of corporate interests and their links with government. It is not necessary to resolve this issue here and I would regard both models as offering important insights into power and the policy process, with the emphasis varying according to time and conditions. The important point to make here is that the 'corporate constitution' is as territorially centralized as the Westminster one. Business was increasingly centralized after the first world war, with locally and regionally based firms being taken over by national and multinational conglomerates. This discouraged the emergence of regional networks of economic decision-makers which are a feature of other European countries. Trade unions also centralized over the same period, with an increase in national and industry-wide wage bargaining, at least until the 1970s. In the political sphere, trade unions pressed for equalization of welfare standards and uniform legislation on work-related matters. So the incorporation of economic interest groups into the national policy process served as a centralizing factor. Corporatism may have challenged the Westminster model of accountable party government but not its centralist bias.

Pressures on the Regime

Two sets of pressures on the unitary/centralist regime in the 1960s and 1970s called forth a variety of responses. The first was a revival of peripheral nationalism. The multinational nature of the United Kingdom had always carried federal implications and created some tension with the centralist Westminster regime. So, in Scotland, it is arguable that the terms of the Union of 1707, described in England as an Act and in Scotland as a Treaty, owed something to compact theory. Scotland had accepted the loss of its Parliament (as had England) but the terms on which the new Parliament of the United Kingdom had been established included respect for Scottish institutions and traditions, notably the separate legal system. The main problem was that, short of a written constitution or federalism, there was no way in which the settlement terms could be guaranteed. Ireland, following the Union of 1800, presented more severe problems, with a lack of popular support for the regime. In Wales, dissent from the established state religion, language and economic grievances had led to periodic discontent.

The traditional response to territorial discontent had been a limited degree of policy differentiation and an extensive system of administrative devolution. In Scotland, the Secretary of State could deliver London policies in a Scottish format which was usually distinctive more in administrative style than in substance. At the same time, the Scottish voice in the Cabinet, able to argue Scotland's case in expenditure matters, provided a powerful form of territorial representation as compensation for having to endure centralist government. In Parliament, Scottish legislation was handled in special Scottish committees, without detracting from the right of Parliament as a whole to the final decision. From 1964, this type of administrative devolution was extended to Wales, with a Secretary of State and a Welsh Office. Scots and Welsh co-operated by giving their votes overwhelmingly to the two main parties, thus endorsing the constitutional status quo.

Administrative devolution was as far as governments felt able to go before the 1970s in accommodating territorial distinctiveness on the British mainland. By defusing federalist and Home Rule demands, it helped preserve the unitary regime while covering the politics of territorial bargaining with the blanket of Cabinet secrecy and collective government. In the case of nineteenth century Ireland, administrative devolution took a more colonial form. With a minister sent over from England and with Irish voters rejecting the British party system, Irish affairs proved a disruptive influence at Westminster. The settlement of 1922, giving effective independence to the larger part and legislative devolution, together with under-representation at Westminster, to the smaller part of Ireland, removed this non-conforming presence from Parliament. In turn, this allowed the modern two-party competitive model of politics, with its downplaying of territorial issues, to emerge.

The constitutional debate of the 1960s and 1970s arose from the failure of this system of territorial management.[4] In Northern Ireland, the Stormont regime proved unable to guarantee law and order. In Scotland and Wales, separatist parties threatened the unitary state directly through their policies of secession and indirectly, by challenging the two party system on which the Westminster regime was based. First, the issue was redefined as non-constitutional and efforts made to assuage Scottish and Welsh discontent with economic concessions and more administrative devolution. Then, when this failed to stem the tide, a form of political devolution was offered, which ostensibly maintained the essentials of the existing constitution, notably parliamentary sovereignty and omnipotence, while establishing elected assemblies for Scotland and Wales. The objective was to satisfy Scottish and Welsh demands for some autonomy while avoiding federalization, which would have placed limits on the autonomy of central government. Northern Ireland was regarded as a case apart, as indeed it was, given the sectarian divide, the irredentist rather than separatist nature of the nationalist case, and the fact that, as neither British party had a stake there after 1974, it did not threaten the two-party system.

The second set of pressures on the system of territorial government in the 1960s and 1970s arose from central government's own need for regional institutions, especially in England, where the territorial administration provided in Scotland and Wales by the respective Offices was absent. Britain's early efforts at anti-disparity policy involved minimal intervention, consisting of a series of incentives to divert industry into unemployment blackspots. By the early 1960s, diversion of large, state-aided plants was being undertaken as part of the 'growth pole' philosophy and industrial assistance was gradually extended to whole regions. By the mid 1960s, this had matured into a policy of regional development, presented as a means of rectifying the injustice of unequal living standards while simultaneously contributing to national modernization, international competitiveness and growth. Since this could be presented as a non-zero-sum game, questions of priorities, control and power in regional development policy were side-stepped. Nor, as long as policy had consisted merely of grants to blackspots, were serious administrative issues raised. Regional policy, like the rest of economic policy, was a matter for the centre, with no input from local government. Regional planning, however, required a spatial machinery and a means to link it to the environmental planning of local government and its Whitehall sponsors.

So, under the Labour government elected in 1964, moves were made to institutionalize regional planning with a threefold purpose: to provide a spatial dimension to the national indicative planning to which the government was committed; to provide a framework for the diversionary regional economic policy; and to link national policies with local government land-use strategies. At the same time, government wanted to encourage the emergence of new regional élites, committed to development and growth. Local government was rejected as a partner in this project because municipal boundaries were too restricted and because municipal elites were seen as insufficiently production-minded, too committed to the old municipal politics of distribution (this issue resurfaced in the late 1960s in the arguments about 'councillor calibre'). Serious regional planning, with its cross-functional and spatial perspectives would challenge the old central-local division of responsibilities and the functionalist basis of central government itself. To succeed, the centre would need either to regionalize its own operations under a dominant department of territorial government (as exists in Scotland) or to resign its monopoly of economic and industrial policy making, sharing it with regional elites. It proved willing to do neither.

The outcome was the Regional Economic Planning Councils, a corporatist device, intended to co-opt regional, industrial and union leaders as well as sundry experts and local government representatives, a territorial version of the corporatist mode of policy making which was becoming so important at national level. Along with these went Regional Economic Planning Boards, representing deconcentrated arms of central government and intended to transcend the functional divisions of government to produce a coherent spatial perspective. Almost identical devices were introduced around the same time in France and Italy, the other large unitary European democracies[5] but while, in those countries, they were to develop into elected regional government, the British experiment foundered.

Much has been written about the experience of the economic planning machinery and it is appropriate here only to make some remarks on their political weaknesses. The representative composition of the councils implied that they should articulate a distinct regional interest, yet their function was to carry out a central policy, the National Plan. In the development regions, councils easily adopted the role of lobbying for local interest; those in areas like the West Midlands found it more difficult to co-operate in a policy of diverting industry away from their own region. Functionalism in central government prevented a coherent central perspective, with the Ministry of Housing and Local Government insisting on retaining its land-use responsibilities.[6] While some ministers saw the new machinery as the basis for an eventual system of regional government, others resisted.[7] The councils lacked political standing, formal powers or finance and many members, disillusioned with their ambiguous role, resigned. The demise of the National Plan removed a major task of the councils and boards, while the abolition of the Department of Economic Affairs deprived English regional economic planning of its sponsor. Co-ordination of local land-use planning, the 'regional strategies' of the 1970s, moved to consortia of local authorities, with some involvement by the regional economic planning councils in some regions. The councils lingered on until 1979, without a clear role, though in some regions, they helped maintain a network of regional economic decision-makers. In Scotland, the council was retained, since there it had a significant interlocutor in the Secretary of State.

Proposals for Regional Government

The 1970s saw a shoal of proposals for regional reform, inspired by the two factors examined above and the contemporary movement for local government modernization. It is very significant that 'devolution' and local government reform were treated as separate issues, though both raised the question of regionalism. In 1966 Royal Commissions on local government in England and in Scotland were established, followed in 1969 by the Royal Commission on the Constitution (Kilbrandon Commission). Each interpreted its remit as largely excluding matters falling to the other, with the result that there was no comprehensive review of territorial government and the reform of English regional structures was largely prejudiced by local government reform before the Kilbrandon Commission report. Arguably, devolution and local government reform are analytically distinct, the former involving transfers of power from the centre, the latter the discharge of functions already delegated but this does not justify their separate treatment. That stemmed partly from the very functionalist basis of central government itself, with the Department of Economic Affairs concerned with regionalism, the Ministry of Housing and Local Government with local government reform, and the Scottish and Welsh secretaries and the Prime Minister with the need to contain nationalist pressure. A large part, too, was played by calculation. The commissions on local government were set up with a serious purpose, to produce the reforms desired by the centre. The Kilbrandon Commission was set up to buy time. It was political events which ensured that, when Kilbrandon finally reported, the issue of Scottish nationalism should have gone away only to return with even greater force. A breakdown of the two-party duopoly and the election of a parliament in which territorial parties held the balance of power is one of the few means, short of the breakdown in governability, by which the issue of territorial devolution can reach the agenda in the Westminister constitution. Under other circumstances, it is prone to be overtaken by other priorities or defeated by centralist pressures. Rather than attempt a chronological account of the various proposals canvassed and attempted in the 1970s, I shall present them under thematic headings and try to explain why all were ultimately unsuccessful in changing the traditional British mode of territorial government.

Regionalizing the State

A series of proposals aimed at satisfying the various pressures within a single scheme, so providing uniformity and political equity while transforming the unitary state. There are two problems with this approach. First, the strength of demand for constitutional change varied, being much greater in Scotland than elsewhere. Secondly, the existing structures and procedures of government differ in ways which would make adaptation to a common format difficult. In particular, the Scottish legal system, and the existence of Scottish legislation at Westminster, mean that real devolution to Scotland would have to be legislative, otherwise Westminster would have to continue to pass separate Scottish laws or to assimilate Scottish law to English, in contradiction to the spirit of devolution. For English regions, however, nobody has argued for distinct criminal laws or separate provision for divorce.

The most radical form of regionalizing the state would be federalism and, while this was advocated by the Liberal Party, *The Scotsman* and, for a time, *The Economist*, the proposals were vague, particularly on responsibility for economic policy and finance. The main problem with federalism, however, is that it would strike at the heart of the Westminster regime, since federalism implies limits on the power of central government and an abridgement of parliamentary sovereignty. No government and neither of the main parties was prepared to countenance this and there was, in any case, no popular constituency, except perhaps in Scotland, for such radical change.

Two other proposals for comprehensive regionalism are worth noting. In 1968, John Mackintosh[8] published a scheme for uniform regional government aimed at reforming the local government system, devolving power from central government and satisfying Scottish and Welsh aspirations. There would be eleven regions, including Scotland and Wales, with powers derived from both central and local government and which would be free to organize second tier local government at their discretion. The thrust of Mackintosh's argument was the need to decentralize power, to reinvigorate local democracy, and increase accountability by transferring functions to regions. The proposals of the minority report of the Kilbrandon Commission, from Lord Crowther Hunt and Alan Peacock,[9] were in some respects similar, insisting on equality of status for all regions and a devolution of power, though their general tenor was somewhat more centralist than Mackintosh. Emphasizing the limits which EEC entry posed for devolution, they denied regional assemblies legislative powers, except for the ability to pass ordinances, and stressed the need for central regulations. Analytically, the main problem with their scheme is its institutional bias, being largely premised on the 'existing tier' of regional government, by which they refer to the miscellaneous boards and field offices set up by various ministries many of which, it may be argued[10] have no inherently regional function at all. By contrast, Mackintosh emphasizes the functions of government and their most appropriate location. Neither Mackintosh nor Peacock and Crowther Hunt, however, provide a satisfactory scheme for dealing with Scottish legislation. Indeed the latter illustrate their proposals with two acts of Parliament which do not apply to Scotland at all.

One proposal for uniform regionalism which has surfaced periodically is to reproduce in the English regions the machinery of Scottish and Welsh Offices. The premise is that regional economic planning policies are essentially the province of central government so that political devolution is inappropriate. On the other hand, the centre's operations in the regions are ill co-ordinated and sometimes in conflict, while mechanisms are needed to reconcile local and national land use and development strategies. The proposal for regional ministers has the attraction of apparently leaving the Westminster model of unitary government intact. Advocates of the model, however, rarely understand that the Scottish and Welsh offices are not field offices of the functional Whitehall departments but independent departments in their own right, with separate representation in Cabinet and their own expenditure programmes. As examples of the territorial principle of organization, they can exist within a unitary government only because they are exceptional. To extend the principle to the English regions would mean abandoning the functional principle altogether over large parts of government and replacing the whole of the Department of the Environment, and the Ministry of Agriculture, most of the Departments of Education, Health and Transport and a large part of the Home Office with separate regional departments. Such a departure would be considerably more radical than the establishment of elected regional assemblies, with the central departments remaining in their tutelary role.

Proposals for regionalizing the state have consistently met with opposition from local government, which values its direct links with the centre. They have also been opposed by central civil servants brought up in the centralist/functionalist system. On the other hand, the experience with regional planning did affect a generation of civil servants based in the regions, especially in the north of England, many of whom came to look favourably on proposals for regional government as a means of ensuring greater policy coherence and increasing the weight of regional interests in bargaining with Whitehall. Proposals for comprehensive regionalization, however, never reached the political agenda because there was no point at which territorial government as a whole was officially considered. Instead, the issue of English regionalism, local government reform and Scottish devolution were considered separately and sequentially. This, as I have already stressed, was no accident. Central governments were no more interested in comprehensive constitutional reform than in devolving real power. Rather, they responded to a series of pressing administrative and political needs. This produced the second set of responses to be examined.

Exceptionalism for the periphery

Ever since the Union of 1707, British governments have practised a policy of exceptionalism for the peripheral nations of Scotland, Ireland and Wales. The strategic aim has been twofold: to assuage discontents on the periphery and discourage seccession; and to do this in a way which leaves the essentials of the Westminster regime intact by limiting devolution to selected areas and restricting it functionally.

The first exceptionalist proposals of the 1960s came from the Conservative Party, following Edward Heath's Declaration of Perth. As elaborated by the Douglas-Home committee, these proposed an elected Scottish assembly which, to preserve the principle of the unitary state would be part of the parliament, taking the committee stage of Scottish bills which would complete their progress at Westminster. The obvious potential for conflict between the two assemblies was brushed off with a typically British call for 'commonsense, objectivity and tolerance'.[11] In government, the Conservatives made no moves to implement the scheme, which was formally abandoned by the Scottish Conservative conference in 1973.

The Labour Party devolution scheme, derived from the majority report of the Kilbrandon Commission,[12] was no less concerned with maintaining the unitary state but by a different route. The Scotland and Wales Bill of 1976 and its successors the Scotland Act and Wales Act of 1978, emphasized parliamentary sovereignty and the fundamental political and economic unity of the United Kingdom, though offering little guidance on what the latter meant in practice. Separately elected assemblies were proposed, the Scottish one to have legislative powers, but the change which this represented in the traditional pattern of territorial government should not be exaggerated. The old implicit trade-off of self-government for privileged representation at the centre was skipped by retaining the secretaries of state and the full complement of Scottish and Welsh M.P.s along with the assemblies. The retention of the 108 M.P.s, which already over-represented Scotland and Wales in relation to population, owed not a little to Labour's need of them to form governments but was presented as essential to safeguard Scottish and Welsh interests at the centre. Economic and financial powers were to remain centralized and the assemblies' powers were described in narrow terms, in relation to individual pieces of legislation, rather than broad functions. A unified civil service was to be retained and Westminster's powers to legislate in devolved fields would be unabridged. This approach, tacking on assemblies to the existing system rather than transforming it, was a typical product of the British approach to constitutional reform. It reflected both the attitudes of ministers in the Labour government and of the major interest groups which it consulted. In Scotland, there is a marked tendency for groups to favour devolution in principle but seek to keep their own field centralized. This reflects a preference for retaining policy networks in which the groups have established a role. In the case of business and the trade unions, historical and partisan factors incline the former to oppose and the latter to favour Scottish Home Rule but both are united in wishing to exclude trade, labour legislation and most industrial policy from its remit.

There is no space here to recount the history of the Scottish and Welsh proposals but several important factors contributed to their failure. The essential one is that they lacked a parliamentary majority, hence the imposition of the referendum with its restrictive rules and the failure to implement the Scotland Act following the small YES majority. In Wales, as devolution came to be seen as a concession to nationalist pressure rather than a measure for better government, opinion turned against it. Among English M.P.s, there was deep opposition to exceptionalism as creating political injustice and the Scottish M.P. Tam Dalyell relentlessly pressed the 'West Lothian Question', which listed places in his constituency on whose affairs Scottish M.P.s would have no vote and places in England on whose affairs they would. After the accession of Margaret Thatcher to the leadership, the Conservatives turned decisively away from devolution while support from other parties was muted by Labour's insistence on reproducing the Westminster electoral system and pattern of executive government, which would serve to give the party a monopoly of power under the new arrangements.

The attempt at exceptionalism for Scotland, and, less seriously, for Wales, though unsuccessful, did have repercussions for the issue of English regionalism. The devolution debate had alerted English M.P.s to the benefits which Scotland derived from having its own minister in Cabinet and the regional distribution of public expenditure became an issue. In an attempt to still criticism of the devolution proposals, too, the government issued in 1976 a discussion paper[13] on possibilities for regional government in England. While this did little more than dismiss all the possibilities canvassed, as well as playing down the significance of the Scotland and Wales proposals, it did serve to keep the debate on English regionalism going, to be picked up in the context of local government reform.

Regionalism and Local Government Reform

The third type of proposal for regional government can be characterized broadly as arising from the debate in local government reform in England and focussing on improved local government rather than devolution of power from the centre. We can usefully distinguish here between proposals for indirectly elected regional bodies, whether chosen by local government or the economic interest groups, and directly elected councils. Indirectly elected bodies would have no independent standing and would function mainly as forums for discussion and mechanisms for co-ordination of policies among the agencies represented. Directly elected authorities, on the other hand, would have their own political standing. As a result, indirectly elected councils have frequently been dismissed as ineffectual talking shops, while directly elected councils have been seen as a threat by existing power holders in central and local government and in the networks of corporate interest representation which became so important in the 1970s.

The Redcliffe-Maud Commission on local government in England was restricted to examining the structure in relation to existing functions, thus formally excluding a consideration of devolution. Evidence from government departments further guided it away from a regional solution which central civil servants clearly saw as a potential challenge to Whitehall.[14] Yet both the majority report and the memorandum of dissent from Derek Senior recognized a need for broader areas than proposed local authorities for the co-ordination of land use and other policy matters. For the majority,[15] these should take the form of provincial councils, indirectly elected but with power to co-opt additional members, which would draw up strategic land use plans and co-ordinate education and children's services. Similar proposals were made by a majority of the Kilbrandon

Commission. Senior's memorandum[16] went wider, to consider not merely local co-ordination but central-local linkages in planning and proposed two models. On the assumption that central government was not prepared to devolve major powers, there would be five indirectly elected provincial councils advising ministers of state in the production of regional strategies. Were central government prepared to countenance devolution, Senior suggested there could be some twelve to fifteen elected provinces to serve as the top tier of local government as well as receiving powers from the centre, an echo of Mackintosh's proposals.

Having consigned the issue of regional government and devolution to the Royal Commission on the Constitution, both Labour and Conservative governments before and after the 1970 election were able to argue that decisions should await its report. Meanwhile, local government reform should not be delayed. The 1972 legislation for England consequently had nothing for regions, though contemporaneous reforms in the health and water services produced regionally based structures. These were justified on technical grounds by reference to the specific needs of the services involved but the effect was to reduce political control over them since the region lacked either elected territorial government or strong deconcentrated arms of central government.

The 1972 reforms settled neither the future of local government nor the question of regionalism. Within the Labour Party, there was resentment at the loss of powers by cities to the counties under the Conservative reform and the unaccountable status of the regional health and water authorities. An obvious solution was to establish large regional councils to take over the regional agencies, with county powers dispersed between them and the cities. At the same time, pressure was mounting for some compensation in England for Scottish and Welsh devolution. After a vague commitment in principle in the party's 1976 programme, more detailed proposals were unveiled in 1977.[17] These included a 'local government' model, in which regional authorities would have limited powers and local government would retain its direct links with the centre; and a 'Welsh model' of executive devolution similar to the Crowther-Hunt and Peacock proposals. After intensive discussion, which revealed a growing regional consciuousness in the party, especially in the north, the proposals foundered on the vested interests within the Labour movement. Local councillors resisted any solution which would sever their direct links with Whitehall. Trade unions pressed for corporatist rather than elected bodies at regional level - the health service unions argued for an 'industrial democracy' which would allow them to join the medical profession in control of the system. Ministers resisted any dimunition of their powers.

These factors were consistently to bedevil any attempt by the Labour Party to produce a coherent regional strategy.[18] By the end of the Labour Government, all that had appeared was a commitment to 'organic change', an incremental strengthening of city councils which might eventually cause the counties to fade away. By 1983, this had firmed up to a commitment to abolish the shire counties, but with only the vaguest approval in principle to the idea of regional authorities which might eventually replace them. A similar fate befell the proposals of Labour's regional spokesman John Prescott.[19] These, starting from a policy rather than an institutional base, recommended regional governments to engage in economic planning as part of a return to interventionist government. Again, local government interests, the party leadership and the unions combined to prevent the proposals becoming policy.

Regionalism in the 1980s

The 1980s has not been a decade of institutional reform in Britain as political attention has focussed on more pressing issues and the government in office has pursued a centralization of power. Yet, there has been a steady stream of proposals for regional reform, spurred by a number of factors. The abolition of the metropolitan counties both opened the issue of territorial government and removed a possible obstacle to regionalism, especially on the part of Labour councillors. Experience of centralization under the Thatcher government has raised doubts about the doctrine of unlimited central authority while the lack of alternation at central level has removed the feature which reconciled centralized government with pluralist democracy. So, among the various opposition forces, interest in the dispersal of power has grown, as it has among the European left and centre generally. The Liberal/SDP Alliance made constitutional reform a major plank of its platform, though finding as much difficulty as Labour in agreeing on a scheme. A new generation of politicians in the Labour Party, capitalizing on the weakness of the parliamentary leadership in the early 1980s, was able to use local government as a platform for gaining national attention. In the north of England, many of the new generation are more sympathetic to regional reform and less tied to the centralist/municipalist tradition than their elders. All the opposition parties are committed to the creation of an elected Scottish assembly. Increased economic and political division in Britain has led to calls for a revival of regional policy[20] while the rate and location of economic change have prompted calls for a return to strategic and regional planning.[21] It seems likely that a future non-Conservative government will have to give serious attention to the regional question. Yet, a series of obstacles remain to any solution.

None of the British parties has seriously faced the implications of dispersing power. Labour continues to see Scottish devolution and proposals for Wales and the English regions as something to be granted by a sovereign parliament and, usually, limited to Labour-supporting areas (Scotland, Wales, the north of England). The Democrats emphasize the need for devolution yet have consistently linked this with a model of consensual decision-making which neatly removes the conflicts inherent in this. Neither party leadership has shown itself ready to contemplate a real territorial negotiation such as took place in Spain in the late 1970s and early 1980s. Yet Labour (and in their time the Conservatives) have easily accepted negotiation as a mode of policy making within the corporate constitution.

Another key obstacle is an inability to talk seriously about equity and its implications. Labour in insisting on the unitary Westminster mode of government, has emphasized the need to maintain the 'political and economic unity of the United Kingdom' without ever defining just what this involves. Often it has simply been identified with the Westminster mode of government itself rather than with any programme for territorial economic or political equality. At the same time, it has resisted proposals to entrench civil rights constitutionally on the grounds that Parliament, not the courts, are the basis of civil liberties - a notion so shaken by the events of recent years, that many Labour politicians are reluctantly abandoning it. The Alliance parties have been on firmer ground here, in wishing to combine devolution with a written statement of the rights of citizenship to give substantive meaning to the 'United Kingdom'.

Finally, there is the question of how economic powers can be divided. Any government embarking on a more interventionist programme will need to have regard to its spatial articulation yet, with the possible exception of Scotland, the administrative machinery to do this is absent. Should spatial planning be combined with political devolution, in Scotland or elsewhere, the administrative problem will be combined with the political one of power and influence within regional government and the relationship of devolved political power to national economic policy.

The balance of organized economic and political interests in Britain remains against a radical reform of territorial government. European experience shows that movement is most likely where there is a change of regime or a party realignment,[22] breaking old power structures. In Britain, constitutional change has usually been prompted by a crisis of the party system at Westminster and this remains the most likely route for a reorganization of the territorial power structure.

References

1.   Jones, B. and Keating, M. (1985) *Labour and the British State*, Oxford: Clarendon.
2.   Bulpitt, J. (1983) *Territory and Power in the United Kingdom*, Manchester: Manchester University Press.
3.   Gyford, J. and James, M. (1983) *National Parties and Local Politics*, London: Allen & Unwin.
4.   Keating, M. (1988) *State and Regional Nationalism. Territorial Politics in Western Europe*, Brighton: Harvester.
5.   Keating, M. *State and Regional Nationalism*.
6.   Lindley, P. (1982) The Framework of Regional Planning 1964-82, in Hogwood, B. and Keating, M. (eds.) *Regional Government in England*, Oxford: Clarendon.

7.   Crossman, R.H.S. (1975) *Diaries of a Cabinet Minister* vol.1, London: Hamish Hamilton.

8.   Mackintosh, J.P. (1968) *The Devolution of Power*, Harmondsworth: Penguin.

9.   *Royal Commission on the Constitution 1969-73, Volume II. Memorandum of Dissent* by Lord Crowther-Hunt and Professor A.T. Peacock, Cmnd 5640-1, London: HMSO, 1973.

10. Keating, M. and Rhodes, M. (1982) 'The Status of Regional Government. An Analysis of the West Midlands' in Hogwood, B. and Keating, M. (eds.) *Regional Government in England and Wales*, Oxford: Clarendon.

11. *Scotland's Government. The Report of the Scottish Constitutional Committee*, chairman Sir Alec Douglas-Home, Edinburgh, 1970.

12. *Royal Commission on the Constitution, 1969-73 Volume 1 Report* Cmnd 5640, London: HMSO, 1973 (known as the Kilbrandon Commission).

13. *Devolution: The English Dimension*, London: HMSO, 1976.

14. Wood, B. (1976) *The Process of Local Government Reform* 1966-74, London: Allen & Unwin.

15. *Royal Commission on Local Government in England 1966-9, Report, vol 1*, Cmnd 4040, London: HMSO, 1969 (known as the Redcliffe-Maud Commission).

16. *Royal Commission on Local Government in England 1966-9, Report, vol 2*, Cmnd 4040, London: HMSO 1969 (Memorandum of Dissent by Derek Senior).

17. *Regional Authorities and Local Government Reform. A Discussion Document for the Labour Movement*, London: Labour Party, 1976.

18. Keating, M. (1984) 'Labour's Territorial Strategy' in MacAllister, I. and Rose, R. (eds.) *The Nationwide Competition for Votes*, London: Frances Pinter.

19. Prescott, J. (1984) *Alternative Regional Strategy*, London: Parliamentary Spokesman's Group.

20. Regional Studies Association (1983) *Report of an Inquiry into Regional Problems in the United Kingdom*, Norwich: Geo Books.

21. Royal Town Planning Institute (1986) *Strategic Planning for Regional Potential*, London RTPI.

22. Keating, M. (1988) 'Does Regional Government Work? The Experience of France, Italy and Spain', *Governance*, 1.2.

11

Britain in a Europe of Regions

Michael Hebbert

Introduction

The reader who has stayed the course may by now see British regionalism in much the same light as the Esperanto movement: a plucky cause, destined for obscurity. Despite its long history, the regional idea has left little mark. Today even more than when the Royal Commission on the Constitution took evidence, the United Kingdom remains 'the largest unitary state in Europe and among the most centralized of the major industrial countries of the world'.[1] The chronicle since the last regionalist upsurge of 1960 to 1975 has been especially unpromising. At the institutional level, the dismantling of the Regional Economic Planning Councils in 1979 was followed by abolition of the quasi-regional Metropolitan Councils in 1986. Politically, the 1987 general election confirmed the inability of the Scottish National Party and Plaid Cymru to recapture the ground lost after the debacle of the Scotland and Wales Acts in 1978-9. Three of the smaller regionalist parties - Mebyon Kernow, the Cornish National Party, and the Wessex Regionalists - could not raise the increased election deposit and withdrew from the contest.[2] The initial passionate commitment of the Campaign for Social Democracy in 1981 to build a new party of government on a platform of constitutional decentralization ended in disarray. The Social and Liberal Democratic Party was notably more circumspect at its launch in 1988, and deferred discussion of the devolution issue for more than a year thereafter.

The idea of regionalism, undeterred by these setbacks, springs up irrepressibly. Specialist groups such as the Regional Studies Association and the Royal Town Planning Institute have kept it in good currency, against all tendencies of government practice.[3] Since 1980 the Regionalist Seminar has provided a new and lively network for small groups of active campaigners for political regionalism in the North, Cornwall, Orkney, Shetland and Wessex.[4] Closer into the political mainstream each of the opposition parties continues to toy with a commitment to devolution in Scotland and Wales and some form of political regionalization in England, though the 1987 election manifestoes were cautiously worded and decentralization was hardly mentioned during the campaign by politicians.

What are the prospects for regionalism in Britain - continued exile at the political margin, or a national rediscovery of that federal tradition discerned earlier by Michael Burgess? The question can no longer be answered in purely insular terms. When regional devolution returns to the political agenda in Britain, the European Community will be moving to the next decisive stage of integration under the provisions of the Single European Act. Because the achievement of a single internal market necessarily involves a shift of sovereignty from state to supranational levels of government, it puts a question mark over the primacy of Westminster, and that in turn may be thought to open up new perspectives for the regions and nations under the hegemony of London. As the Scottish National Party stressed in their successful campaign for the Glasgow Govan byelection in November 1988, the outlook for British regionalism has to be seen in wider, European terms.

The Regionalization of Europe

Regionalism, as a movement, has as long a history in most European countries as in Britain, involving much the same incongruous combination of technical, cultural, political and administrative elements.[5] Unlike its British counterpart, though, it has made its mark on the government. If we take a comparative view of territorial organization and politics over the past twenty years, the British experience of centralization contrasts strongly with that of her European partners. Though generalization about trends in government is difficult, there is widespread agreement among commentators that a significant downward shift of power has occurred from national capitals to intermediate and local government level.[6] Broadly speaking, the northern European democracies have proceeded by the merging and strengthening of existing local governments: in the Napoleonic states of southern Europe, lower levels have been left unreformed and a new level of elected government inserted at the regional tier.[7]

The Conference of Local and Regional Authorities of Europe (CLRAE) sees the latter reforms, and the grouping of local governments in Scandinavian countries, as aspects of an underlying trend towards the *regionalization* of Europe[8] defined by the following six characteristics:

a. the establishment and reinforcement of large-scale territorial authorities on the level immediately beneath the central government;

b. their endowment with a comprehensive regional sphere of activity, within which they operate largely on their own responsibility and have broad rights of participation, particularly in regional and economic planning, cultural policy and the provision and promotion of such facilities as are required by the regional community;

c. extensive combination of existing state authorities of equivalent level with these highest regional units of government and the transfer of appropriate central government functions to these units;

d. the establishment within these authorities of popularly elected representative assemblies which participate directly in the decision-making process and of an adequate administrative apparatus of their own;

e. their endowment with legislative powers in as far as the national interest, and in particular legal unity and conformity to common legal standards, does not necessitate legislation by the national parliament;

f. their endowment with independent budgetary powers, including a share of general tax revenue.

Regionalization in this sense is not a remote reformist vision, but could rather be described, without exaggeration, as a description of normal institutional arrangements at the intermediate level within western democracies. Its normality might be thought surprising in view of the mixed ancestry of the regional idea, which as its critics have often observed, has meant all things to all men, reflecting in its time, technocratic concerns of national policy elites for efficient deconcentrated decision structures; autonomist demands of peripheral ethnic minorities; counter-culture movements against the modern industrial state; backward-looking right-wing traditionalism; forward-looking left-wing progressivism; administrative modernization of local governments; the electoral rewards to be won by the promise of new territorial structures.[9]

The literature of regionalism is full of these distinctions: 'top-down' versus 'bottom-up'; and of course the planning-inspired regionalism that has featured in many previous chapters,[10] 'political' versus 'functional' regionalism[11], 'regionalization' versus 'regionalism'.[12] The traditional fear of regionalists was that the different impulses would cancel each other out, with minority ethnic claims diluted by generalized decentralization schemes and grass roots initiatives absorbed into central planning systems.[13] In the event the various forms of regionalism seem to have had a mutually reinforcing effect. Political regionalism has fed off its administrative counterpart. Concessions of autonomy to ethnically militant Region X have stimulated demands for general decentralization of government in Regions Y and Z. Modest shifts of electoral support towards regionalist parties have levered substantial concessions out of national mass parties.

The key to Europe's regionalization has been its pragmatic character. Unlike federalism, the political concept of the region has not been surrounded by any penumbra of *a priori* doctrine; that indeed has always been one of its chief attractions. In countries accustomed to the certainties of a Roman law tradition, the frankly experimental character of institutional devices such as the Belgian constitutional amendment of 1970 or Title VIII of the Spanish Constitution of

1978 has come in for severe criticism.[14] The 'regional state', lawyers have argued, is neither fish nor fowl, neither properly federal nor fully unitary, and thus inherently unstable.

To political scientists, however, the development of an intermediate tier in such contrasted unitary states as Italy, Belgium, France and Spain, reveals the practicality of regionalism as an evolutionary solution to certain common structural problems facing the late twentieth century European state. Devolution, like privatization (to which it is linked in constitutional theory)[15] relieves the state of a burden of policy commitment it had become less and less able to fulfil, with consequent problems for its own legitimacy. In Mény's analysis, regionalism indicates 'the maturity and sophistication of political systems able to assimilate changes which on the face of it presented a serious threat to their very existence'.[16] Regional power has grown largely, if not entirely, by absorption of functions hitherto held by the state centre. Typical subjects for devolution have been health and social policy, public works and planning, water and environmental protection, housing, culture and local economic development. The central state's traditional 'regional policy' role, distributing grants for industrial development in peripheral areas, has - as the monitoring of Kevin Allen's team at Strathclyde University clearly shows - increasingly been devolved to the regions themselves.[17]

A consequence of the regionalization process has been the growing cohesion and confidence of the new regional elites. That the German Länder control 40% of public expenditure and the French regions less than 2% seems to count for less than their common intermediate (and intermediary) status between central and local governments. The consolidation of this intermediate tier across Europe confirms Vernon Bogdanor's argument of the relative unimportance in practice of juridical distinctions between federalism, which divides power, and regionalism, which merely devolves it.[18] In political reality the majority of European states have shifted towards a quasi-federalism, and the shift will not be lightly reversible. To cite once again the Conference of Local and Regional Authorities of Europe:

> '... regional government is no longer a somewhat vague intermediate level of little direct concern to the citizen which can be administered as an extension of either the national or the local level, dependent on them and with hardly any independent significance'.[19]

The history of the Conference is telling in itself. Originally set up by the Council of Europe in 1955 as a Conference of Local Authorities (made up of representatives of national local government associations) it changed its title in 1975 in recognition of the growing importance of the intermediate, regional level. In 1982 CLRAE was elevated into a Standing Conference of the Council of Europe. But the distinctiveness of the regional as opposed to local tier of government generated pressures for a separate representative organization, leading in April 1986 to the setting up of a Council of European Regions, under the Presidency of Edgar Faure, President-General of the Franche-Comte. Next on the agenda is the establishment of a formal parliamentary representation of the eighty or so elected regional assemblies of Europe. The Council of Europe envisages CLRAE developing into a Senate of Regions, alongside the Parliamentary Assembly in Strasbourg which represents national parliaments. The stronger view of the regions themselves, as laid down in their 'Bordeaux Declaration' of 1978, is that they should constitute a Second Chamber of the European Parliament and so participate directly as a legislature in the building of a sovereign Europe.[20]

Towards a 'Europe of Regions'

In a European perspective, regionalism transcends the state and joins forces with the larger movement for continental integration. At its strongest, for example in the passionately anti-statist writings of Denis de Rougemont and Guy Heraud, the vision of a "Europe of Regions" implies the abolition of nation states:[21]

'Europe and the regions are natural political allies against the feudal power of the sovereign nation-states in much the same way as the king and the communes once were ... The nation-state, which is too small to carry out certain jobs in modern industrial societies and too large to carry out others, is nowadays challenged on both fronts. The centralized, sovereign nation-state is the heir to the concepts and problems of the pre-technical era, but it has been incapable of tackling the major objectives of our time, and it is this which has finally cast doubt on the legitimacy of its historical attempt to monopolize politics and to arrogate to itself all powers and rights and the allegience of individuals and groups'.[22]

A "Europe of Regions" implies integration of sovereignty on the continental scale and its disintegration to levels corresponding to the real ethnic and geographical units suppressed by the arbitrary (because in origin military) boundaries of states.[22] This perspective is especially attractive to ethno-linguistic minority regions - Scotland, Catalonia, Brittany - which see in European integration a realistic alternative to militant go-it-alone nationalism. European and regional loyalty displace state-nationalism:

'We are more and more Tuscans, Sicilians, Walloons and Welshmen, and less and less Italians Frenchmen and Englishmen, or in other words we are becoming more and more Europeans'.[24]

The actual construction of European institutions, however, has followed another logic, based upon close protection of the interests of the central governments of member states. Under the Treaty of Rome, federal, regional or unitary states are all treated as constitutional monoliths. National governments monopolize access to the Commission, even on matters - such as the European Regional Development Fund - of primarily subnational significance. As a special concession to their federal status, the German Länder have a single 'observer' attached to the Commission, but regional administrations elsewhere have no such privilege.[25]

Nevertheless, the regionalization trend discussed earlier does undoubtedly owe something to the changing institutional context at the European scale. In its typically slow, modest way the twenty member Council of Europe (in Strasbourg) has, as we have seen, provided regional governments with a forum and helped to build up a comparative documentation on the legal and fiscal bases of regional autonomy.[26] The Council's *Outline Convention on Transfrontier Co-operation between Territorial Authorities or Communities* has stimulated a remarkable proliferation of transfrontier agreements along all the major frontier zones of mainland Europe. The European Parliament (also in Strasbourg) has repeatedly taken up the regionalist cause, most notably in its resolution of 1984 which called upon the governments of all member states without an elected intermediate tier to make good the omission, and requested the Commission and Council of Ministers to draft legislation enabling the regions to establish and maintain direct relations with the Community institutions, with due safeguards for member states' constitutional powers.[27]

Besides, the growth of Community intervention and funding has a significant regional dimension. As shown in the detailed studies published by Michael Keating and Barry Jones the bureaucracy of the Commission in Brussels has a natural interest in cultivating the development of a regional tier.[28] For administrative purposes the region offers a more uniform and rational territorial framework than states. The Commission established the statistical documentation for Europe on a regional rather than a national basis. In certain respects, as John Banks recently noted, the 'essentially managerialist-functionalist' concerns of the centralizing Eurocrat have been convergent with those of peripheral regionalist.[29] The European Community has facilitated the establishment and consolidation of regional governments, particularly in Spain, both by providing an intangible reassurance of a stable macro-political environment, and more concretely, as a source of subsidary funding for projects conceived at the regional level.

However, the benign relation between Brussels and the regions conceals a serious paradox. As many observers have commented, further progress towards political and economic integration under the Single European Act, with its provision for the abolition of all internal barriers to trade by 1992, is rather more likely to weaken than reinforce regional autonomy. It will necessarily involve a substantial expansion of Community legislation in important regional functions such as economic development, technical training and infrastructure. Now, the proliferation of EEC regulations and directives on such matters directly threatens regional autonomy. Regions are not represented in the legislative body, the Council of Ministers, which passes its measures behind closed doors. The legal duty to comply with community law lies with the central governments of member states, even if the topic has been devolved to a subnational (regional) legislature. In the event of non-compliance, it is the member state, and not the region, that will be taken to the European Court. Inevitably, matters of interest to the Community tend to become more centralized at the national level within member states.[30] So the relation between Europe and the regions has a strange twist. The two tiers of government, subnational and supranational, have emerged over the same period and out of the same idealism. Though mutually reinforcing in some respects there is also a basic tension between the development of the Community as actually constituted and the interests of substate governments. The more progress towards economic and political integration, the greater that tension is likely to become. Nevertheless, the regions are now firmly established as building blocks of Europe. In the 1990s it will no longer be possible, as it was in the 1970s, to treat the politics of integration exclusively as a matter of state interest.

John Banks, surveying the European scene in his book *Federal Britain?* (1971) looked forward to the emergence of a younger, post-war generation whose vision of the Community as a federation of small nations and regions of large nations would be the antithesis of de Gaulle's "Europe des Patries". He foresaw popular mobilization for European unity linked to a new radical regionalism and a decline of the old and chauvinistic national patriotisms. In the United Kingdom, he detected a growing disenchantment with what he called 'the myth of unionism':

'... by the end of the 1960s Great Britain was the only major political entity in Western Europe north of the Pyrenees that had neither undergone nor attempted a decentralization of governmental power along regional lines. It had become clear that the introduction of regional government on an elective basis, far from being a retrograde step, would do no more than put Britain into the mainstream of European developments, and by assimilating her economic planning machinery to that of her continental partners would make eventual entry to the Common Market that much easier'.[31]

Britain breaks step

The evolution of British regionalism in 1965-1975 initially fitted the general European trend rather well. We find the same bundle of factors as in France, Belgium and Spain; a nationalist revival of home-rule demands on the ethnic periphery; a central policy preoccupation with macro-economic development planning and its implementation on the ground; a diffused administrative interest in regions as the basis for land use policy and local government modernization; and a fresh concern amongst political elites for the contribution of structural reorganization to making government less remote and so stimulating democratic participation. As elsewhere, it seemed that these diverse factors might be mutually reinforcing. John Mackintosh, M.P. argued strongly in *The Devolution of Power* (1968) for regionalism as a workable solution both to Scottish and Welsh aspirations and to England's need for local government reform.[32] The impression formed by the majority of the Kilbrandon Commission, after four years' investigation of regionalism in all its aspects, was that 'while the people of Great Britain as a whole cannot be said to be seriously dissatisfied with their system of government, they have less attachment to it than in the past and there are some substantial and persistent causes of discontent which may contain the seeds of more serious trouble. We think that devolution could do much to reduce the discontent. It would counter over-centralization and, to a lesser extent, strengthen democracy. It would be a response to national feeling in Scotland and Wales'.[33]

In contrast to this somewhat lukewarm endorsement the minority *Memorandum of Dissent* by Lord Crowther-Hunt and Professor Alan Peacock powerfully restated the model advocated by John Mackintosh, with provincial authorities in England having devolved powers so as to ensure an equality of political rights with autonomous national assemblies in Scotland and Wales. Like Mackintosh, they argued for a single, drastic constitutional reform of the U.K. as a simultaneous solution to its multiple ills of regional imbalance, policy overload at the centre, and antiquated arrangements at the local level. Their scheme was a intellectually more coherent than the majority of the Royal Commission (itself internally divided in matters of detail) but as Jim Sharpe well puts it, in home-rule-all-round 'it is difficult to avoid the conclusion that ... we are not dealing with an issue that has any firm foundations in the realm of practicable politics'.[34] The more pragmatic model recommended by Kilbrandon, combining legislative devolution to Scottish and Welsh assemblies with advisory English regional councils on the lines also recommended by the Redcliffe-Maud Commission was closer to the model of regionalism pursued in the first instance in France and Belgium.[35] Had the recommendations of the Kilbrandon Commission been implemented, initially weak regional advisory bodies might in due course have generated their own allegience and territorial demands, evolving as on the continent towards a tier of uniform elective representation for new regions and old alike.

Instead, for reasons well analyzed by Michael Keating in the previous chapter Kilbrandon was shelved and the dynamic process of cumulative reinforcement by which Scottish and Welsh examples might have stimulated English regional aspirations was never set in motion. The potential centrifugal challenge of regionalism was managed by piecemeal measures.[36] Regional economic decline was tackled with a battery of ad hoc policy devices - the Hunt Committee, Regional Economic Planning Councils, Regional Employment Premium,

Temporary Employment Subsidy and the Manpower Services Commission - until interest waned with the surprising discovery that regional unemployment had become politically tolerable. For two years before the arrival of Mrs Thatcher the policy focus had already shifted elsewhere, to the 'inner city' and more localist approaches to economic regeneration. Meanwhile, the devolution issue had been, for the while, defused by legislation which took up the best part of the 1976-77 and 1977-78 parliamentary sessions before collapsing at the referendum hurdle in 1978 and bringing the government down with it.

The reform of local government, an important component of regionalization in European countries, was tackled in Britain as a separate matter from the devolution issue. As the Kilbrandon Report noted, the 1973 reorganization spiked a principal argument for regional devolution, by creating a 'modernized' system of fewer and larger lower-tier units. 'Many of the matters generally considered most suitable for regional devolution relate to services for which operational responsibility has already been conferred on local authorities. In all parts of Great Britain local government is being reformed and strengthened to enable it to provide those services more effectively and economically without being subjected to excessive regulation through financial and other controls'.[37] No matter that these words have an ironical ring in retrospect. At the time, the great upheaval of local reorganization put paid to thought of further structural reform. The energy spent on region-building in France, Italy, Spain and Belgium was in Britain absorbed into adjustments at municipal and county levels, without, however, any of the decentralizing measures to strengthen county government that characterized the Scandinavian reforms of this period. The Government received fewer than 100 responses from the public to its Green Paper *Devolution, the English Dimension* (1976) which argued that Scottish and Welsh devolution might imply a need for major change in England. The only change that did occur, three years later, was the dismantling of the last vestigial trace of regional institutions.

Could the course of events have gone otherwise? Without that crystallization of unlike elements that occurred in Europe, British regionalism remained stillborn, never winning hearts and minds to a politically significant degree. It commanded 'some degree of intellectual assent, but not that kind of committed assent which leads to action'.[38] So, Britain missed the opportunity to ride with the tide of regionalization. As Sir Meredith Whitaker said when the resolution "On Regional Institutions in Europe" was adopted by CLRAE,

'We of the U.K. very much hope ... [for] exemption from the spirit of the resolution that there must be regionalization in all the member states. It is not necessary for the U.K., we do not want it ... What other countries wish to have for themselves, that is fine. We do not impose any of our views on them, we equally do not wish to have the systems of other countries imposed on ourselves'.[39]

Britain was duly excused, by the insertion of a clause that regionalization was not necessary 'in states, e.g. the U.K., (sic!) which already have a system of local government comprising units comparable in competence and powers to the Länder or the Swiss cantons'.[40]

Resurgence of the Regional Idea

That robust dismissal of regionalization in 1980 rings less true nine years later. As we approach the Single European Act's deadline of 1992 for the removal of internal frontiers, a number of factors have combined to bring regionalism back into the public eye. Those various strands of thought and action which we have followed through these pages - town planning, industrial development, local government structure, and national-level territorial politics - seem once again to be recombining into a reform agenda based on the unifying idea of regional devolution. The impetus has come less from the Berlaymont Building than Downing Street. Mrs. Thatcher's third term has handsomely restored regionalism to the political agenda in at least three different ways.

First there are the reverbations of two critical measures, both reputedly pursued against Cabinet doubts at the personal insistence of the Prime Minister, the abolition of the Greater London Council and the six Metropolitan Counties (Local Government Act 1985), and the abolition of rates and introduction of community charge or poll tax (Community Charge Act 1987).

The first measure destabilized the entire system of local government by lopping off the top tier of county government from the seven largest cities while leaving it intact elsewhere. Bottom-tier councils inside the metropolitan areas became unitary authorities, responsible for the entire range of local government services in their boundaries. Though small in number the metropolitan districts and boroughs have created an anomaly with repercussions throughout the local government system. The arbitrary subdivisions of a few big cities now have full stand-alone status whilst great free-standing towns with centuries-old traditions of municipal autonomy remain buried as lower-tier units under the county councils. 'If Bury or Sandwell or North Shields are fit enought to run their own services' Jack Straw MP asked in 1985, 'then why not Portsmouth or Plymouth or Hull or Nottingham? *Further major change in local government is therefore inevitable*'.[41]

After the 1987 general election the Conservative government embarked on a further round of local government legislation. The Education Reform Act in particular deepened the shadow over the County Councils. Education is by far the most important function at county level. This service was allocated to them as upper-tier authorities in 1973 in the conviction that an efficient standard of provision could not be achieved by smaller more localized councils. But the abolition of the Inner London Education Authority - inserted as an afterthought into the Education Reform Act - set a precedent for public education provision by authorities as small as Kensington and Chelsea, with only 9,000 children and one secondary school. London example again established an anomaly with repercussions through the entire local government system. Besides, the Act's general provision for schools to opt out of local government system, is bound to diminish the role of the countries. Were schools to shift in substantial numbers into a direct grant relationship with central government, county budgets and manpower would rapidly deplete. Nor will it be easy for the counties to compensate for their declining involvement in direct service provision, with a stronger role in strategic policy-making. Their most important medium-term policy instruments, the structure plans prepared under the 1971 Town and Country Planning Act, have themselves been under threat of abolition since the government published a Green Paper in 1986.[42]

The Association of District Councils concludes from the structural precedent of the big cities, and the functional trend of present legislation, that unitary, one-tier local government should be the model throughout England and Wales.[43] Professional and specialist groups such as the Royal Town Planning Institute have followed the same line of argument, envisaging a simplified system of all-purpose district councils together with a new regional tier of government, larger and stronger than existing counties.[44] There are indications that a slimmed-down unitary system also best matches the Conservative Government's thinking about the evolution of local government in Britain - a model of 'enabling' not 'providing' government.[45] The keystone of this system is the Community Charge or poll tax, a system of local government finance biased against spending. Its logic will be to reinforce the argument for a pulling back of local government into a single, simple system of local councils.

The poll tax has also given a direct and powerful impetus to regionalism. The use of Scotland, where Conservative support is minimal, as a testbed for this unpopular measure was a great stimulus to nationalist feeling and brought the issue of devolution right back to the top of the political agenda. With polls indicating 77% support amongst voters for some measure of home rule, all except Conservative politicians joined forces during 1988 in the Campaign for a Scottish Assembly. Following the earlier recommendations of a Constitutional Steering Committee under the chairmanship of Sir Robert Grieve plans were laid for an all-party Scottish Constitutional Convention.[46] The nationalist revival was linked with a campaign of civil disobedience against the poll tax in which 100 prominent Scots, including Labour front-bench M.P.s, pledged themselves to non-payment. The resounding SNP victory in the Glasgow Govan by-election of November 1988 confirmed the strength of political alienation in Scotland from a Westminster government in which only 10 out of 72 Scottish seats were held by Conservatives, though there were doubts whether the mutual desire for change would prove strong enough to hold opposition forces together in the lead-up to the proposed Convention.

As in the 1970s, the movement for devolution north of the border had immediate repercussions to the south. In January 1988 a northern group of Labour M.P.s published a Bill for the establishment of a Northern Regional

Assembly with devolved powers, and a Northern Development Agency on the model of those in Scotland and Wales. Traditional scepticism within the Labour Party about regional decentralization seemed, in the later 1980s, to be outweighed by fear that England's industrial regions would be doubly disadvantaged if the Celtic periphery were to win political autonomy on top of its existing financial advantages through the centrally endowed Development Agencies.

In its style as well as its substance, the evolving programme of Thatcherism has prompted revived interest in the issue of regional devolution. Measures supposed to transfer choice from elected local governments to consumers and shareholders have in practice involved a substantial accumulation of power at the centre, in Whitehall and Westminster. This paradox was especially apparent as the cutting edge of Conservative reform moved into local education and housing, and finance in the third Thatcher term - all measures involving a direct challenge to the principle of local self-government and a still further involvement of central government ministers in decisions about local public services. Faced with these laws, and the manner of their implementation, many pondered the legitimacy of a constitution that entrusted such all-encompassing legislative and executive power to a government possessing less than half the vote in the country as a whole, and less than a quarter in Scotland. By stretching the British Constitution to its limit, Mrs. Thatcher returned the issue of constitutional reform to the political agenda.[47]

The concentration of power in London, and its use in an autocratic manner, is associated with another increasing salient issue of the late 1980s, the concentration of wealth and investment in London and its broad geographical sphere of influence, which extends from the Wash to the River Ex. In the period of rapid economic growth since 1985, the south-east of England has the lion's share of all growth sectors within the economy, especially financial services and high-technology industry. It has the highest property prices and the lowest unemployment. It is also the heartland of the Conservative vote. Across a broad range of indicators, the map of Britain polarizes into a stark pattern of north-south division.[48] Many have drawn the contrast with the dynamic, polycentric economic geography of West Germany. Economic and political considerations are seen to combine in favour of a thorough-going strategy of decentralization in Britain.[49]

Pulling the strands together, we find regional reorganization exerting its now-familar attraction as an icon of reform, offering a simultaneous solution to a variety of discontents, from infrastructure and land use planning and industrial development, through questions of cultural identity, to the central issues of power and politics in Britain. In its broad outlines the favoured reform solution favoured by most of those who call for regional devolution generally resembles that in the minority report of the Kilbrandon Commission (1973) by Lord Crowther-Hunt and Professor Peacock, with regional assemblies for the English provinces balancing national devolution to Scotland and Wales. The main task of the regions would be to bring under direct regional accountability the quangoes and branches of central government already active on the regional level for a range of functions such as industrial promotion, the NHS, health, rural development, the arts and sports; in other words, to draw power down from the centre, not up from the local level. Nevertheless, local change is also anticipated. Abolition of the English county councils is now seen, particularly on the left, as an essential element of the decentralization strategy, both so as to meet the criticism that regionalization would involve an excessive growth of bureaucracy, and to resolve the anomaly of the metropolitan areas.[50] Also, concern to entrench the powers of devolved assemblies has revived interest in the abolition of the House of Lords and its replacement with an Upper House representing the regions.[51]

Conclusion

What most marks the new surge of interest in regionalism from earlier episodes described in these pages is the sense of a European dimension.[52] Exponents of regionalism in the late 1980s place more and more emphasis on two propositions: first, that Britain is an odd man out in Europe for want of a regional tier of government; second, that this tier will continue to grow in importance as a consequence of economic and political integration in the European Community. Yet as we saw at the outset of this chapter, neither proposition is reliable.

When we compare the degree of decentralization of government in the United Kingdom and her Western neighbours we may well conclude that local government in this country is exposed to central interference and control to a unique degree, and that its position relative to the centre has deteriorated more sharply than anywhere else. What we cannot say is that this country is anomalous in its degree of regionalization. There is no standard model of intermediate, regional-scale government in Europe. If we broadly generalize between northern and southern patterns of local government reform the British case falls with the large, reformed county units of Denmark, Sweden and Norway, rather than the newly-inserted regional assemblies of Belgium, France, Italy and Spain.[53] If there is an anomaly in Britain it lies not at the regional but the local scale, where the large district authorities created in 1973 contrast remarkably with the intimate, face-to-face scale of communes and municipalities elsewhere.[54] After drastic amalgamations in the 1970s, the Swedish communes are large by European standards yet their population averages less than 30,000; the English district council has an average population in excess of 130,000. If the purpose of reform were to align Britain more closely with patterns of decentralization elsewhere, it would begin at the bottom, with the subdivision of district authorities into their constituent communities, rather than pursue a novel, and so politically artificial grouping of counties that are themselves territorial communities with strong historical and cultural roots.

As to the prospective balance between regional, national and supranational tiers of government, it would be rash to assume that the accelerating economic and political integration implicit in the Single European Act necessarily enhances the prospects for regional self-government in Britain. As we saw earlier in this chapter, the reverse is more likely true. The extension of European legislation reinforces national, not regional, jurisdictions, for it is the governments of member states of the European Community whose representatives jointly make directives and regulations and it is they who are legally answerable to the Court of the European Community for their implementation. Community membership, as Sir Bernard Burrows and Geofrey Denton have observed, already constrains the scope of regional or federal devolution in Britain and the constraint has tended to tighten over time.[55] Moreover, 1992 will erode the legitimacy of regions as well as their powers. An explicit objective behind the removal of internal barriers is to make European industry less fragmented and encourage the emergence of 'Euro-champions' capable of competing for world markets. Whilst this policy may conceivably bring benefits for consumers in general and the European economy as a whole, it involves painful readjustment to the economies of all but the most-favoured regions. It is regional governments who will bear the heaviest political cost of the 1992-induced wave of mergers, acquisitions, closures and rationalization.[56]

As this book goes to press, the issue of regionalism seems to be climbing back into the political agenda. The Labour Party, engaged in a major reappraisal of its policies on all fronts, is contemplating a commitment to 'home rule all round', the Democrats likewise. Some redoubtable opponents of regionalism, such as Professor George Jones of London School of Economics, are making warning sallies into print.[57] Appeal to European example is not altogether reassuring for the regionalist cause. It is true that a tide of regionalization ran in 1965-85 in Italy, Belgium, Spain and France - all states with a Napoleonic model of public administration. The process of decentralization was lubricated by comparative example, the solidarity between regional elites, and the supportive role of Europe-wide agencies. The United Kingdom dallied simultaneously with regional devolution and a northern-European model of local government reform, opting for a watered down version of the latter - fewer and larger authorities but with fewer and smaller responsibilities. In retrospect this certainly seems to have been the wrong path, but it will be no easy matter to change it. Europe in the 1990s, dominated by struggles over political and economic integration, will offer a less hospitable environment for regional reform, as and when political circumstances next allow it.

Acknowledgement

I have been helped by the comments and ideas of many colleagues inside the LSE, particularly George Jones, Tony Travers and John Sellgren. Outside, John Banks, Isobel Lindsay (SNP) and Gordon Prentice (Labour Party) responded most helpfully to queries about present and future developments.

Notes and References

1. Kilbrandon (1973) *Royal Commission on the Constitution 1969-1973* Volume 1 Report Cmnd 5640 London: HMSO.

2. Banks, J. (1987) 'Regional Britain and the 1987 General Election' *The Regionalist* No. 10, pp.45.

3. See Regional Studies Association (1983) *Report of an Enquiry into Regional Problems in the United Kingdom* Norwich: Geo Books, Royal Town Planning Institute (1986) *Strategic Planning for Regional Potential* London: RTPI; Wannop, U. (1988) 'Do we need Regional Local Government and is the Scottish model relevant?' *Regional Studies* 22, 6, 439-452.

4. *The Regionalist* (twice yearly) Published by John Ellis, Sancroft House, 6a Church Street, Houghton-le-Spring, Tyne and Wear DH4 4DN. The best review of the movement's activities is Bennett, R.J. (1985) 'Regional movements in Britain: a review of aims and status' *Government and Policy* III pp.75-96.

5. For instance, the French movement for regional autonomy described by Flory, T. (1966) *Le Mouvement Régionaliste Français*, Paris: Presses Universitaires de France.

6. See Dente, B. and Kjellberg, F. (1988) *The Dynamics of Institutional Change - Local Government Reorganization in Western Democracies* London: Sage; Page E.C. and Goldsmith, M.J. (eds.) (1987) *Central and Local Government Relations, a Comparative Analysis of West European Unitary States* London: Sage; Morgan, R. (ed.) (1986) *Regionalism in European Politics* London: Policy Studies Institute; Mény, Y. (1982) *Dix Ans du Regionalization en Europe* Paris: Cujas; Vandamme J. (1981) 'Regionalism in Europe' in Cameron, D. (ed.) *Regionalism and Supranationalism* London: Policy Studies Institute; Sharpe, L.J. (ed.) (1979) *Decentralist Trends in Western Democracies* London: Sage.

7. See Sharpe, L.J. (1988) 'Local Government Reorganization: General Theory and U.K. Practice' in Dente, B. and Kjellberg, F. op cit, pp.89-129, and Keating M. (1988) 'Does Regional Government Work? The Experience of Italy, France and Spain' *Governance* 1,2, 184-204..

8. CLRAE (1980) 'Resolution 117 on regional institutions in Europe' *Proceedings of the Conference of Local and Regional Authorities of Europe* Fifteenth Session 10-12 June 1980 Strasbourg: Council of Europe.

9. See Keating, M. (1988) op cit.

10. Top-down and bottom-up theories of regional development are compared in Stöhr W. and Taylor, D.R.F. (1981) *Development from Above or Below?* Chichester: John Wiley.

11.   Burdeau, G. (1976) *Traité du Science Politique* Vol. IX p.131.

12.   Massart, Pierard F. (1974) *Pour Une Doctrine de la Région en Europe: Régionalisation et Régionalisme* Brussels: Bruylant pp.14-19.

13.   A fear most vocally expressed by Basque and Catalan nationalists over the decentralization measures in the 1978 Spanish Constitution. See Hebbert, M. (1987) 'Regionalism, a reform concept and its application to Spain' *Government and Policy* 5, pp.239-250.

14.   ibid, p.242.

15.   See Burdeau, G. (1980) *Traité de Science Politique*, Paris: Pichon et Durand Anzias Third edition, Vol. II, pp.388-390.

16.   Mény, Y. (1986) 'The Political Dynamics of Regionalism: Italy. France and Spain' in Morgan, R. (ed.) (1986) op cit, p.25; Bogdanor V. (1979) *Devolution*, Oxford: Oxford University Press pp.4-6.

17.   Yuill, D. and Allen K. (1986) *European Regional Incentives* Strathclyde: Centre for the Study of Public Policy.

18.   In Morgan, R. (ed.) (1986) op cit, pp.43-64.

19.   CLARE (1980) Resolution 117. 'On Regional Institutions in Europe'.

20.   *Regional Contact* (1987) Volume 1 [containing Bordeaux Declaration] Foundation for International Understanding, Copenhagen.

21.   For the "Europe of Regions" see MacFarquar, R. (1978) 'The Community, the State and the Regions' in Burrows B. et al. (ed.) (1976) *Federal Solutions to European Issues* London: Macmillan pp.17-24; or, more sceptically, Rhodes, R.A.W. (1974) 'Regional Policy and a Europe of Regions' *Regional Studies* 8, pp.105-114.

22.   J. Buchman cited in Cameron, D. (1981) op cit, p.40.

23.   Ronen, D. (1979) *The Quest For Self Determination* Methuen: Yale University Press pp.100-116.

24.   CLRAE Proceedings 12 June 1980, p.76; his words were echoed by Heribert Barrera, Leader of the left-wing nationalist Esquerra Republicana de Catalunya, who rejoiced at Catalonia's entry to the EC 'because the more we become Europeans the less we shall be Spaniards' (*El Pais*, 30.VI.85).

25.   Malanczuk, P. (1985) 'European Affairs and the Länder of the Federal Republic of Germany' *Common Market Law Review* 22, pp.237-272.

26.   Council of Europe (1979-) *Länder, Cantons and Regions of Europe - Constitutional and Legislative Provisions Concerning the Organization of Regional Government* (series of documents) Strasbourg: Council of Europe.

27.   Debates of the European Parliament (1984-5) April 12th 1984, *Official Journal of the European Communities Annexe* No. 1-313, pp.259-271, pp.307-308.

28.   Keating, M. and Jones, B. (1985) *Regions in the European Community*, Oxford: OUP.

29.   Banks, J. (1986) '40 Years of European Regionalist Movements' *The Regionalist* Issue 8, 9-12.

30.   Three publications of the Policy Studies Institute London, are helpful: Coombes, D. (ed.) (1979) *European Integration, Regional Devolution and National Parliaments*; Cameron, D. (ed.) (1981) *Regionalism and Supranationalism: Challenges and Alternatives to the Nation State in Canada and Europe*; and Morgan, R. (ed.) (1986) *Regionalism in European Politics* see also Kolinsky, M. (ed.) (1978) *Divided Loyalties - British*

Regional Assertion and European Integration, Manchester: Manchester University Press; Crowther Hurt, Lord and Peacock A.T. (1973) *Royal Commission on the Constitution 1969-1973 Vol. II Memorandum of Dissent*, London: HMSO Cmnd 866 5460-1 Ch.III 'The Common Market Dimension'.

31. Banks, J. (1971) *Federal Britain? The Case for Regionalism* London: Harrap Chapter 12 "Britain in Europe".

32. Mackintosh, J.O. (1968) *The Devolution of Power*, Penguin: Harmondsworth, especially pp.187-207 'Conclusions: A Workable Regionalism for England, Scotland and Wales'.

33. *Royal Commission on the Constitution 1969-1973 Vol.1 Report* London: HMSO Cmnd 5460 p.331.

34. Sharpe, L. J. (1982) 'Regional Government in Britain - the furtive tier' in Meny, Y. (ed.) *Dix Ans du Régionalisation en Europe* Paris: Cujas.

35. *Royal Commission on Local Government in England* (1969) Cmnd 4040 London: HMSO Ch X.

36. Parsons, W. (1980) *The Politics of Regional Policy* London: Croom Helm.

37. op cit, p.253.

38. Johnson, N. (1983) 'Decentralization in Britain: a critique of the case in the light of West German experience' *Government and Policy* 1, pp.5-16.

39. CLRAE Proceedings 12 June 1980, p.70.

40. CLRAE Resolution 117 (1980) 'On Regional Institutions in Europe'.

41. Transcript of speech by Jack Straw MP to the Association of Metropolitan Authorities September 19, 1985.

42. Department of the Environment (1986) *The Future of Development Plans* London: DoE.

43. Association of District Councils (1987) *Closer to the People* London: ADC; and the follow-up study, Stewart, M. and Tolan, F. (1988) *Feasibility Study into the Transfer of Functions from County to District Councils - Report of research carried out in Cheshire for the Association of District Councils*, Bristol: School for Advanced Urban Studies.

44. See note 3 above.

45. Ridley, N. (1988) *The Local Right*, London: Centre for Policy Studies

46. Scotland's Claim of Right to Self-Determination, Kilmarnock: Scotland - U.N. Committee, 1979.

47. Federal Trust (1987) *Against the Over Mighty State* London: The Federal Trust.

48. Osmond, J. (1988) *The Divided Kingdom* London: Constable; Green, A.E. (1988) 'The North-South Divide in Great Britain: an examination of the evidence' *Transactions of the Institute of British Geographers* 13, pp.170-198; Town and Country Planning Association (1987) *North-South Divide - a New Deal for Britain's Regions* London: TCPA.

49. Social Democratic Party (1983) *Decentralizing Britain* Green Paper No 3; Marquand, J. (1988) 'Economic Benefits of Regional Government' *Town & Country Planning* April, pp.117-9. But for a caution over the West German parallel, see Johnson, N. (1983) 'Decentralization in Britain: a critique of the case in the light of West German experience' *Government & Policy* 1, pp.5-16.

50.   Labour Party (1987) *Local Government Reform in England & Wales* London: The Labour Party; Labour Party (1988) 'Urban and Regional Policy - A National Strategy: Richard Caborn, M.P.'s Submission to Labour's Policy Review', unpublished typescript.

51.   e.g. Roy Hattersley's article 'Devolution to defend the nation against elective dictatorship' *The Independent*, December 30th 1988.

52.   Contrast John Banks' comment in 1971 that 'the connection between European unity and regional government is still largely unperceived by intellectuals, let alone by ordinary people' *op cit*, p.297.

53.   The north-south distinction emerges clearly in two recent comparative volumes, Dente, B. and Kjellberg, F. (1988) *The Dynamics of Institutional Change: Local Government Reorganization in Western Democracies* London: Sage; and Page, E.C. and Goldsmith, M.J. (1987) *Central and Local Government Relations: A Comparative Analysis of West European Unitary States* London: Sage.

54.   Sharpe, L.J. (1988) 'Local Government Reorganization: general theory and U.K. practice' in Dente, B. and Kjellberg, F. op cit, pp.107-115.

55.   Burrows, Sir B. and Denton, G. (1980) *Devolution or Federalism, Options for a United Kingdom* Chapters 7 and 8.

56.   The complete omission of the regional dimension from EC's own report on the economic effects of 1992 is ominous: Cecchini, P. (1988) *The European Challenge, 1992, The Benefits of a Single Market* Aldershot: Wildwood House.

57.   e.g. Jones, G.W. (1988) 'Against Regional Government' *Local Government Studies* September-October pp.1-11.

Index